*Lyric Descent
in the
German Romantic Tradition*

Lyric Descent
in the
German Romantic Tradition

BRIGITTE PEUCKER

Yale University Press
New Haven and London

Designed by Nancy Ovedovitz and set in Garamond No. 3 type by
R/TSI. Printed in the United States of America by
Thomson-Shore, Inc., Dexter, Michigan.

Library of Congress Cataloging-in-Publication Data

Peucker, Brigitte.
    Lyric descent in the German romantic tradition.

    Bibliography: p.
    Includes index.
    1. German poetry—History and criticism.   2. German
poetry—18th century—History and criticism.
3. German poetry—19th century—History and criticism.
4. German poetry—20th century—History and criticism.
5. Romanticism—Germany.   I. Title.
PT571.P48   1987   831'.04'09145   86-23393
ISBN-0-300-03714-7 (alk. paper)

Excerpts from the poems "Sonnets to Orpheus," "Seventh Elegy,"
"Orpheus. Eurydice. Hermes," "Lament," "Wendung," "Es winkt
zu Fühlung," "O wo ist der . . . ," and the complete poems "An
Hölderlin," and "Pont du Carrousel" are reprinted with permission
from *Selected Works, Volume II: Poetry by Rainer Maria Rilke*,
translated by J. B. Leishman. Copyright © 1960 by the Hogarth
Press. Reprinted by permission of the Hogarth Press and New
Directions Publishing Corporation. Excerpts from Friedrich
Hölderlin's *Poems and Fragments*, translated by Michael Hamburger,
are reprinted with the permission of Cambridge University Press.
Excerpts from *Faust*, by Johann Wolfgang von Goethe, translated
by Walter Arendt, edited by Cyrus Hamlin, are reprinted by
permission of W. W. Norton and Company, Inc. A Norton
Critical Edition. Copyright © 1976 by W. W. Norton and
Company, Inc.

The paper in this book meets the guidelines for permanence and
durability of the Committee on Production Guidelines for Book
Longevity of the Council on Library Resources.

10   9   8   7   6   5   4   3   2   1

For Paul

Contents

Acknowledgments

My greatest debt of gratitude is to my husband, Paul H. Fry, whose endless generosity and unfailing patience made this project possible. I have benefited enormously from his example, from his wise counsel, and from the critical spirit of his thinking.

To my colleagues and former teachers—among whom I wish to single out Peter Demetz, Ingeborg Glier, Geoffrey Hartman, Jeffrey Sammons, and George Schoolfield—I owe special thanks for continued, sustaining encouragement and aid. My students, too, have provided encouragement and both influenced and challenged my ideas.

For their friendship and conversation over the years I wish especially to thank Maria DiBattista, Laurie Fendrich, Jocelyne Kolb, Alfred and Barbara MacAdam, Michael Seidel, Marilyn Fries, John and Karen Danford, Thomas and Martha Hyde, Richard and Cynthia Brodhead, Candace Waid, David Marshall, Norton Batkin, Julie Iovine, Lise Davis and Edward Mendelson.

An earlier and shorter version of my Droste-Hülshoff chapter appeared in the *Journal of English and Germanic Philology*, and I thank the University of Illinois Press for permission to reprint. For permission to print material from an earlier version of the Eichendorff chapter which appeared in the *Germanic Review*, volume LVII, number 3 (Summer 1982) I thank Heldref Publications and the Helen Dwight Reid Educational Foundation.

I am grateful to the Trustees of Yale University for granting me a leave of absence while on a Morse Fellowship and, at a later date, a Mellon Fellowship at the Whitney Humanities Center. Thanks are in order also to the A. Whitney Griswold Foundation for partial subsidization of the manuscript, and to Elisabeth Strenger, who cheerfully and efficiently helped to prepare it. I am very grateful also to Anthony J. Niesz and Lloyd Suttle, both of Yale University, who so generously helped to solve many a computer problem.

Special thanks go to Ellen Graham of the Yale University Press, whose kindness, proficiency, and sound advice helped me to circumvent numerous obstacles.

I feel very fortunate indeed to have had the assistance of so many; needless to say, they are not implicated in my errors.

Chapter One
Lyric Descent:
Tradition and
Authority

*Insofar as the past has been
transmitted as tradition, it possesses
authority; insofar as authority presents
itself historically, it becomes tradition.*
—Hannah Arendt, "Introduction,"
Walter Benjamin's *Illuminations*

The uneasy tension between ascent and descent, the yearning for the transcendent and the search for natural origins, is surely among the most compelling dynamics of lyric poetry, especially in the Romantic lyric that has predominated since the later eighteenth century. This book presents an account of the personal fictions whereby the German Romantic poets and their descendants figure forth the powers that enable writing. The poets I have chosen to discuss at length, Joseph von Eichendorff, Annette von Droste-Hülshoff, Rainer Maria Rilke, and Georg Trakl, are among the most prominent inheritors of German Romanticism, a tradition which, as most comparatists would argue, in its broadest sense includes Goethe.[1] As the title suggests, it is my view that the celestial longings of the Romantic lyric are overborne by intimations about sources of inspiration that are nearer to hand and literally more radical than the poetic myths about divine origin and stellar influence. What takes precedence is a buried site that is at once the underworld and the unconscious; and the descent to that natural origin, from which the poet is estranged by language and culture, typically proves at the same time to have been a descent through the literary tradition, from the origins of which the poet feels equally estranged by the mediation of intervening poets.

Perhaps the most continuous theme of the present study, then, is the appropriation and revision of Romantic tropes and postures by poets whose inability to escape the gravitational pull away from transcendence essentially defines the Romantic predicament. What is chiefly embattled in this perpetual crisis is the status of nature and the natural image. Simultaneously origin and end, mother, midwife, and devourer, the nature represented in these poets' figural descents

1

is the object of longing and repugnance at once. At one extreme, the irreducible priority and permanence of nature—permanent if only in its process of universal decay—inspires in the poet, even beyond the longing for reunion, the spirit of emulation, with the resultant attempt to impart the substantiality of things to poetic words. At the other extreme, descent becomes burial and nature is confronted as death itself—but with the perplexing intuition that in the meeting of extremes it is nothing other than death, the fact of mortality, that constitutes the being of poetry. In the case of the female poet, as we shall see, these themes are even more prominent than in male poets, but crucially realigned. Although the four poets featured in the ensuing chapters do not for the most part approach the moment of descent in ways that are paradigmatic of their period or generation, each does pose the problem anew, in each case over against the approach of predecessors. While my two pairings of contemporaries cannot be said to comprise a chronological sequence, I nevertheless view their divergent treatments of the descent theme when arranged in the present sequence as a kind of "progress" of the subject— progressive both because of the increased complexity within the sequence with which descent itself is confronted, and also because of the increased complexity with which the mediation of the German lyric tradition is negotiated.

The theme of descent is of course subject to generic as well as to authorial influence. The generalization that lyric descent is the subjective miniature of epic descent will prove helpful in this regard, but only if it is borne in mind, in fairness to the self-consciousness and subtlety of epic, that descent in Milton, Dante, Virgil, and even Homer is already motivated at least as much by psychological as by cultural concerns and is set apart within the narratives of those authors as the moment in which the essentially social definition of destiny is permitted an individual dimension. Lyric descent in turn retains traces of narrative, and with it a persistent interest in the social, if only as a lost idyll: the decay and abandonment of aristocratic milieux, the social function of the *Sänger*, the connection between nationalism and native voice, the displacement of social criticism as the theme of madness (in Droste-Hülshoff), and perhaps most pervasively, the *Abendland* problematic in which the nostalgia of lyric and of historiography seem to merge—all of these related themes play in and around the discussions that follow. It is interesting, though, and perhaps the best measure in this context of the irreducible distance between epic and lyric, that lyric descent borrows its traditional narrative material not from epic but from folklore, from the native ballad tradition and from the classical myths, most notably that of Orpheus. (We may take it as emblematic that lyric poets could find Orpheus in Ovid or in Virgil's *Georgics*, but nothing about him in any classical epic apart from the *Argonautica* of Appolonius.)

These remarks will already have made it sufficiently clear that my understanding of the term *lyric* is not, for the purposes of this study, a morphological one. I do not refer to a kind of poetry as distinguished, say, from satire, but to an orientation of the imagination that is at once (ambiguously or simultaneously) inward-looking and epiphanic, connected with the lyre only in that its cast of voice is achieved in part by resonances of tone and mood. Thus without attempting my own definition within the tripartite scheme of narrative, dramatic, and lyric that one finds variously subdivided in German genre theory, I shall follow this school of thought in using the term *lyric* metaphysically and psychologically rather than formally. For this reason, although much of the time I shall dwell at considerable length on individual texts, I am not concerned primarily to offer "readings" of them as self-contained entities, but rather to bring poetic and prose texts alike to bear on an imaginative event: to isolate the characteristic moment of descent in each successive author and to describe it typologically.

Goethe, Novalis, and Hölderlin as their successors interpreted them are the poets—or poetic figures—in rivalry with whose myths of descent the four poets mainly considered here shaped their own. The chapters that follow have much to say about received images: the convenient reductions of—and occasionally shrewd implicit criticisms of—Goethe, Novalis, and Hölderlin by their poetic descendants. But for the moment, as models for comparing the accomplishments of Eichendorff, Droste-Hülshoff, Rilke, and Trakl, it is best to look at the descendental themes of these earlier poets as nearly as possible on their own terms.

In Goethe, the dialectic of transcendence and descent is already extremely complex, but the exaggeration of his naturalism into a univocal position by the poets who followed him is understandable and to some extent even justifiable. Except with reference to the deluded Faust's "zwei Seelen" and other such passages (in which the author's ironic distance is perceptible even as early as his *Sturm und*

Drang phase), it is very difficult to map an antithesis between imagination and nature in Goethe's writings. His doctrine of organicism entails a "profound harmony between the laws of the mind and those of nature."[2] Accordingly, Goethe tends to evoke the themes of nature and of consciousness at one and the same time, whether in narratives of growth or symbols of presence. This is equally true of poems as early as "Mahomets Gesang" (Winter, 1772–73) and as late as "Um Mitternacht" (1818) and the "Dornburg" poem of 1828. When "der Herr" in the "Prolog im Himmel" compares himself with a gardener and Faust (as well as, implicitly, *Faust*) with a tree, suggesting that works of art and human characters alike grow to maturity like things in nature, he insists that the creative principle is grounded, immanent within the organic sphere. And thus even poems centered on tropes conventionally associated with celestial influence, like the moon, are drawn into the orbit of the poet's growth.

"Um Mitternacht," for instance, narrates a progress of the imagination and of poetry reflected in the poet's changing response to the nighttime sky. In the first stanza, the reaction of the poet as a young boy to the starry skies is touched with a thrill of Gothic horror; the shining forth of the stars is experienced in the graveyard setting common to English and German poetry of the previous century, and the mood of the stanza is fully in keeping with supernatural ballads in the mode of Bürger. The second stanza renders the beloved, a Laura figure, as a star whose shining affects the poet tidally. He was one who

> Zur Liebsten musste, musste, weil sie zog,
> Gestirn und Nordschein über mir im Streite,
> Ich gehend, kommend Seligkeiten sog;[3]
>
> [Must go to my beloved, must, because she pulled, / Stars and zodiacal light above me struggling, / I going, coming bliss enjoyed.]*

These lines recall the young poet of the *Sesenheimer Lieder*, for whom the pathetic fallacy prevails and nature becomes a setting that always reflects the vagaries of his passion. This merger of Petrarchism with the enthusiasm for nature indicates the turning of the poet away from the morbid inwardness of ready-to-hand literary models to the more other-directed egoism of the pathetic fallacy that typifies traditional conceits. The third stanza then records the significance of the moon's light for the mature poetic self: now light is enlightenment,

Unless otherwise noted, all translations are mine.

the illumination of the mind, in contrast with the superstitious *Geisterwelt* of the previous stanzas. This moon also represents the synthetic power of mind asserting itself as an implied narrative in "Um Mitternacht" as a whole, the power of making an abstract overview or summing-up vividly metaphorical, transcending temporality by remaining in its midst. In short, this moon is a symbol of Goethe's mature lyrics:

> Bis dann zuletzt des vollen Mondes Helle
> So klar und deutlich mir ins Finstere drang,
> Auch der Gedanke willig, sinnig, schnelle
> Sich ums Vergangne wie ums Künftige schlang;   [I, 373]

> [Until at last the full moon's brightness / Clearly and distinctly penetrated my darkness, / And thought willingly, judiciously, quickly / Entwined itself around past and future.]

Even at its most transcendent, then, serenely fixed in its place like the thoughts of a sage, the moon remains, indeed most constructively becomes, the inward action of poetic consciousness. Goethe's three responses evolve naturally toward maturity like an organism; and the growth of his own imagination in turn reflects the growth of poetry—Goethe's own and also, as he now proudly supposes, the poetry of Germany, from northern supernaturalism to "Classicism."

Even in the much earlier "An den Mond," the later version of which was published in 1789, this celestial trope descends to become an activity of mind. The moon effects an intermingling of self and world typical of the early Goethe, a dissolving of boundaries which is, in fact, the theme of the poem:

> Füllest wieder Busch und Tal
> Still mit Nebelglanz,
> Lösest endlich auch einmal
> Meine Seele ganz;   [I, 129]

> [Once again you fill bush and valley / Silently with foggy luster / Dissolving finally also now / My soul totally.]

The diffusion of the moonlight through the fog obscures the valley's contours, making a region of light so congenial to the inward man that it draws the soul out of itself and into the world of experience which, beneath its penumbra, the valley continues to represent. At the same time, reciprocally, the diffusion of poetic thought brings the scene to life in the world of the poem. The blurring of distinctions that allows this interchange of landscape and imagination appears again in the ambiguous language of the second stanza: the moon spreads its humanized glance "lindernd" over "mein Gefild," rendering subject and object continuous. The moon's palliative gaze in this stanza is compared with the mild eye of a friend who watches over the speaker;[4] all that is left of its traditionally sublime otherness is its capacity to encompass the whole of the speaker's life, his "Geschick," but this power in turn has been reduced by Goethe's appropriation of it to the scope of human abilities. At its most distinct the moon remains a mediatory presence, moving the solitary speaker, now suspended between joy and pain, to a "Nachklang" or echo of past memories.

An abrupt and initially puzzling change enters the poem in the fourth stanza. Until then unity is everywhere preferred to outline, and everything is covered by the "Nebelglanz" of the first stanza, which dissolves the shapes of the landscape just as it softens the emotions of the alienated speaker. But in the fourth stanza an obtrusive image comes into sharp focus:

> Fliesse, fliesse, lieber Fluss!
> Nimmer werd' ich froh,
> So verrauschte Scherz und Kuss,
> Und die Treue so.
>
> [Flow, flow, dear stream! / Never will I be glad, / In this way rolled on jest and kiss, / And faithfulness passed on so.]

This new image, if we take it to refer to an actual flowing stream, would be difficult to find either in the indistinct vista without or in the speaker's cherished selfhood within, and thus suddenly evokes the natural world as a place apart. That is what finally takes place, as we shall see in a moment, but in the meantime a confusion of reference is sustained for the purpose of making the border between self and world still less distinct. The "Fluss" defines itself as the continuation of a flow of images, and will preliminarily be interpreted in any case as the flooding of the landscape by the moonlight which has precipitated the speaker's memories; indeed, the "Fluss" can be understood to symbolize the eighteenth-century doctrine of associationism which appears thus far to govern the poem. The next stanza, on the impossibility of forgetting a now-lost, still-treasured possession (no doubt the love of Frau von Stein), does nothing to alter one's sense that "fliesse, fliesse, lieber Fluss" addresses the flowing inner landscape of memory. But then, as if to yoke inner and outer together more firmly in the very act of separating them for the first time, in a stanza that is indented to mark its importance, Goethe purports to resolve all ambiguity by returning the river to the real world: "Rausche, Fluss, das Tal entlang" (I, 130).

With this expansive gesture Goethe completes the eclipse of the tranquil moon by its figuration as a never-quiet river, which now occupies the entire territory as it were from within—memory, the temporal flow of experience, a nocturnal landscape, and the unifying sheen of light—that is traditionally overseen from above by the celestial trope the poem never names. There is unity in nature as well as from the transcendent perspective, the poet suggests, and what is gained by absorbing the moon into the immediate world is a transfusion of vital energy; unlike the moon, the river is subject to seasonal change and natural process, and becomes, in the seventh stanza, a true "Quelle" from which the poet hopes for the budding of poetic thought:

Wenn du in der Winternacht
Wütend überschwillst,
Oder um die Frühlingspracht
Junger Knospen quillst.

[When you in the winter night / Angrily overflow, / Or round the springtime glory / of young buds swell.]

And thus the "Fluss," at the point of its most concrete naturalization (humanized only by apostrophe), becomes, at the same time, the flow of poetry, perhaps poetic language itself. A "Quelle" which gives forth only its own element, water, but which is given to the reader self-referentially as an instance of poetic language, the river furthermore tempts one to conclude that the origin of poetic language is poetic language. (I have elsewhere reached a similar conclusion concerning the "reifende Frucht" of "Auf dem See."[5]) With this ultimate subversion of dualism, eclipsing all transcendent priority and inspiration, Goethe concludes that that poem which is wholly natural and thus originary is also wholly lexical, growing out of its own element like a bud on a tree. We shall return more than once in later chapters to Hölderlin's better-known, overtly expressed *hope* to find "Worte," which "wie Blumen entstehn" ("Brot und Wein"), but no other poet shares Goethe's spontaneous assumption that he has found them already. For Goethe alone, the movement of descent is not a gesture staged even in part against the priority of another German writer. In the serene confidence that he has reinvented German poetry,[6] Goethe finds language only in nature.

Faust's unremitting dualism, exemplified by his frustrated conclusion that the sign of the macrocosm is merely a sign, is the essential intellectual blindness, finally made literal at the end of Part II, which keeps him in a state of restless yearning.[7] In contrast with his imbalance and restlessness we can observe the final, serene stage of the lyrics we are considering here. In the final two stanzas of "An den Mond," the image of the river disappears; as in the moonlit, Romantic valley of the poem's opening, the speaker again isolates himself, evoking the pleasures of withdrawing from life, "ohne Hass," in the company of someone who can share all that passes through "das Labyrinth der Brust." Eichendorff borrows this expression in his "Anklänge" to describe the solipsism of the imagination. But in doing so he misreads Goethe's poem, the end of which differs from its calculatedly solipsistic beginning in being a retirement from experience rather than an avoidance of it. Perhaps it is implied that the poetic impulse in this final phase, and thus the impulse that shapes the overview of poems like "An den Mond" and "Um Mitternacht," lacks the immediacy of the overflowing evoked in the middle stanzas; as detached retrospect, it produces meta-poetry rather than poetry. But this distinction points all the more definitely to the importance of the middle stanzas and their announcement that for Goethe the site of poetry must always be the in-between world of process, neither deep within nor high above, Faust's descents and final ascent notwithstanding.

Faust is absent, as he always is at such revelatory moments, when in Part II the philosophical dispute between Thales and Anaxagoras concerning the question whether life began in water or fire is resolved in favor of Thales and water. The climax of the descent down the Lower Peneios to the Aegean comes when Homunculus, seeking a natural origin, douses his artificial flame in the element of Venus-Galatea, an avatar of "das Ewigweibliche." The whole vast poem repeats this pattern, always in mockery of Faust's understanding, from the contrast between the midnight oil of the *Studierzimmer* (to which Faust is drawn like a moth) and the brightly colored costumes that merge with the landscape on Easter morning (none of which can hold Faust's attention for long) to the monstrous assault on the oceanic origins of life by the land-reclamation project that brings Faust to the end of his own life. The pattern is most marked at moments of actual descent or ascent. The tedium of Auerbach's Cellar is summarized in the fact that in Faust's presence the unnatu-

ral wine turns into flame. The ersatz youth recovered from the
witches' concoction is tempered by fire, and the forms of beauty
recovered through the mystification of the descent to the Mothers go
up in smoke when they are touched by life. Euphorion's plunge into
the sea, in some ways recalling the happier plunge of Homunculus,
is doomed by its motive, his attraction to the battle-lines of history,
which in calling him "Ikarus" the chorus compares with a flight too
close to the sun.[8]

Most problematic according to this view, of course, is the ascent
into the heavens with which Goethe "saves" Faust in the end. The
motives of this ascent can perhaps never be quite reconciled by
interpretation with Goethe's situation of the poetic moment within
the process world as described here. A few reconciliatory comments
can be made, however. The defeat of Mephisto by the flaming roses
marks the redemption, the transmutation, of fire, so that its function
is fused with that of the baptismal water Faust has always avoided in
favor of this or that devilish potion. His salvation accomplished, the
ascent of Faust begins in a region (to be frequently recreated both in
language and setting by the authors who follow Goethe in this
study) that is *rooted* in earth and water—

Wurzeln, sie klammern an,
Stamm dicht an Stamm hinan.
Woge nach Woge spritzt,   [II, v, 11846–48]
[Tree roots entwine and close, / Tree trunks in serried rows. / Gushing
up, wave on wave.][9]

—suggesting that the purification of Faust's mortal remains is a
gradual process, a kind of half-life in decay that takes its origin not
in ascent but in descent, and not at all a dualistic separation of soul
from body. The "Pater Ecstaticus," whose name evokes that very
separation, speaks admittedly of the "Dauerstern, / Ewiger Liebe
Kern" (II, v, 11864–65), but, "auf und ab schwebend," he may be
accorded less than full insight in contrast with the "Pater Profundus,"
in the "tiefe Region," who continues the descendental theme by
celebrating the transformational energy of the mountain gorges, and
the "Pater Seraphicus," in the "mittlere Region," who interestingly
inhabits precisely that border region where body and spirit merge
that characterizes the valley of "An den Mond":

Welch ein Morgenwölkchen schwebet
Durch der Tannen schwankend Haar!

Ahn' ich, was im Innern lebet?
Es ist junge Geisterschar.   [II, v, 11890-93]

[What a wispy dawn-cloud hovers / in the spruces' swaying hair; / Do I
fathom what it covers? / A young spirit-band is there.]

Of the ascent from here, it is worth noting that Faust henceforth
disappears (unless we can infer something of his condition from the
erstwhile Gretchen's announcement that he is *still* blind: "Noch
blendet ihn der neue Tag" [II, v, 12093]) while the less perfected
angels ("Nebelnd um Felsenhöh'" [II, v, 11966]) adjust themselves to
immateriality by speaking of a higher world (II, v, 11977) resembling this one. And in any case, finally, "das Ewigweibliche," the
creative principle to which all our poets will characteristically *descend*,
with varying emotions, was first a daisy in *Faust* (Margarete) and
then the water-nymph in whose presence that spark of life whose
intelligence was so much keener than that of Faust has desired to
begin anew.

There are other instances in Goethe of what Geoffrey Hartman has
termed, referring to similar moments in English poetry, a "downward displacement of the stars."[10] One of the more conspicuous
occurs in "Auf dem See" (published 1789), in which the rising sun is
brought down from the sky and converted by the medium of poetic
language into a ripening fruit; it is always the ambiguity of poetic
language (in this case suggesting either fruit in the landscape or fruit
of thought) that allows the poet to draw even the sublime into his
preferred world of growth and decay. Indeed, Goethe's belief in the
organic action of the mind, mediated by and expressed in language,
leads him at moments even to enter into rivalry with nature. In a
letter of June 1787 to Frau von Stein he theorizes about his *Urpflanze*
(the prototype of all flowers theoretically merging the *Geist* with the
flora Goethe had been observing scientifically) and proceeds to declare:

Die Urpflanze wird das wunderlichste Geschöpf von der Welt, über
welches mich die Natur selbst beneiden soll. Mit diesem Modell und
dem Schlüssel dazu kann man alsdann noch Pflanzen ins Unendliche
erfinden.[11]

[The *Urpflanze* is becoming the most remarkable creation in the world,
for which nature itself shall envy me. With this model and the key to it
one will be able to invent plants *ad infinitum.*]

At less hubristic moments (even Goethe is at pains to insist that the

Urpflanze is not a construct of the poetic mind, but an inference of the scientific mind), but also perhaps less characteristic ones tending back in the direction of dualism, Goethe believes simply that the divine spirit finds its finest expression in nature and that man can learn from that expression to be its worthy communicant. Thus in his poem "Die Metamorphose der Pflanzen" (1798; I, 199–200), the leaf feels "die göttliche Hand" and the plant develops toward "Vollendung" and "das Vollkommnere," these being likewise the goals of man's ethical striving.

But the doctrine of organic form remains, if not precisely the denial, certainly a drastic reorientation of matter-spirit dualism; for Goethe the "shaping spirit," in Coleridge's phrase, is immanent within things and not superimposed on them by a transcendent power. It is this organicism, again, for which his poetry comes to stand in the eyes of later poets. A passage from Heine's *Romantische Schule* (1838) uncannily expresses my reading of Goethe figuratively as follows:

Das grosse Publikum aber verehrte diesen Baum [Goethe] eben weil er so selbstständig herrlich war, weil er so lieblich die ganze Welt mit seinem Wohlduft erfüllte, weil seine Zweige so prachtvoll in den Himmel ragten, so dass es aussah *als seien die Sterne nur die goldnen Früchte des grossen Wunderbaums*. [italics Heine's][12]

[But the greater public venerated this tree precisely because it was so self-sufficiently magnificent, because it filled the whole world with its fragrance so pleasingly, because its branches towered up so gloriously into the heavens, so that it looked as though the stars were merely the golden fruit of this great and wonderful tree.]

Writing in 1851, Eichendorff expressed this reading of Goethe figuratively as follows:

Goethe ist uns immer wie ein herrlicher Baum erschienen, der, mächtig in der Erde wurzelnd, gar nicht in den Himmel *mag*, und doch weil er eben nicht anders kann, mit allen Zweigen und Knospen durstig von dem Lichte trinkt, das durch sein kräftiges Laub zittert.[13]

[Goethe always appeared to us as a magnificent tree which, powerfully rooted in the earth, does not even *want* to grow heavenward, and yet because it simply cannot do otherwise, drinks thirstily of the light that shivers through its rich foliage.]

The tree, a favorite metaphor of Goethe that becomes his emblem in the critical tradition, is perhaps not accidentally prominent in

Rilke's poetry, coming to stand for the poem itself—of a certain kind, as we shall see—as well as for the Orphic poet and, intermittently, for the poetics of the *Sonette an Orpheus*.

As his critics, poetic or otherwise, have always pointed out, Goethe does not emphasize the negative aspect of the organic analogy, the fact that growth must terminate—or, as Novalis would have it, culminate—in death. As his indifference to the charnel-house potential of poems like "Um Mitternacht" indicates, Goethe was not moved by this aspect of Young's *Night Thoughts* or of other poems of the English graveyard school that so strongly appealed to the sensibilities of Klopstock and Novalis. Death plays its part in Goethe's poetry, but its meaning, as in the death and redemption of Faust, is not fully consistent with the implications of organicism. Death verges on the spiritual in Goethe, which is to say, it is sublimated; and even though in Goethe the imagination is more triumphantly continuous with nature than it is for those Romantics afflicted by *Sehnsucht*, it is not inspired, as it is for these others and perhaps logically should be for him, by the immanence of death. For Goethe almost alone, death is not what Wallace Stevens calls "the mother of beauty": "das Ewigweibliche" is eternally alive. But in taking death for a source of inspiration, the other poets in this study carry Goethe's organic doctrine to its logical conclusion.

Novalis is preeminent among the poets for whom descent leads not to the vitality and immediacy of nature but to the—equally inspirational—region of death, a region figurally presented as an aspect of nature but literally understood as an inner space, a state of consciousness. As the mystical space in his *Hymnen an die Nacht* (1800), night is the goal toward which the "Weg nach Innen" tends, and the entry into this space, in accordance with the "dark night of the soul" in the mystical tradition, is most often effected by a descent: "Abwärts wend' ich mich"; "Hinunter in der Erde Schoss"; "Hinunter zu der süssen Braut"; "Und senkt uns in der Erde Schoss."[14] At once the earthen "Schoss" or womb itself and also the place where the vision of the mother appears, "night" is clearly the originary source for Novalis. But it is also the point of ultimate return, the region where beginnings and ends are symbolically fused in the poet's reunion with the beloved woman who got there first. For Novalis, then, the quarry of the poet's descent is a prototype of the Freudian unconscious; and essentially for this reason one critic has made the claim that his underworld is Novalis's most far-reaching legacy to the imagination: "it [the mythical elaboration of the underworld] is the modern poetic Mythos *par excellence*."[15] The significance for Novalis of this reunion with the earth and its merciful release from estrangement is something Trakl evidently understood in beginning the two last versions of his poem "An Novalis" with the line: "In dunkler Erde ruht der heilige Fremdling."[16]

Novalis's *Hymnen* celebrate the descent into the self as an enviable act of imaginative power which is thus far Orphic, but depart from the Orphic pattern when the poet is happily united with his Eurydice-Sophie in an underworld of the self from which he has no desire to return into the light. Because the "earth" in the *Hymnen* contains the grave of the beloved but is simultaneously transformed into a mystical inner space, it is at once the abode of memory and of Eros, desire and its sublimated fulfillment. The death of the beloved is redeemed by the death of Christ, the guarantor of everlasting life, and the poet's erotic feelings toward Sophie are absorbed by the mystical "Wollust" he feels toward Christ and toward death itself— or almost absorbed, as the lingering suggestion of vampirism indicates: "O! sauge Geliebter, / Gewaltig mich an" (fourth *Hymn*; 159). In his central imaginative achievement, reversing Goethe's intimation in "Bergschluchten" that transcendence faintly replicates the mountain gorges whence it originates, Novalis transforms the underworld abode of death by endowing it with the most positive characteristics of Heaven, until it becomes the "Heimat," home of God the Father and of the soul. Novalis trusts his God-given imagination not to mislead him as he partially inverts the upper and lower regions— only partially in that he does not make the heavens seem like an underworld; it is enough to make them seem remote and secondary in value by equating them with the exterior world in contrast with the immediate interiority of the world below.

Another important instance of descent in Novalis belongs here: the episode in *Heinrich von Ofterdingen* (1802), Novalis's *Bildungsroman*, in which the young poet-to-be meets a miner and later descends with him into a series of caves, there to learn the significance of descent and of the past for poetry. Just as the miner plumbs the depths of the earth in order to bring up precious metals and stones, so the poet descends into the self in order to release past experience into poetry. As if to affirm this parallel, the miner tells Heinrich that "Gesang und Zitherspiel gehört zum Leben des Bergmanns" (293). In *Heinrich von Ofterdingen* as well as in the *Hymnen*, the descent into the earth is represented as a return to the Mother—and to the beloved, as the miner's song plainly shows:

> Der ist der Herr der Erde
> Wer ihre Tiefen misst,
> Und jeglicher Beschwerde
> In ihrem Schoss vergisst.
>
> . . . .
> Er ist mit ihr verbündet
> Und inniglich vertraut,
> Und wird von ihr entzündet,
> Als wär' sie seine Braut.   [294]

[He is the lord of the Earth / Who measures her depths, / And forgets all complaints / within her womb. // He is allied with her / And sincerely intimate, / And is inflamed by her / As though she were his bride.]

To emphasize its resemblance to the unconscious mind, this mine is called a labyrinth, an "Irrgarten von Gängen," and differs from the many other caves in *Heinrich von Ofterdingen* only insofar as it is explicitly a scene of human action and therefore more closely parallels the site of poetic creation. So volatile is the relation between the way down and the way up that the hermit who inhabits one of the caves will say of miners, "ihr seyd beinah verkehrte Astrologen" (307). The stars' place among the regions of light discredits them in the eyes of Novalis, however, and so the miners in quest of divination look to the vasty deep and extend the strength gained from descent even to the prophetic mode of poetry.

Streams in Novalis, the fountainheads of poetry and carriers of imagination, often have their origin in one or another of the many caves in his landscape. Through this association among others, the series of caves into which Heinrich descends in the company of the miner serves as a poet's initiation by stages. The first cave is manifestly a place of death: its floor is littered with bones and teeth, some of which bear the marks of decomposition, "Spuren der Verwesung" (300). In *Heinrich von Ofterdingen*, which differs in this respect from the *Hymnen*, this setting is significant because it harbors signs of an ancient, possibly prehistoric time—the antediluvian "uralte Zeit" of Romanticism—showing how the underworld, like the night in the *Hymnen*, takes priority in time over the surface, daylit world. Entering a second cave where once again traces of previous life can be found, Heinrich wonders whether a second, submerged world exists under the crust of the earth, and whether "unerhörte Geburten" (300) inhabit such a world, creatures "die das innere Feuer des dunklen Schosses zu riesenmässigen und geistesgewaltigen Gestalten auftriebe" (300) inhabit such a world, creatures "die das innere Feuer des dunklen Schosses zu riesenmässigen und geistesgewaltigen Gestalten auftriebe" (300). The cave is transformed by Heinrich's Orphic imagination into a place where the earth, being at once a maternal refuge and a repository of the dead and of the past, nourishes unheard-of forms of life. Having come to understand the priority of death, darkness, and interiority in the first cave, then, Heinrich now learns that this procreative womb may bring forth monstrous births not only resembling the chthonic dragons of Christian quest-romance but also the more disgusting monsters that appear in literary satire as tropes for the unnatural in poetry.

As Heinrich's experience becomes more and more directly a lesson in the writing of poetry, he comes to a third and final cave harboring the hermit and a "Geschichtsschreiber"—better translated as writer of history or of stories than simply as "historian" because there is little difference in Novalis's scheme of things between a historian and a poet. Here again in accordance with the theme of the *Hymnen*, the poet is a historian in the sense that he must encounter the past as an otherness made continuous with the present only by death. To do this, he must descend into memory, which can internalize the dead; "Er-innerung" is the term that dominates the poetics of Novalis and resonates still in the poetics of Rilke.[17] Again like a poet in this regard, and like the "Astrologe," the "Geschichtsschreiber" is able to "write" the future because it merely recapitulates the past in different guises; because all stories have the descent to death in common, they have all been enacted previously. In perusing the hermit's book, Heinrich is able to recognize himself in a wide variety of situations, some familiar from the recent past and others that anticipate his future as a poet. Because the future must be extrapolated from the memory of the past, the quest for knowledge becomes subjective, the stuff of elegy, and the imagination, with its elastic power of sympathy for all the dead, becomes the supreme poetic faculty.

Whereas in the *Lehrlinge zu Sais* (1802) Novalis claims that it is the poet's function to interpret nature, in *Heinrich von Ofterdingen*, following Fichte, Novalis understands nature to be but a projection of the self and, ultimately, of the origin of the self, the absolute or God.[18] Echoing Herder, Novalis wishes to see nature as a "Chiffrenschrift" or "Wunderschrift" (201), and believes that although one can sense in the things of nature an interpretive guide to this writing—a "Sprachlehre" or linguistics, as it were—it never becomes an infallible key but remains an intimation, an "Ahndung" (201).[19] In hoping that the world of nature will be released by poetry into that of the spirit, Novalis does not depart from the thinking of Fichte, Schelling, or the Schlegels; but what sets him apart, once again, is the direction taken for this transformation, the descent into "Gottes Tiefe," which ultimately derives from the mysticism of Jakob Böhme, as Novalis's poem "An Tieck" in particular would suggest. In this respect at least, Novalis does not in effect revise Goethe at all. It is a commonplace of Novalis criticism that for him everything is poetry or else must be poeticized; that poetry, as René Wellek has written, simply *is* "the peculiar mode of action of the human spirit."[20] What poetry decidedly does not do—and herein arises one point of dispute with Goethe—is in any way to imitate, to follow the lead of, external nature, because to do so would be to admit the priority of nature to the action of the spirit. Arguably the teacher in Novalis's *Lehrlinge zu Sais* is a Goethe figure, at least insofar as he collects stones, flowers, and other objects of nature, organizing them in artistic arrangements.[21] His "grosse bunte Bilder" are the products of his senses: "er hörte, sah, tastete, und dachte zugleich" (202). In order to distinguish himself from his teacher, whose song is informed by nature and seeks to interpret it, the apprentice who is the speaker of the *Lehrlinge* says, "So wie dem Lehrer ist mir nie gewesen. Mich führt alles in mich selbst zurück" (203). Novalis embraces a poetics of metamorphosis, but it is neither Ovidian nor Goethean: for him each thing is transformed into something else in order finally to be conjoined in an *unio mystica*. As one might expect, again unlike Goethe, Novalis has no interest at all in form. In fact, it is his express purpose, especially in the *Hymnen*, to achieve the liquidity of an ever-changing series of images that supplant each other. This is appropriate because, as the apprentice says in the *Lehrlinge*, all images are merely "Bilder, Hüllen, Zierden, versammelt um ein göttlich Wunderbild" (204). Novalis's interest centers "im Flüssigen, im Dünnen, im Gestaltlosen" (206), but decidedly without the mediatory function these qualities are accorded in Goethe's "An den Mond."

Like Goethe in *Faust*, Part Two, Novalis affirms in the *Lehrlinge* that the Ancients correctly located the origin of all things, the

"Ursprung der Dinge" (228), in "dem Flüssigen." But the Ancients
meant more by this, he contends further, than that life came forth
from existing bodies of water. Thinking perhaps of Heraclitus, Novalis propounds an underlying principle of liquidity, "das Urflüssige"
(228), of which we can gain an intuitive understanding from the
state of mystical disorientation induced by wine, "in der goldenen
Flut der Trauben" (second *Hymn*; 153), and which is, essentially, a
life principle: "Die Berauschten fühlen nur zu gut diese überirdische
Wonne des Flüssigen, und am Ende sind alle angenehme Empfin-
dungen in uns mannigfache Zerfliessungen, Regungen jener Urge-
wässer in uns. Selbst der Schlaf ist nichts als die Flut jenes
unsichtbaren Weltmeers, und das Erwachen das Eintreten der Ebbe"
(228). But death, too, is drawn into the current of "das Urflüssige";
Novalis defines the death drive ("Todestrieb" is a word Hölderlin
uses in "Stimme des Volks"[22]) as the "gewaltige Sehnsucht nach dem
Zerfliessen" (228). He frequently envisions death as a submersion in
water, the maternal element, "mütterliches Gewässer" (228), which
it is tempting to interpret as an escape from paternal oppression, the
exalted surveillance, for example, of a sky god.

Novalis anticipates the Freud of *Beyond the Pleasure Principle* in so
many ways that his essentially Freudian revision of his own Christianity, drawing God down to a place where archaeology and eschatology
are united under the sign of death, should not seem surprising. The
paradoxical identification of life with death—"Im Tode ward das
ewige Leben kund" (fifth *Hymn*; 167)—is after all entirely Christian,
figuratively true in orthodox belief and literally true for the mystic.
Death for the Christian and the Freudian alike is a return to the
"Heimat," and it remains only for Novalis, before Freud, to locate
that home in the earth rather than in the sky. More broadly considered, in any case, the paradoxes on which the works of Novalis turn
simply comprise a version of the poetic project of Romanticism in
general, which students of literature have repeatedly identified as the
reconciliation of opposites. As the "Jüngling" states in *Lehrlinge*:

Es ist nicht blos Wiederschein, dass der Himmel im Wasser liegt, es ist
eine zarte Befreundung, ein Zeichen der Nachbarschaft, und wenn der
unerfüllte Trieb in die unermessliche Höhe will, so versinkt die glück-
liche Liebe gern in die endlose Tiefe."   [229]

[It is not simply reflection that causes Heaven to lie in the water; it is a
tender friendship, a sign of proximity, and if unfulfilled passion strives

to attain the immeasurable heights, then happy love willingly sinks into the endless depths.]

Although Novalis joins the heavens and the waters—and the underworld—dialectically, he directs the focus and energy of his work toward descent, in which he finds a fulfillment that is at least partly erotic, thereby disparaging what one might suppose to be the typical Romantic impulse, the self-sustained condition of yearning for the inaccessible.

In turning to Hölderlin, whose swans like the "Jüngling" of Novalis gaze into the water "wo silberne Wolken sich spiegeln, / Und ätherisches Blau unter den Schiffenden wallt" ("Menons Klagen um Diotima"; I, 103), among the many complex assertions that can be hazarded concerning the topic of descent alone, the present discussion requires only that two be put forward and as far as possible clarified. The first is that although Hölderlin is characteristically read as a poet for whom ascent is a mission—if not quite an accomplishment—and although the chief among such readers are in fact the great poets who succeed Hölderlin in the German Romantic tradition, the gravitational pull of descent, specifically a commitment to the natural world inherited from Goethe and from the Greeks, is as strong in his writings as it is in the poets and critics who suppose themselves to have demystified him from their own comparatively earthbound perspectives.[23] The second point, which in the ensuing remarks will grow out of the first, is that Hölderlin's contribution to the theme of descent, without which the work of Rilke and Trakl especially would have a very different character, is his emphasis on the problem of poetic language. Goethe in the confidence of having founded German poetry takes it for granted that language descends to him as a gift from nature; Novalis with his indifference to form views language as a necessary evil that can reflect his view of phenomena only if it dissolves itself in an ever-flowing series of images and, as it were, permits the imagination to descend beneath it. But Hölderlin approaches the theme of descent with the acute—and uneasy—sense that what one descends *for* is a mode of poetic speech that is not given from on high.

The characteristically Romantic quest for and fear of origins, both in their transcendent and buried forms, occasions an ever-present tension in Hölderlin's poetry, one that he constantly reformulates, most often with the wish to resolve it in "das Harmonischentgegengesetzte." Perhaps the most prominent personifications of this tension are the "Mutter Erde" and "Vater Äther," whose erstwhile union (as Gaea and Uranus, and in other forms in other cosmogonies) comprises a link between the recesses of earth and the ethereal heights. Hölderlin criticism has frequently emphasized the upward movement of transcendence, and one finds this emphasis still implicit in such interesting and innovative recent studies as that of Rainer Nägele, who links the realm of the fathers with Hölderlin's socially oriented quest for utopia. Especially in the later poetry, Nägele argues, Hölderlin's ties to fathers, both actual and literary, are transformed into a forward-looking dynamic.[24] In the present remarks concerning this extraordinarily complex issue, however, I shall emphasize the persistence of the tension between ascent and descent rather than its resolution in any direction. In "Der Mensch," for example, where the parental pair is "Vater Helios" and "Mutter Erde," their offspring is man, who inherits the father's "hohe Seele" and the mother's "Lust" and "Trauer" (I, 46). But this couple is as profoundly estranged as the incompatibility of their characters would indicate, and their offspring becomes aware of himself as a consciousness divided, perpetually in disequilibrium and bent on mediating between his dwelling-place and his vision of home. Cyrus Hamlin has explained how Hölderlin accommodates this doubleness rhetorically as "a fundamental tension or opposition between statement and attitude, or expression and point of view, in any moment of the poem. . . . Meaning is defined as the interaction of these opposing elements, an interaction which is *metaphoric* or *hyperbolic*, through which the poem attains its seriousness, its solidity, and its truth."[25]

Like Goethe in "Bergschluchten," though doubtless with a more acute sense of the difficulty of unifying polar opposites, Hölderlin naturalizes the paternal and maternal figures of origin in the single image of the mountain or, more tellingly, of the volcano, its fiery depths connecting it with the germinal recesses while its summit remains in the region of the sublime. A horizontal equivalent of the volcano, the river in Hölderlin also complicates the problem of the "source" as Goethe and Novalis render it. In flowing away from its wellspring (in nature), it also flows toward it (in the Absolute), connecting origin with endpoint both as wanderer and as path. "Der Neckar," for example, associates the river with childhood and thereby sets in place the constructively ambiguous theme of "Heimat"; and *Der Rhein*, similarly, capitalizes on the pun in "Reinentsprungenes" to present the source in all its metaphysical complexity. The

Rhine—a "Halbgott"—is expressly descended both from the heavens and the earth, "Aus günstigen Höhn . . . / Und so aus heiligem Schosse" (I, 148–49), and the river is enjoined always to remember this ancestry:

> Doch nimmer, nimmer vergisst ers.
> Denn eher muss die Wohnung vergehn,
> Und die Satzung zum Unbild werden
> Der Tag der Menschen, ehe vergessen
> Ein solcher durfte den Ursprung
> Und die reine Stimme der Jugend.   [I, 149–50]
>
> [Yet never, never does he forget. / For sooner the dwelling shall be destroyed, / And all the laws, and the day of men / Become iniquitous, than such as he / Forget his origin / And the pure voice of his youth.][26]

Mankind also, whose memory is likewise celebrated in this hymn, and in particular the poet, here the exemplary figure of Rousseau, must share with the river the obligation to keep alive in memory the bipolarity of "das Beste"—

>   bis in den Tod
> Kann aber ein Mensch auch
> Im Gedächtnis doch das Beste behalten,
> Und dann erlebt er das Höchste [I, 152]
>
> [but until death / A mortal too can retain / And bear in mind what is best / And man is supremely favoured.]   [421]

—but with a cross-current of emotion superadded: although man's ties to his origins should be "Liebesbande" (I, 150), they can also become "Stricke," fetters, and when this occurs, they are threatening signs of mortality.

As in Novalis, but with only a trace of his joyful anticipation, to look back and down for Hölderlin is to confront death, this being perhaps one of the reasons why Rilke associates Hölderlin with Orpheus. Even the Rhine itself was "lichtlos," "in Fesseln," and "im kältesten Abgrund" (I, 148) at its point of origination, and its wellspring was a site of death,[27] of separation in exile until the time of implied "return." There is a measure of "Todeslust" in this theme, but unlike Novalis, Hölderlin warns against man's indulgence of his Dionysian tendency toward self-annihilation. In the Empedokles ode, although the poet confesses that the descent into "die Tiefe" (I, 67) holds a temptation for him, he also makes it clear that his Empedokles should not have sacrificed himself to nature by throwing himself into the "gärenden Kelch" (I, 67) of Mount Aetna. In "Stimme des Volks," the downward surge of a river is a metaphor for the death-wish of an entire people; that which is mortal, the poet says, is all too ready to resist differentiation and is drawn, despite resistance by the progressive Spirit, "Ins All zurück" (I, 86):

                                    . . . so stürzt
Der Strom hinab, er suchet die Ruh, es reisst,
  Es ziehet wider Willen ihn, von
  Klippe zu Klippe, den Steuerlosen,

Das wunderbare Sehnen dem Abgrund zu[.]   [I, 86-87]

[So rivers plunge—not movement, but rest they seek— / Drawn on, pulled down against their will from / Boulder to boulder—abandoned, helmless— / By that mysterious yearning toward the chasm;]   [179]

In "Stimme des Volks," the "Todeslust" activated by looking backward is also interpreted socially as the blind adherence to precedent. In Plutarch's story of the city of Xanthos, the sons follow the bad example of the fathers (the example, that is, that is recommended by legends concerning their forefathers' actions), resulting in the release of Dionysian frenzy—"alle waren ausser sich" (I, 88)—in the city for a second time. But Hölderlin concludes that the legends themselves are not responsible; they are not bearers of a racial death-wish but stand in the service of "dem Höchsten" (I, 88). The problem lies rather, he says, in their having been inadequately interpreted without the benefit of memory, "Gedächtnis": "doch auch bedarf es / Eines, die heiligen auszulegen" (I, 88)—a problem Hölderlin in turn seeks to remedy in retelling Plutarch. The question, then, whether the descent into the natural and human history stored by memory restricts the possibility of cultural and spiritual development or rather provides a millennial future with a proleptic image of itself, is at bottom finally for Hölderlin, as I have said, a question of language, "das strömende Wort" ("Brot und Wein," I, 115), the purity or corruption of which depends on the nature of its origin.

In *Tod des Empedokles* (first version), the decision of Empedokles to follow "den heiligen stillen Todespfad" (II, 479) is meant to atone for his desire to control nature, to become her master, "Herr." He submits himself to that which he had intended to subjugate:

Ich kannt es ja, ich hatt es ausgelernt,
Das Leben der Natur, wie sollt es mir

Noch heilig sein, wie einst!   [II, 477]

[Of course I knew it, I had exhausted it, / The life of nature, how could
it still be as holy for me / As it once was!]²⁸

What is suggested only to be qualified in "Stimme des Volks," that
the articulation of a deed in language can be seen to incur more guilt
than the deed itself, is reasserted in this drama. Empedokles confesses: "ich allein / War Gott, und sprachs im frechen Stolz heraus"
(II, 477), implying that having asserted his mastery of nature in
language is what makes his death imperative. Pausanias replies that
it was precisely the sign of his access to divinity, his election, that
Empedokles, understanding more fully than anyone before him "die
ewige Welt" through an act of the *Geist*, was able to speak "das
kühne Wort": "Was? Um eines Wortes willen?" (II, 477). But for
Empedokles it is human language that has constituted his knowledge
rather than the other way around, and because he knows that in
arrogating the understanding that is fraught with spirit to himself he
has alienated himself from the world-spirit he feels the more acutely
the censure implicit in the intended praise of Pausanias: "wie du mit
Einer stolzen Silbe / Vom Herzen aller Götter dich gerissen" (II,
477). In speaking his syllable proclaiming mastery, Empedokles has
brought estrangement into the world; in exalting man he cast him
out of the bosom of nature. As one who knows, he no longer is, like
nature, but merely refers. What he has needed was a language *of*
nature rather than about it. Unlike Empedokles, however, Hölderlin
does not despair over this central Romantic difficulty, but hopes
more modestly for a language accessible within the fallen condition
brought about by "das kühne Wort," a language in which a trace of
the *Ursprache* may be transmitted even though it is not the *Ursprache*
itself. In "Natur und Kunst oder Saturn und Jupiter," Jupiter has
banished his father Saturn to the abyss—"Abgrund"—taking the
high ground for himself by implying that nature, the Golden Age of
Saturn, was pre-linguistic, mere sound, while his language of
knowledge has introduced "Kunst" to the world. But the poet, the
putative beneficiary of Jupiter's founding act, feels the need, not to
fall silent in deference to this gift, but rather to descend backward
on his own terms, to name Saturn and thereby at least nominally to
reestablish the authority of nature over art. And Jupiter in his turn
is called upon to acknowledge that his power derives from Saturn:
"so kömmt / von ihm, was dein ist, siehe!" (I, 79).²⁹

Recurrently in Hölderlin, then, there is an apparent impasse be-

tween natural beings and the gods that arises from the appropriation
and functional definition of language by the latter. Nature resists
being authorized by words that are secondary to its own pure vocality. In "Der gefesselte Strom" and in "Ganymed," the river and the
youth, respectively, are at first unwilling to respond to the denomi-
native, beckoning word of the father because that word, simply as a
word, calls to mind the rival authority of their own partially divine
origins. Perhaps "Ganymed," a revision of "Der gefesselte Strom,"
turns from the river to the mythological figure in order more clearly
to justify the vertical movement of the poems in which the word
clearly descends from on high. After his initial resistance, Ganymede
defers to the father, ascending to him in order to participate in a
privileged conversation: "himmlisch Gespräch ist sein nun" (I, 98),
the same, perhaps, which "we have been" in "Friedensfeier" (I, 163,
166); this mood in Hölderlin reflects the religious humility of knowing that man is a created being.

Human language is god-given also in "Germanien," but with
something more of that trace of autochthony that occasions the
initial resistance of Ganymede to the divine word. The eagle of
"Germanien" brings language—"die Blume des Mundes" (I, 155)—
down from above; but the use of this organic metaphor itself suggests that something comes from below as well, and redefines
language more closely in correspondence with the natural language
described by Empedokles in *Tod des Empedokles*:

> Es sprechen, wenn ich ferne bin, statt meiner
> Des Himmels Blumen, blühendes Gestirn
> Und die der Erde tausendfach entkeimen,
> Die göttlichgegenwärtige Natur
> Bedarf der Rede nicht[.]   [II, 513]

> [When I am far away there will speak in my place / The heavens'
> flowers, blooming stars / And those that sprout by the thousands from
> the earth, / Divinely present Nature does not require speech.]

Flowers and stars, "blühendes Gestirn," are the originary language of
nature, forming a miniature of the conflict between earth and sky
that interestingly draws the sky down within the orbit of natural
things, deciding after all for the likelihood that the language capable
of carrying culture forward in a way that wisely retains nature within
the horizon of "das Gedächtnis" must have had, in certain respects,
an autonomous and natural origin. Here and earlier, when he apostrophizes the stars as "Blumen des Himmels" (II, 494), Empedokles

relocates the "word from on high" in the natural world.[30] The "Worte" that "wie Blumen, entstehn" of the oft-quoted passage in "Brot und Wein" (I, 117) seem to have their place alongside the divine Word and among things that at times appear to take ontological priority even over the gods.

As there is no open, sustained rivalry between these two versions of language, the constitutive language of the gods and the elemental self-expression of nature, it is best to conclude that in the inaccessible spheres where they arise in their pure form they are really not in opposition or even different. Although the poet has access to neither and must rest content with mediation, it is precisely these languages together, neither privileged before the other, that his mediatory language alone can envision, bring into the present, and petition to speak the future. As Lawrence Ryan explains it, the poet's function is to speak an equivalent of the mute language of nature in poetic language, thereby according to the Absolute, which lacks "Bewusstsein," a subjectively mediated consciousness: "That happens in language which forms a 'world within a world,' in which the 'voice of the Eternal to the Eternal' is perceptible (and only there perceptible), but even here, in fact, not in the theoretical abstractness of philosophical discourse, but in the metaphysical unity of language, which makes the autonomous movement of the universal perceptible in the singular."[31] In coming to be identified with this vocation thus defined, Hölderlin became, for modern poets experiencing ever more complex forms of estrangement from received languages and traditions, virtually *the* poet in sympathy and rivalry with whom it was necessary to define themselves.

But even for these poets, as for Hölderlin himself, behind Hölderlin there stands a still more immutable figure, that of Goethe. We have said that Goethe alone seems simply to overwhelm questions of tradition and authority with his own confident inventiveness. He does not deign to revise or alter the traditional sources he uses, but boldly appropriates them as raw materials. (Trakl does the same thing, largely to escape the futility of the kinds of revision and alteration that Goethe had merely disdained.) Novalis's effort to complement Goethe, while revealing the place of death within Goethe's organic world, inaugurates the tradition of poetic revision that is always entailed in the meaning of descent for each poet in turn. As we have seen, in an important sense Novalis proves to have been unable to revise Goethe at all, and in this too he sets a precedent that will never vary. Each poet in turn finds Goethe in his or her path and simply turns aside, like Novalis converting the failure to revise Goethe into a criticism or negation of nature itself— having discovered, to paraphrase Pope, that nature and Goethe are the same. What this means is that for all the talk of *Sehnsucht nach dem Unendlichen*, the German Romantic tradition since Goethe has never produced an unabashedly transcendental voice.[32]

Hölderlin's complex derivation from and revision of Goethe is exemplary for modern poets, so much so that he rather than Goethe becomes the chief ancestral rival of Rilke and Trakl. What Hölderlin does is to represent his attitude toward the past and toward progenitors mythologically, dividing the legacy of the past into sky and earth, father and mother, Jupiter and Saturn, Christian and Greek, Goethe as patriarch-sage and Goethe as child of nature, with the revisionary purpose of suggesting that all these pairings are divided against themselves, leaving Hölderlin the task of reuniting them— without denying either their priority or their irrecoverable purity of expression—into a poetic *Logos*, a single streaming word that will carry culture into the future. If the first two poets to whom I now turn both find Goethe in their path, the first deflecting his rivalry onto the inversion of Goethe by Novalis and the second deflecting her rivalry onto a series of maternal and sororal figures, what the second two encounter and attempt to revise is Hölderlin's definitive division of Goethe's legacy into two parts, the idea of authority as a return to wellsprings and the idea of tradition as the Olympian serenity of the unalterable.

Chapter Two
The Poetry of
Transgression:
Eichendorff's
Venus and the
Voices in the Ground

*Advancement of meaning occurs only in
the sphere of the projections of desire, of
the derivatives of the unconscious, of
the revivals of archaism. We nourish
our least carnal symbols with desires
that have been checked, deviated,
transformed. We represent our ideals
with images issuing from cleansed
desire.*
—Paul Ricoeur, *Freud and Philosophy*

In the late 1950s, Adorno reclaimed Eichendorff for contemporary criticism.[1] His solicitude was necessary because Eichendorff's
poetry had long been mistaken for simple nature poetry, and
because his undeservedly narrow reputation as the poet of "der
deutsche Wald," which had made him popular among conservatives
from the beginning, had been celebrated by Nazi Germany.[2] But the
Romantics in general had come to have a bad name, and Adorno no
doubt believed that if he was to rescue Eichendorff he would have to
separate him from the mainstream of German Romanticism. To this
end, Adorno argued that Eichendorff turns against the hegemony of
the perceiving subject in earlier Romantics such as Novalis; he
speaks of Eichendorff's "anti-subjectivism," of his "stummen Ein-
spruch gegen das dichterische Subjekt," his "Absage ans Herrs-
chaftliche."[3] But Adorno's rehabilitation of Eichendorff, while
admirable in intention, was almost certainly based upon an unten-
able premise. Eichendorff's Romantic inwardness cannot be wished
away. Although he claims rhetorically to transform the subjective
nature of the Romantic quest from exploration of the self into a
heavenward flight, from inward and downward to upward ("nach
Hause" or heavenward) and outward (toward "das ewige Meer" or
Eternity), the Romantic "descent" nevertheless remains the source of
his poetic creativity. Where Eichendorff thinks to celebrate release
from subjectivity through the conversion of the "underworld" into

safer, more conventionalized regions or topoi, he actually celebrates the enchantment and the bondage of the self—bondage to personal memory, to erotic drives, and to a literary past which he is at pains to repudiate. It is my intention to delineate the nature of Eichendorff's underworld, to explain both the enchantment and the fear reflected in his struggle for freedom from the underworld "voices," "die Stimmen im Grund," which haunt and inspire him.

Although Eichendorff's poetry was written over a period of more than forty years, his oeuvre is remarkably unified: it's severely limited stock of recurrent images, descriptions, and poetic situations has often caused critics to speak of his *Urlandschaft*, of one originary landscape in his work,[4] consisting of heights, vast expanses, and labyrinthine enclosures—an "inner" landscape in which regions of the mind are either projected onto the world or mythologized.[5] The world of Eichendorff's poetry is an astonishingly sensuous one, composed of fragrances and colors, movement and metamorphosis—and the sound of voices. For Eichendorff this process world of constant change is unstable and eludes control. The voluptuousness of his natural world is a sign of its corruption, its endless participation in a seasonal cycle that is always revealed, in the final analysis, to have a sexual basis.[6]

Eichendorff's lyrics move back and forth among domains that are more often than not tiered along a vertical axis: an upper region to which he devoutly aspires, a middle region which is the fallen world of Nature, and a subterranean region or underworld.[7] To be sure, Eichendorff's geography is not an altogether vertically tending one. Signs of his desire to scramble this schematization are everywhere. For example, the middle region contains its own "underworld" topography: a labyrinthine forest or a garden. And a horizontal plane is implicitly connoted by the contrast between the "here" and the "beyond." But these apparent aberrations are primarily analogues for and elaborations of the vertically tending regions. Thus the horizontal movement beyond landscape to "das ewige Meer" is obviously the equivalent of the soul's heavenward flight. To effect this identification, Eichendorff adapts a favored metaphor for man, the boat at sea, transforming the traditional wings of celestial ascent into sails, as in "Die Brautfahrt" (1816), where "heisser Sehnsucht Flügel" is parallel to "weisse Segel dort gespannt."[8] The mythological quest by boat is often that of the Argonauts, a choice that can perhaps be explained by the presence of Orpheus, the first poet of descent, in Jason's crew.

Indeed, "Sängerfahrt" (1818) suggests the identification of epic hero and poet: "Am Mast steh ich als Sprecher, / Der für euch alle singt" (120). But what remains important concerning the metaphor of the boat, among others, is not so much Eichendorff's conversion of ascent into a forward movement as his attempt to transfer what is subterranean to the surface, to dissociate his Orpheus from the descent into "der Seelen wunderliches Bergwerk," as Rilke would put it in "Orpheus. Eurydike. Hermes." It is Eichendorff's expressed intention, in general, to sublimate the darker aspects of subterranean knowledge; and Adorno supposes this intention to have been carried out. But Eichendorff lingers in the realm of his personal descent with a far more helpless fascination than Adorno supposes.

The garden, the valley, the sea,[9] the forest, "der Grund"—all these "submerged" regions suggest a dangerous interiority, the "Labyrinth der Brust" of "Anklänge" (I, 59). As labyrinth, the underworld comes to the surface in the metaphor of the forest: "endlos der Wälder Labyrinth" ("Nacht," II, 1837; I, 195). The predominant characteristics of the underworld, "die Stimmen im Grund," "das Rauschen der Quellen," or "die Zauberlieder," have their equivalents in the forest's "Waldesrauschen."[10] Almost inevitably, the poet wanders "too deep" into the wood. As we would expect, the middle realm is the safe center from which Eichendorff makes his imaginative forays into other regions. The situation of countless Eichendorff poems involves a view from a hillside, and although this view may carry the eye into the distance, it most often looks downward. The potential menace of this vantage point has often been noticed: "The abrupt, unbroken, and perpendicular view from the edge of a cliff or precipice is repulsive and frightening to the poet: there seems to be something wild and untrammeled about it," says one reader.[11] This "something" is the lure of the depths or abyss—the recurrent "Grund," with its telltale link to the "Abgrund." The "Grund" is at once abyss, bottom, foundation, background, ground, and earth, and all of these implications are continuously at work in the poet's imagination. Plainly the underworld is a metaphor for the inner self, as when the pain of past experience is expressed in language that anticipates Rilke: "Von üppig blühenden Schmerzen / Rauscht eine Wildnis im Grund" ("Abend," 1837; I, 285). The "Grund," then, the fundamental ground that gives way to reveal an underworld, is also the psyche, the inviting subjectivity which, as Adorno rightly argues, is threatening to the poet.

In the poem "Memento," in fact, Eichendorff describes forces latent in the self as "gebundene Bestien," poetically anticipating the attitude both of traditional psychoanalysis and its critics toward the libidinal; here and elsewhere, Eichendorff describes the unconscious as his own characteristic *Grund* or underworld.[12] If Nature in Eichendorff's lyric is an analog for the psyche—and certainly it is—then there must be an integral connection of sexuality and memory (these are represented by unceasing daemonic voices, "die Stimmen im Grund," or the songs of the sirens), with the imagination. Thus it is hardly surprising that the relationship between muse and poet is intensely erotic, or that, as a result of their liaison, the imagination itself is in some sense "fallen." For this reason, Eichendorff is completely at ease with his imagination only when it produces images of poetic flight that are resolutely confined to the service of an orthodox, mediately inspirational religion: this imagery is somewhat varied but reduces easily to the figure of a soul whose only connection to the natural world (and to the fully present bird or butterfly that normally represent it) is synecdochic, a pair of wings, "Schwingen" or "Flügel"—or "Segel." But the poverty of Eichendorff's imagination in portraying the journey to God, the meagerness of his imagery for the transcendent, strongly suggests that his imagination has sources other than the desire for religious redemption that he pronounces to be the motive of his poetry.

Ironically, although Eichendorff considered solipsism the danger to be avoided, he frequently represents the lure of subjectivity as a seduction by an interiorized other. Each interior region features a "temptress": a Loreley; a "Waldweib"; the sirens of the deep; the fair lady of Romance; Diana, who is divested of her virginity and becomes a huntress of men; and, most often, Venus, who in Eichendorff's lyric is more at home under the earth than she is under the waves. Classical mythology can personify human emotions, just as it can personify and hallow Nature, and Eichendorff makes use of mythological figures in both these ways: as metaphors for the erotic drives he clearly fears, and as devices for depicting the sensuousness of the process world in which such drives may be supposed to arise. Venus is Eichendorff's supreme sorceress in part because she is the deity who presides over Nature's cycle; in the poem "Götterdämmerung," Eichendorff's "twilight of the gods," she and the entire pantheon are banished underground, only to emerge again from their "Göttergrab" with every spring.

The lure of descent is increased yet further by the fact that Eichendorff's temptress is also his muse. As he says in "Schlimme Wahl" (1839; I, 57), he who is not burnt to ashes by the fairy's glance has never been a poet. Poetic power is itself ambiguous, poised between the divine and the demonic: "Musst Gott du werden oder teuflisch enden" ("Memento"). In "Frisch auf!" (1836; I, 100–01) the poet is able freely to admit the link between eroticism and his imagination, perhaps because the poem is playful and humorous; in that poem the poet who "sass am Schreibtisch bleich und krumm" (100) is abducted by a forest huntress on horseback who takes him out into a vital natural world which then rejuvenates and inspires him, so that he "wusste der Lieder noch genug" (101). In this vein, one of Eichendorff's earliest romances, "Die Zauberin im Walde" (1808; I, 323–25), portrays the powerful, solipsistic imagination of a child enchanted by his "schwülen Waldesgarten" (324). The sorceress arrives on a crystal boat and presents him with pearls from her necklace. As he sows these pearls in the earth, one by one, full-blown flowers spring up, resembling the eyes of the lady. The fact that this latter image alludes to Novalis's *Heinrich von Ofterdingen*, in which the eyes of the poet's bride are prefigured by the "blaue Blume" of Romanticism, is characteristic of the relationship between Eichendorff and Novalis.[13] Florimund, the speaker of the poem, "remembers" this paradisal state of childhood "innocence," a state in which he could create organically, as God creates, and in which all of his desires are satisfied. Like Keats's "Belle Dame," the lady has spoken to Florimund in a strange language that resonates in his heart; it is presumably also a "natural tongue," or the "Zaubersprache der Natur" that cannot be translated into ordinary discourse. Florimund's "memory" concerns an imaginative state—or, in other terms, an infantile state—which has itself become a "special place," the garden, a region lost to Florimund as an adult:

> "Fortgespült ist nun der Garten
> Und die Blumen all verschwunden,
> Und die Gegend, wo sie standen,
> Hab' ich nimmermehr gefunden."   [324]

["The garden now is washed away / The flowers they have disappeared, / And that place where once they stood, / I have never found again."]

The sorceress who enchains Florimund with her "Perlenkette" comprises a fantasy evoking his latent sexuality. As his days thenceforth dissolve into one another in sleep and dream, this sorceress with her origin in reverie is transformed into a symbol of the enabling imagination; she becomes a muse. And owing to this merger of the erotic and the visionary, the offspring of the union between Florimund and the sorceress, the exotic flowers that spring out of the ground,[14] derive by implication from an unmediated, originary imagination that can create the *things* of nature rather than merely its *songs*. Clearly this is a difficult advantage for the orthodox, repressive poet to consider giving up. The pull of his memory-dream (not unlike a screen memory in the Freudian schema) is a downward pull; as usual in Eichendorff, the garden and its temptress muse are located in the ground, and when Florimund finally succumbs to its lure, when he is pulled "hinunter zu dem Sange" (324), he is symbolically returning to an infantile solipsism which sees the origin of the world in itself. Florimund eventually plunges to his death, seeking the only possible return to a state of unity with Nature—and with the mother, as we shall see later—from which he had fallen away. Although the seasonal cycle is not interrupted by his death, henceforth Nature is disinspirited:

Und es kam der Winter balde,
Und viel' Lenze kamen wieder,
Doch der Vogel in dem Walde
Sang nie mehr die Zauberlieder.   [325]

[And the winter came soon, / And many springs followed, / But the bird in the wood / Sang no more those magic songs.]

It is Mother Nature herself, in a sense, who had been both "die Zauberin im Walde" and the mysterious muse, and who bemoans the disappearance of her former consort, the poet. And the image of the father—which seems arbitrarily introduced at this point—looking down from his mountain into the *Grund* for his son Florimund, suggests that the son's escape from desire into death, or "Ruhe," is perhaps also an escape from a powerful paternal presence:

Hört die Ströme stärker rauschen,
Sah in Nacht des Vaters Burge
Stillerleuchtet ferne stehen,
Alles Leben weit versunken.
Und der Vater schaut' vom Berge,
Schaut' zum dunklen Grunde immer,
Regte sich der Wald so grausig,

Doch den Sohn erblickt' er nimmer.   [324–25]

[Hears the streams rush more loudly, / Saw the father's castle standing / Quietly lit in distant night, / Far and wide all life submerged. / And the father watches from the mountain, / Looks ever down at the dark valley, / Though the forest arise so ghastly, / Yet the son he'd never see.]

Another romance, "Die wunderliche Prinzessin" (ca. 1811; I, 366–71), attempts a description of the "Grund." At first, the setting of this poem is confusing: the opening lines claim that the princess is a sorceress who lives "Weit in einem Walde droben" (366), but once again the forest proves to be a version of the underworld.[15] The princess is "die ewige Braut der Erde," Persephone or spring itself, and her castle lies in the ground; she complains of having been sent "hier herab" (368). Like the sorceress of the wood, she appears to have enthralled and outlasted her wooers; her underworld contains the dead heroes of epic and quest romance, which are at the same time the stone sculptures that so often come alive in Eichendorff. Among these heroes Don Quixote is given prominence (appropriately making a Dulcinea of the princess), in part because he is a literary figure, the latest-born of the heroes:

Eingedenk der Heldentaten
Und der grossen, alten Zeiten,
Bis er ganz von Wahnsinn trunken,
Endlich so nach langem Streiten
Seine Brüder hat gefunden.   [367]

[Mindful of the acts of heroes / And the great and ancient days, / 'Til he, drunk with madness, / At last, after so much combat, / Has found his brothers.]

Doubtless Quixote is also featured because his quest is precisely the solipsistic quest that is most fascinating and inimical to Eichendorff.

These heroes appear in an underworld of a peculiar kind: it is the residence of Persephone, but not of any conventional Hades. Rather, fittingly, the god of the dead here is the poet of the earlier heroic age, and he is intimately connected with *Phantasie*. The princess "hat ein'n wunderlichen Alten, / Der das ganze Haus regieret" (367), but this Elder wears Eichendorff's "Zaubermantel,"[16] "schillernd bunt in allen Farben" (367), and is himself chameleon-like ("Bunt verwirrend alle Zeiten, / Weinet bitterlich und lachet," 368). The function of *Phantasie*, as expressed through this poet-sorcerer, is to transform the heroes of the quest, the newer poets, into "Spielzeug," or mechanical wind-up toys, when they come to the underworld castle to woo the princess; they lack the power of imagination proceeding from the intimacy with nature to which the poetry of the chameleon and color-theorist Goethe attests. The princess, in the meantime, has transformed the earth:

Und, wo ihre Augen gingen:
Quellen aus der Grüne sprangen,
Berg und Wald verzaubert standen,
Tausend Vögel schwirrend sangen.   [369]

[And where her eyes fell, / Streams sprang up out of the greenness, / Mountain and forest stood enchanted, / Birds by the thousands swarming sang.]

Although they come in search of a bride, this is no Orphic foray into the underworld on the part of the younger generation of poets, for instead of gaining power over the underworld by means of the imagination and of song, they are themselves trivialized by an imaginative force that transcends their will. The power of "der Alte" to degrade the poets is not unlike that of Circe to transform men into swine, yet these poets, unlike Florimund, are ultimately capable of withstanding spring and *Phantasie*. They are wind-up toys only until their Reason triumphs over Imagination ("Bis sie endlich alle müde / Wieder kommen zum Verstande," 371), which has literally worn them out.

But this triumph is to be understood as a retreat, for none of the younger poets has succeeded in liberating the princess from her bondage to "der Alte," or to the seasonal cycle that equally enslaves her. To put this in another way, the younger generation of poets is as yet unable to transfigure Nature, either to release it from the seasonal cycle, or to claim it as their own poetic territory by wresting it from the grasp of "der Alte," Goethe. This identification is virtually confirmed by a poem that Eichendorff wrote on the occasion of Goethe's birthday in 1831, entitled "Der alte Held." In the first stanza Goethe is made to speak as follows:

"Ich habe gewacht und gesungen,
Da die Welt noch stumm lag und bleich,
Ich habe den Bann bezwungen,
Der die schöne Braut hielt umschlungen,
Ich habe erobert das Reich."   [I, 92–93]

["I was vigilant and I sang, / When the world still lay silent and pale, /

I broke the spell, / That held the beautiful bride entrapped, / I have conquered the realm."}

It is Goethe's poetry, the younger poet ruefully concedes, that releases nature into life and language.

"Die wunderliche Prinzessin" is discussed further below, but the emphasis here is on the paradigmatic nature of the poetic situation described in these two romances. Both poems feature a descent into an originary place which is the proper abode of generative Nature, of all natural forces. These places are versions of *der Grund*—abyss and ground—and they are threatening because they are connected with death, as in "Die Zauberin im Walde," or with degradation or trivialization, as in "Die wunderliche Prinzessin." And yet they are clearly also the places from which creativity must derive; although neither Florimund nor the younger generation of poets (read: the Romantics) succeeds in creating poetry here, their quest is well motivated and even in failure exemplifies the quest for inspiration. But "inspiration" and the creative act are evoked in Eichendorff by means of sexual metaphors, and in the situation of both our poems they are connected with regression. Florimund is committed to his "memory" of an erotic childhood idyll, a time in which he was erotically at one with Mother Nature. The only hope of reunion with this Mother for Florimund is through death, which is at the same time—in the imagination—an evasion of the powerful father connected with the potent symbols of castle and mountaintop.

In the metaphors of "Die wunderliche Prinzessin," the younger poets are reduced to childhood—more specifically to the mechanical toys of childhood—when they undertake a quest to separate generative Nature from her mate, "der Alte," and from their own poetic fathers. In other words, they still lack the power to claim Nature as their own poetic domain, and this implies, in Romantic terms, that they are as yet unable to transfigure it and release it into a new Golden Age of poesy. One minor consequence of the position taken by Eichendorff in this poem is that the "Vermählung der Jahreszeiten" in Novalis's *Heinrich von Ofterdingen* is by implication perceived to have been an unsuccessful solution to this poetic problem; what this means for Eichendorff's own poetic enterprise will be taken up later. The following section describes the connection between the daemonic forces and the maternal presence in order to develop a sharper image of the way Eichendorff renders his imaginative processes poetically.

II

"Das wunderbare Sehnen dem
Abgrund zu."
—Hölderlin, *"Stimme des Volks"*

In one of its aspects, the underworld is the place of the *"versunk'ne{n}*
schöne[n] Tage[n]"* ("Nachtzauber," 1864; I, 228; italics mine),
housing memories of the idealized personal past ("die alte, schöne
Zeit" is a refrain throughout Eichendorff); but this is a past that lies
buried as Eichendorff's dead father lies buried in his grave in the old
garden in Lubowitz ("Heimweh. An meinen Bruder," 1837; I, 95).
In Eichendorff's poetry the garden, associated as it is with the "dark
backward and abysm of time" in childhood, is most often a region
into which one descends: it is located in a valley or a hollow or in no
region at all, and it comprises a most important variant of the
underworld or *Grund*. The significance of "der alte Garten" has long
been a favorite topic of Eichendorff criticism,[17] being a recurrent
image that remains substantially the same, whether it is situated in
prerevolutionary France or in ancient Rome, in the earliest poetry or
the later novellas.[18] The resonance of this image complex derives
from its two-fold association in the poet's imagination with personal
and with poetic origins. It is, quite simply, *the* locus of the imagination for Eichendorff.

A passage from Eichendorff's sketches for his memoirs, written in
the years 1839 and 1840 and recounting an experience of early
childhood, describes his first imaginative encounter with the muse in
the garden at Lubowitz. The child's reaction to this muse "die
lächelnd vorüberging, Garten und Täler beleuchtend," is to fall
asleep: "ich war ihr noch zu kindisch. . . und ich schlummerte ein,
träumend von künftigen Liedern." ("who smiled in passing, illuminating the garden and valleys. . . I was till too childlike for her . . .
and I fell asleep, dreaming of songs to come").[19] Another, more
frequently cited passage recounts a later experience—at puberty—
from which the poet's creativity might plausibly have sprung, and
could therefore be, in Eichendorff's imaginative reconstruction, the
myth of his election to poethood:

Da in diesem Toster Ziergarten gehe ich einmal als Kind allein in der
Sommer-Mittagsschwüle, alles wie verzaubert und versteinert, die Sta-
tuen, seltsame Beete und Grotten; da, bei einer Biegung, sah ich eine

prächtige Fee eingeschlummert über der Zither—es war wieder die Muse—ich schauerte. . . .Aber ich konnte nicht schlafen die Nacht, das Fenster stand offen, es ging die ganze Nacht ein Singen durch den Garten: Ein Lied, das ich nimmer vergesse, alt nun bin ich geworden, doch—so alt ich bin, es erwacht noch oft, als rief es mich in Mondschein-Nächten und senkt mich in Wehmut![20]

[There in the ornamental garden at Tost as a child I was walking alone in the enchanted noonday heat. All seemed enchanted, petrified—the statues, strange flower beds and grottos. There at a curve in the path I saw a magnificent fairy asleep over a zither—it was the muse again—I shuddered. . . . But I couldn't sleep that night, the window stood open, the whole night singing penetrated the garden: A song, that I'll never forget, I've grown old, but it still awakens often, as though it calls me in moonlit nights and plunges me into melancholy!]

In the first episode, the muse is benign, and promotes the child's entry into the self-contained, hermetic region of sleep and dream which is a prelude to creativity, but in this second confrontation the muse, in the garden at Tost, provokes awe and fear with her night-time song. This time it is the muse, not the boy, who sleeps in the enchanting and enchanted garden, which is already a metaphorical landscape of "Mittagsschwüle." (This experience finds its poetic embodiment in "Der alte Garten.") The sleeping muse is a reminder that poesy not only lies dormant in the realm of the garden but also in the world of dream. This partially explains why the boy, frightened by the muse—that is, by her invitation to sexual and imaginative awakening—cannot sleep at night; by remaining conscious he can resist the dream, the muse, and his own desires.

This "memory," recorded so many years later, is most probably a screen memory that masks yet more overtly erotic daydreams, as sexual and imaginative awakening are implicitly merged in Eichendorff's garden encounters. Indeed, the nighttime song accounted for by this narrative reconstruction is Eichendorff's "uraltes Lied," or, in the language of our century, "love's old sweet song." What is evoked by the old garden is not only the past but also, quite clearly, "der alte Garten" of paradise, which in Eichendorff is usually a place that is already fallen; it is the "Garten der Sünde," as Oskar Seidlin calls it.[21] The more poetry is connected with the libido, the more the ambiguity of the interior submerged region intensifies, needless to say; and thus the image of the garden is often coupled with the theme of man's entrapment by a state of imagination proceeding from desire. In "Nachtzauber," for example, in which the garden lies in a valley, the plant world is seductive and quite obviously fallen:

> Aus der Knospe, halb erschlossen,
> Junge Glieder blühend sprossen,
> Weisse Arme, roter Mund.   [I, 228]
>
> [Out of the bud, half unfurled, / Blossoming young limbs sprout up, /
> White arms, red mouth.]

These are Eichendorff's *fleurs du mal*, as it were, comprising a fallen revision of Novalis's "blaue Blume." There is usually a female presence in the garden—a maternal figure, the garden being Eichendorff's poetic representation of what Freud calls the primal scene. The garden usually contains a fountain at its center which is, in Eichendorff's myth of origin, the maternal source of both sustenance and inspiration. Related to the Arethusan spring, it is embodied in the many hidden "Quellen" in his poetic topography, and is related, as we shall see, to the "stille Seen."

Hermann Kunisch has most concerned himself with Eichendorff's problematic reflections on his "Quellen", and considers the poet's two basic experiences ("Grunderfahrungen") to have been his deep and painful attachment to his brother and his "Hingezogensein zur Heimat."[22] Joseph and his brother Wilhelm were virtually inseparable until 1813; Joseph's childhood journal in fact purports to be the work and possession of both brothers, "die ein Herz und eine Seele waren."[23] In two letters to Joseph written in 1814, Wilhelm expresses the same sense of danger and threatening presence in connection with Lubowitz that Joseph articulates in his recollection of the Tost garden—and, on this occasion, of the Lubowitz garden as well. Wilhelm writes: "The description of Lubowitz' afternoon languor in your letter rings so true, that it frightens me in the inner depths of my being."[24] And, more expansively: "Are you perhaps already in Lubowitz, staring from the barren heights down into the blue air that in our home is inhabited by dangerous spirits? For it entices and pulls the thoughts out into the desolate emptiness, until they are torn in endless confusion and one collapses weakly as though in a fever." We can assume that it is not the realism of Joseph's description that frighten his brother "im innersten," and we wonder what motivates the embarrassed perplexity, the emotional turmoil, that has its climax in collapse. Some of the poems that Eichendorff dedicated to his brother shed light on the nature of their mutual fascination with this place. Interesting too in this context is Kunisch's observation that "It belongs to Eichendorff's peculiarity that singing about the dangers of the depths occurs particularly in those poems that are connected with Lubowitz and his brother."[25]

"Die Heimat. An meinen Bruder" (I, 79) contains much that is already familiar to us: the castle stands elevated above an "Abgrund," the sound of a horn entices ("lockt"), and the wood "rauscht verwirrend" out of the depths.[26] It is in the depths that the unspeakable—or unmentionable—pain ("unnennbar Weh") sleeps and must not be awakened. From this quintessential Eichendorff moment in the first stanza the poem unfolds, in the second stanza, to encompass the garden moment, complete with a girl who awakens a stream of magical sounds ("Strom von Zauberklängen"). Once more there is a conflation of sex and imagination, and the "Zauberklänge" sound as though a now-fallen Nature were singing of the idealized past, the "alte, schöne Zeit." This second stanza, unlike the first, contains no overtly threatening images, but the final stanza takes a negative turn and reveals that "das geheime Singen," which is associated with the female figure of the poem—as the sketch for the memoirs shows—is what will bring about the brothers' ruin. The song, the "Strom von Zauberklängen," had been *awakened* by the girl, and it is therefore connected also to the "unnennbar Weh" that the poet is so reluctant to awaken. This "unspeakable," perhaps "unmentionable" pain is the awareness of precocious sexuality, its object forbidden, that is imperfectly repressed in the poet's recollection of the childhood garden.[27]

Seidlin tells us that "Die Heimat" was later edited by Eichendorff, or possibly by the poet's son Hermann.[28] A word in the last stanza was changed to read, "Wohin du auch in wilder *Lust* magst dringen, / Du findest nirgends Ruh," instead of "wilder *Flucht*" (italics mine); and the last two lines of that stanza were rewritten as follows: "Ach, dieses Bannes zauberischen Ringen / Entfliehn wir nimmer, ich und du!" The original lines were stronger: "In dieses Sees wunderbaren Ringen / Gehn wir doch unter, ich und du!" These revisions force upon us the issue of the brothers' doom in relation to the "wunderbaren Ringen" of the lake. Seidlin's comment about the reworking of the poem—"it almost appears suggestive, that such a central Eichendorff poem is ambivently transmitted"[29]—points to the taboo nature of the mystery that enshrouds the garden and *Heimat*. As there is no lake in Lubowitz,[30] the special significance of the rings in the water cannot be glossed over. In other poems their meaning becomes unmistakable.

The mysterious song, the "Zauberklänge" of "Die Heimat," is featured in "Heimweh. An meinen Bruder" as well, although here it is attributed to the garden itself—that is, to Nature directly. The magic spell or "Bann" of the revised version of "Die Heimat," though a common image in Eichendorff, may have been taken from this poem, in which Nature is said to be under a "Zauberbann." On the whole, in contrast with "Die Heimat," this poem expresses more conventional feelings of homesickness in an unvarying tone of gentle melancholy. Although it omits the female figure, the poem contains the seminal image of nighttime singing in the garden. Here the brothers are bound together not by a curse or a mysterious fate, but simply by their shared past: "so fremd sind die andern" (I, 95). The poet exhorts his brother to join him in a pilgrimage into the past, which in effect, in this poem, is a pilgrimage to the father's grave. At the grave they will kneel to the sound of the old "Zauberlied." The garden as underworld is the place of ominous song, of "Rauschen" and of the "Stimmen." Some of these voices emanate from the dead. As "Heimweh. An meinen Bruder" implies, the garden of childhood which fascinates the poet gains its power in part from the presence of the dead father in the ground. Thus the ground is once more the place of origin—and also the place of return, or death; it is the origin of "voice," which is to be understood, of course, as poetry itself, and that voice seems to be enabled by the presence, once more, of nature and an old man.

The last of the poems supposedly written at this time, Number Six of "Nachklänge," begins with the situation of the garden, and evokes the ruined castle and the dead past in the form of the dead loved ones. Like "Heimweh," this poem mourns the brothers' separation and the fact that the castle has new inhabitants.[31] But here, too, the wood "rauscht im Grunde" and its rushing attests to the brothers' shared youth; the poem ends on a more authentic note than that on which it begins, as it redefines "das Rauschen," or "das alte Lied":

Bald mächtiger und bald leise
In jeder guten Stund'
Geht diese Waldesweise
Mir durch der Seele Grund.

Und stamml' ich auch nur bange,
Ich sing es, weil ich muss,
Du hörst doch in dem Klange
Den alten Heimatsgruss.

{I, 247}

[Now more powerfully, now softly / At every available hour / This forest melody / Penetrates to the depths of my soul. // And though I stammer anxiously, / I sing it, because I must, / Still you hear in the sounds / The old greeting from home.]

Shaken "durch der Seele Grund," the poet is compelled nevertheless to sing the "Waldesweise": "ich sing es, weil ich *muss*." The forest song, "das alte Lied," and his own are identical, and it is implied that his poetry is both obsessive and therapeutic. But this confessional moment is deprived of its force by the final trivializing turn in which he calls his poem a "Heimatsgruss."

The last of the Wilhelm poems to be discussed, and in many ways the most interesting, "Nachruf an meinen Bruder," opens rhetorically with the exclamation "Ach, dass wir schliefen!" The desire that the "unnennbar Weh" not be awakened in "Die Heimat" becomes the desire *for* death in this *Totenopfer.*[32] Generally speaking, this *earlier* poem seems a fulfillment of the threats that are edited out of "Die Heimat." Here the voices in the ground are those of the "blühenden Tiefen," of generative Nature, "die Ströme, die Auen," which seem to be saying that the poet's brother is dead (I, 254). In this case, the poet looks into the *Grund* and sees not his origin—poetic or otherwise—but his brother's end.[33] The voices of Nature express empathy with the brother—" 'ach, dass wir auch schliefen' " (I, 254)—but "der Abend" makes mock of the poet by claiming that he lacks the poetic power to transform the experience of his brother's (imagined) death, and thus in part to transform the voices in the depths, into a heavenward poetic flight:

"Hast doch keine Schwingen,
Durch Wolken zu dringen!
Musst immerfort schauen
Die Ströme, die Auen—
Die werden dir singen
Von *ihm* Tag und Nacht,
Mit Wahnsinnesmacht
Die Seele umschlingen."   [I, 254]

["You don't have any wings, / To penetrate the clouds after all! / You must constantly look at / The streams, the meadows— // Those will sing to you / Of him day and night, / Will entwine your soul / With the power of madness."]

This is a problem that, as it turns out, Eichendorff is unable to solve poetically. His ultimate recovery and conversion of the voices and the upward-tending direction of his song are conventionally effected by a studied turning toward religious orthodoxy ("Der Herr wird dich führen," I, 256) which does not at all resolve the presence of the voices, but simply denies them. This tellingly arbitrary turning from the depths to the heights is a common pattern in Eichendorff's poetry, and it is rarely convincing because it is accompanied by a diminution of poetic power made evident by his reversion to a conventional, uninspired imagery.[34] Of course, the other means of coming to terms with the oracular *Grund*, that of being reunited with the voices in the ground by death—an alternative which the poet here imagines his brother to have taken—remains open. This is the course taken by "der irre Spielmann" in Eichendorff's poetry, the figure whose desire to silence the voices becomes a death-wish culminating in suicide ("Der irre Spielmann," 1837, I, 51–52). This death-wish, which is at the core of "Die Heimat," is imagined by Eichendorff to have overcome his brother in "Nachruf," where he portrays himself as having resisted its pressure. In this latter poem and elsewhere (and here we can begin to explain the significance of Eichendorff's emphasis on the fraternal), the brother is presented as a double or alter ego, and thus his death displaces and helps to repress the poet's wish for his own. It is the aim of the death-wish to restore the past, but as a recent critic has argued, commenting on Freud, "the path backward is blocked by the resistances that maintain the repressions, . . . [T]his blockage of the past suggests that the desired and unattainable 'earlier' state might be the same as the Oedipal desires."[35] For himself, the poet has chosen a version of the death-wish that is acceptable and that connects him with a future rather than a past: the teleological death-wish of Christianity.

The lure of the lake's "magischen Ringen," an image often found in connection with Venus in Eichendorff, is the attraction of the dark, feminine center, the imagined aspect of death that represents a return to the primordial sexual unity of earliest childhood memories. The desire for oblivion is never separate from the desired return to the point of departure. Kunisch perceives this connection: "This longing for the past is not only a search for satisfaction but the wish to extinguish, to perish"["unterzugehen"]. Or again: "It is not only homesickness that is expressed in all of these documents, the songs addressed to Lubowitz and to the brother . . . but a sense of existence that experiences the disintegration of the personality, of the ultimately personal, in the powers of the origin."[36] Eichendorff's fascination with the "magischen Ringen," and the accompanying desire for oblivion and dissolution in their midst, carry over to the structure of "Nachruf an meinen Bruder," a chain of images that causes the reader, too, to circle around a mysterious center. "Die Ströme, die Auen" which sing in the first stanza dissolve into "der Abend" in the third; "der Abend," at that point is first said to sing like the sirens, then in fact takes on their metaphorical characteristics, and finally *becomes* the sirens itself:

> So singt, wie Sirenen,
> Von hellblauen, schönen
> Vergangenen Zeiten,
> Der Abend vom weiten
> Versinkt dann in Tönen
> Erst Busen, dann Mund
> Im blühenden Grund.
> O schweiget Sirenen!   [I, 255]

[So sings, like the sirens, / Of light-blue, beautiful / Days gone by, / The evening distantly / Submerges then in tones / First breast, then mouth / In the blooming abyss. / O be silent, sirens!]

The syntax of this stanza allows the easy dissolution of one image into another; the ambiguity of the referent continues into the next stanza, for when the poet pleads, "O wecket nicht wieder," he is referring either to the sirens or to the original "singers," "die Ströme, die Auen," and not to "der Abend." But what is the sirens' song— supposing that it is theirs—likely to awaken other than the "zaubrische Lieder," which lie dreaming over the fields and trees? And is there really any difference between the sirens' song—we recall its close association with the evening—and the "zaubrische Lieder" that lurk in the rest of the landscape? The strategy of the poet in these stanzas is to obscure the source of voice. The voices come to him from all sides, remarkably like echoes from a central source; but this central source is finally unidentifiable: it is the voice at the bottom of the lake from whence the "magische Ringe" issue:

> Du kanntest die Wellen
> Des Sees, sie schwellen
> In magischen Ringen.
> Ein wehmütig Singen
> Tief unter den Quellen
> Im Schlummer dort hält

Verzaubert die Welt.   [I, 255]

[You knew the waves / Of the lake, they swell / In magical rings. / A melancholy singing / Deep under the sources / In a slumber holds there / Enchanted the world.]

In one sense, the magical rings represent the song that travels outward from its source; with reference to the imagined death of the brother, they are also the waves which proceed from the spot where he has drowned, and thus a bond with the brother forged by song. "Nachruf an meinen Bruder," then, is not so much an abstractly expressed wish for reunion with the brother in death—although this feeling is to some extent a mask of which the poet willingly makes use—as an imagined act of suicide. This reading of the poem would connect Wilhelm closely with the many instances of the "dark brother" (a form of the Romantic double) that occur in Eichendorff's oeuvre, the most notable of these being the figure of Rudolf in *Ahnung und Gegenwart*.

"Nachruf an meinen Bruder" was written around the time of the letters from Wilhelm that express his troubled feelings about Lubowitz; and the evasiveness of this poem deepens the mysterious obscurity of the bond that ties Eichendorff to "die vergangenen alten Zeiten" and to Lubowitz. As the narrator says in *Ahnung und Gegenwart*: "Denn die Erinnerungen an die Kindheit sind desto *empfindlicher und verschämter*, je *tiefer und unverständlicher* sie werden." (II, 54; italics mine). It seems clear that in his life Eichendorff suffered from none of the neuroses associated with mother-fixation: he married early and seems to have led a remarkably happy life as husband and father. But I would still suggest that as a poet Eichendorff derives his power, and, indeed, much of his imagery, from an obsession with his origin that derives from unresolved Oedipal feelings toward his mother and, by extension, toward the setting of Lubowitz. It is natural that Lubowitz should be associated with his childhood, since it was the family residence, but it is also understandable that there be a particular tie between Lubowitz and the mother, because it was she who brought the estate into the Eichendorff family, and it was sold when she died. It has been pointed out that the Romantic *Sehnsucht in die Ferne*, which is particularly strong in Eichendorff, is at bottom a passionate attachment to one's *Heimat*. As one critic has put it: "That which rises resplendent in the distance, simultaneously points back to the primordial home of man." This same critic recognizes a connection between this yearning and the attachment to the mother.[37] It is, too, a displacement of a temporal fixation (with the past) into geographical terms (the distance); and it is, in Schiller's terms evoking the temporal and the spatial together, the Sentimental longing for the condition of Naivety, or the state of at-oneness with Nature. In *Das Marmorbild*—to instance other Oedipal moments in Eichendorff— the statue of Venus simultaneously holds a sexual fascination for Florio and is emblematic of birth and origination. And the poem "Frau Venus" presents Mother Earth in a double aspect as "die schöne Mutter" and as the springtime bride in bridal array: "Die schöne Mutter grüssen tausend Lieder, / Sie wieder jung, im Brautkranz süss zu sehen" (I, 225).

Eichendorff's commentators have a natural reluctance to "psychologize," and while Kunisch, for example, notes the peculiar emphasis the brother and *die Heimat* receive in Eichendorff's work and even notes their association with "die Tiefe"—and is himself interested enough in the subject to have devoted several articles to it—he is unwilling for the most part to explain how this image cluster comes to be. And Kunisch, indeed, is less evasive than most. One critic speaks of the mythological significance of Eichendorff's "uralte Erinnerungen," and even suggests that 'these ancient memories,' which ascend from the chthonic depths, point to a connectedness with a perpetually self-renewing Mother Earth, who in Eichendorff has the features of a beloved," but ventures no farther.[38] Even an essay that overtly concerns itself with matters of a Freudian nature, such as Lothar Pikulik's "Die Mythisierung des Geschlechtstriebes in Eichendorffs *Marmorbild*,"[39] avoids drawing conclusions about its findings. The voices of the critics encircle this taboo area much as the voices of nature encircle, yet point to, the voice in the magical center of "Nachruf."

It seems hardly necessary to point out that Eichendorff's psychic drama stands before us in the array of a personal mythology. The ambivalence of the poet's—and his brother's—feelings about their origin is explained, from a Freudian perspective, by the fact that the attachment to the mother, which is pleasurable to the infant, becomes repulsive to the adult male, whose repressions have converted this pleasure into horror. Even so, *Wilhelm* Eichendorff is able to write a romance in which a newly-wed man leaves his bride for a statue of Venus at the water's edge; speaking of the "Zauberquellen" that have lured him from his bride, the young man says: "Und noch keinem ist's gelungen, / Ihren Ursprung zu belauern."[40] For Joseph, too, Venus in all her variants—Mother Earth, generative Nature—is the principal object of Oedipal feelings. *Das Marmorbild*, whose centrality in Eichendorff's oeuvre as a whole has been hitherto remarked,[41] contains Eichendorff's most exhaustive treatment of the Venus figure. And it is in this novella, fittingly, that the garden finds its most frightening form.

The "dark knight" Donati begins to gain an influence over Florio, the young poet and central character of *Das Marmorbild*, by recalling to him with unaccountable accuracy the events of his childhood: "Auch war er so genau bekannt mit der Gegend seiner Heimat, dem Garten und jedem heimischen Platz, der Florio herzlich lieb war aus alten Zeiten" (II, 314). It is Donati who leads Florio to the garden of earthly delights which is also the garden of childhood. When Florio first sees the Venus statue that so fascinates him, it is with the feeling that he has known her from the time of his earliest youth: "denn ihm kam jenes Bild wie eine langgesuchte, nun plötzlich erkannte Geliebte vor, wie eine Wunderblume, aus der Frühlings-dämmerung und träumerischen Stille seiner frühesten Jugend heraufgewachsen" (II, 318). Florio's feeling of resignation, his "Ahnung" or intimation—ironically—of a past state of bliss, is a recurrent motif in Eichendorff. In presenting the encounter between Florio and the statue he seems to recognize, Eichendorff makes use of the Pygmalion theme: as Florio gazes upon the statue, it begins to come alive, and his delusion clearly results from his projection of repressed desire onto the marble statue. Placed at the edge of a pond or *Weiher*, the sculpture reminds Florio of the birth of Venus, her emergence out of the water: "als wäre die Göttin soeben erst aus dem Wasser getaucht" (II, 318). Water being the originary medium at once of life and of its reflection, Florio's preoccupation with the Venus figure at this point in the novella suggests a narcissistic preoccupation with his own origin. This suggestion is reinforced by the narcissism of Venus, who is fascinated by her own image in the pond; and in comparing her to a "Wunderblume," furthermore, Eichendorff alludes not only to the other instances of the "Wunderblume" in his own work (we recall Florimund's garden), but also to the myth of Narcissus, who was transformed into a flower.

The circle motif—"die magischen Ringe"—of "Nachruf an meinen Bruder" again occurs in conjunction with water in *Das Marmorbild*. Swans circle around the reflection of Venus in the pond:

"einige Schwäne beschrieben still ihre einförmigen Kreise um das Bild" (II, 318).[42] Of course the swans primarily suggest interiority and solipsism, being symbols of the imagination; and their circular motion would seem to intensify this connection, especially considering that they encircle an idealized representation, implicitly condemning the statue as an artistic expression that is too far removed from reality. But the swan was also frequently associated with Venus in Classical mythology; and its "song" is an emblem of the common and relevant theme of poetic expression as dying breath. (Eichendorff himself evokes the swan song in his poem "Todeslust," I, 312). Finally, if we remember that the swans are inscribing their circles on the surface of a pond, and that circles themselves are female symbols, it becomes apparent that origination, sexuality, and death have been brought together here with unusual compression. Perhaps the swans not only suggest the Venus statue's preoccupation with her image on the water—in other words, with her birth—or Florio's passion for a "woman" whom he has created at once from a self-projection and from his displaced desire for another, but also constitute, through their connection with the circularity of art, an emblem for Eichendorff's art as it persistently encircles his origin, a center he dare not name because that would mean his (poetic) death. To break through repression would be, ironically, to destroy one's mythology—a fact of which Rilke, as we shall see, was fully aware.

Eichendorff's Venus herself brings death in her train. Donati, one of the "enthralled knights" in her service, is characterized by his deathly pallor, which reminds the company of "der stille Gast" (death) in Fortunato's song. Like the pale knights of Romance in Keats's "La Belle Dame Sans Merci," he seems to have been the victim of a vampire; as Fortunato implies at the conclusion of the novella, Donati is one of the living dead whose curse it is not to be released into death. A dream Florio has shortly before his experience with the statue of Venus connects him in turn with both Donati and the swan image; he dreams that he is sailing on a moonlit sea in a boat with "swan-colored" sails, evoking the knights of romance, knights who are carried over the water to their death. During this dream excursion Florio is surrounded by sirens whose song fills him with "Wehmut," while his boat begins sinking deeper and deeper into the water's depths.

In one sense, *Das Marmorbild* is a quest romance. At the beginning of the novella Florio is in a condition that might be compared to Parzival's "tumbheit"; indeed, the narrator calls him "den Blöden" (II,309). This is a quest of whose object Florio is not wholly aware. He speaks of his *Sehnsucht* for *die Ferne*, but, as is so often the case in Eichendorff, his quest is only converted into the quest for God after much postponement, and meanwhile pursues the fulfillment of regressive desires. As Florio tells Fortunato ("der christliche Sänger"): "Ich habe jetzt das Reisen erwählt und befinde mich wie aus einem Gefängnis erlöst, alle alten Wünsche und Freuden sind nun auf einmal in die Freiheit gesetzt" (II, 307–08). Like most other quest romances, Florio's includes a descent into an underworld; his entry into the Venus garden, another version of the *Kindheitsgarten*, is presented, characteristically, as a descent into a sunken realm: "Florio betrachtete verwundert Bäume, Brunnen und Blumen, denn es war ihm als sei das alles lange versunken, und über ihm ging der Strom der Tage mit leichten, klaren Wellen, und unten läge nur der Garten gebunden und verzaubert und träumte von dem vergangenen Leben" (II, 321). The proximity of Florio's dream is evident here; in a sense, he has entered the realm of the dead, as the "Strom der Tage" not only evokes the passing of past time, but also alludes to the poet of death, Novalis—to the dream of Heinrich von Ofterdingen in which that wan hero must first drown in order to be united with his Mathilde in death.

This visit to the garden and the palace of Venus is the final stage of Florio's negative quest; it is the scene of seduction and near-consummation, all of which is linked in turn to his attraction to riddles. He had wanted to solve "alle Rätsel, die so schwer auf ihm lasteten" (II, 328), and although their exact nature remains unclear, we can guess what they are with some confidence. In Eichendorff, the riddles that preoccupy men nearly always have to do with the identity of women. His women are veiled, masked, have doubles, or are disguised as boys. Certainly disguises and mysteries are commonplaces of the *Trivialliteratur* of Eichendorff's time, but, after all, Gothic fiction is itself generally understood to be built up around metaphors for the psyche. "Rätsel" in any case are unusually prominent in Eichendorff, for reasons presumably related to the role of sexuality in his poetic cosmos. So great is the dominance of the Western imagination by the riddle of the sphinx that we can suppose possession of the answer to any pressing riddle to involve sexual knowledge, whether transgressive or licit.[43] It is just on the threshold of such knowledge that Eichendorff shies away, rescuing his hero, and perhaps himself, for another order of knowing altogether. When he is about to gain sexual knowledge of Venus, Florio forcefully denies the "Rätsel" by appealing to God, or conscience; and, as though the true object of the quest had all along been its denial (which is, indeed, the object of its positive, religious counterpart), Florio emerges from his ordeal "neugeboren" (II, 346). One critic recognizes that Florio's rejection of the Venus statue marks an advance beyond his former self: "What is really at stake is human development, in particular the crisis which terminates the first phase of life, when the human being is faced with the task of superceding himself in order to make room for a new phase of life."[44] But he does not specify what it is from which one must break off ties, or what defines and determines these phases. Florio has successfully escaped from an infantile stage of sexuality which finds its fulfillment in the mother into a stage at which he has been released from the mother (again, "neugeboren") sufficiently to be united with the young Bianca—to whom, however, he had been attracted because of her "fast noch kindliche Gestalt" (II, 308), and to whom he declares his love while she is in boys' clothing. Evidently, then, the encounter with Venus leaves its mark.

Florio's descent carries him into the unconscious, and his final encounter with Venus, from which Eichendorff turns him away, is no less than an almost-realized sexual union with the mother. The Venus figure in this novella merges with images of narcissism: she is fascinated with her own reflection, first in the pond and later in the mirror at her palace. Florio initially imagines her as a narcissistic "Wunderblume," a flower which is, like the other exotic flowers in Eichendorff's poetry—such as the "Nachtblume"—at least vaguely sexual. Flower imagery surrounds Venus in *Das Marmorbild*; flowers fill her garden, her gowns and veils are flower-bedecked, and more than once she is described as "blühend." And finally, to tighten the link between Oedipal fixation and narcissism, Florio's own name ("floreo," to bloom or blossom—and hence to "develop," but only in the retrospect of a happy ending) shows his intimate connection with the temptress, suggesting perhaps even that she is a self-projection. In falling in love with her, he falls in love at once with a representation of the mother who had loved him in the "schöne, alte Zeit" of infancy and also with that former self who was loved by her.[45]

Again, this Venus is the muse in Eichendorff's garden. She is the woman with the lute:[46] "es war ihm, als hätte er die schöne Lautenspielerin schon lange gekannt und nur in der Zerstreuung des Lebens wieder vergessen und verloren" (II, 323). Later on, this sense of recognition is given another explanation which is, like this one, attached to the theme of art: Florio thinks that he recognizes the Venus figure from one of the paintings he knew in his childhood. These paintings were located in the *Lusthaus* of the garden and had the effect, Florio explains, of filling him with longing for an erotic future; his father, who would often join him in looking at the paintings, would tell stories from his erotic past. Afterward the father would pace up and down the garden in agitation, while the son would assume a Werther-like position in the grass.[47] In bringing to bear the issues of visual art and narrative, Eichendorff has here suggested a myth of creative generation, the son awaiting his turn, which revolves around the figure of Venus in the center. When the Venus figure is most clearly a projection of Florio himself—at the masquerade in which he sees her as Bianca's double—she says to him, speaking as a censor: "forscht nicht nach den Wurzeln im Grunde" (II, 330). It is almost as though Eichendorff recognizes his myth of generation for what it is, a bid for imaginative independence which runs the risk, dependence being unavoidable, of embracing the barren earliness of solipsism.

The two other central characters of *Das Marmorbild*, Donati and Fortunato, are also worth examining in their relation to Florio. Both of them can be associated with Florio's childhood: Donati is able unaccountably to describe places and events from it, and Fortunato "saves" Florio by singing a song he recognizes from his childhood days. Fortunato's song is "eines von jenen ursprünglichen Liedern, die, wie Erinnerungen und Nachklänge aus einer andern heimatlichen Welt, durch das Paradiesgärtlein unserer Kindheit ziehen" (II, 344). We already know how ambiguous Eichendorff's feelings about the "Paradiesgärtlein" are; it is often idealized in his work, but usually a serpent lurks in the grass. Eichendorff does not share the widespread Romantic insistence upon childhood innocence. In fact, it is an earlier song of Fortunato's that has called Florio's "alte Jugendträume" to mind, and although one realizes that Fortunato is allied with the forces of good, one also knows the "alte Jugendträume" to have had dubious origins.

But how have both the "evil" Donati and the "good" Fortunato gained information concerning Florio's childhood? Concerning this question it is interesting to note that Fortunato shows himself to be a master at disguises; at the masquerade he changes his costume often, each time looking "immer neu und immer unbekannt" (II, 329). Donati, on the other hand, who is virtually featureless, is compared with a "Nachtschmetterling"—"wie aus einem phantastischen Traum entflogen" (II, 315). "Donati" means "hingegeben," a devotee, no longer in possession of oneself, and, indeed, he is enthralled by Venus. As befits one who is repeatedly described in connection with death, one of his favorite pursuits is hunting; in other words, Donati is a *Triebwesen*, a creature of the id dominated by the death instinct as well as by sexuality. Fortunato, on the other hand, performs all the functions of the superego. As Florio flees from the palace of Venus, he thinks that on the pond near which the Venus statue had stood he sees Fortunato standing upright in a boat, strumming his guitar. Although Florio assumes that he is seeing a "Blendwerk der Nacht" (II, 339), this vision is clearly a positive counterpart to the dream in which he himself was threatened with drowning in a boat. Fortunato's upright position in the boat evokes a mast, which in Eichendorff frequently represents the cross, and Fortunato can therefore be identified as a Christian singer or poet. As a well-known artist, he functions as a role model for the young Florio, an idealized self.

It is Fortunato who manages to free Florio from his obsession with his origin, but in doing so he deprives Florio of his creative myth. In demythologizing Venus, he denies the imagination—specifically Florio's imagination—any direct access to Nature:

> Florio warf einen Blick nach dem Berge. In einer grossen Einsamkeit lag da altes, verfallenes Gemäuer umher, schöne, halb in die Erde versunkene Säulen und künstlich gehauene Steine, alles von einer üppig blühenden Wildnis grünverschlungener Ranken, Hecken und hohen Unkrauts überdeckt. Ein Weiher befand sich daneben, über dem sich ein zum Teil zertrümmertes Marmorbild erhob, hell vom Morgen angeglüht. Es war offenbar dieselbe Gegend, dieselbe Stelle, wo er den schönen Garten und die Dame gesehen hatte.   [II, 341]

> [Florio cast a glance toward the mountain. Old decaying walls lay scattered about in great desolation, columns half sunk into the earth and artfully hewn stones—everything covered over with a voluptuously blooming wilderness of green entwined vines, hedges, and high weeds. A pond was to be found next to it, above which a partly ruined marble statue rose, brightly illuminated by the morning. It was obviously the same region, the same spot, where he had seen the beautiful garden and the lady.]

It is questionable whether Florio, whose imagination has been deprived of its authentic ground, can continue to be a poet. Considering that his bachelorhood is made to seem an admirable state at the beginning of the novella, it seems likely that in the end he will probably marry the pretty Bianca and relinquish his art for the life of the *Philister*. Of course the Christian poet Fortunato for his part *does* have a lady, but she is the Virgin Mary, the beloved mother of Christ who is the counterpart of Venus.

Freud argues that in infancy the male child's unconscious has already split its mother image into two opposite types, the virginal Madonna and the sensual Jezebel available to everyone. This split is everywhere apparent in Eichendorff's work, and it seems clear that of the two the temptress image is the most poetically productive for him. It is widely agreed that for Eichendorf Venus is associated with vegetative nature,[48] that she plays a part in the natural cycle and in generation. In *Das Marmorbild* she is simply pressed down—and finally repressed—into the earth, from which she struggles to emerge; the ruins at the end of the novella are covered with an "üppig blühende Wildnis." Donati claims that the Venus figure is ubiquitous, "bald da, bald dort" (II, 323); she is Mother Nature herself, taking her form in each man's imagination from that man's mother. As she tells Florio: "Ein jeder glaubt mich schon mal gesehen zu haben, denn mein Bild dämmert und blüht wohl in allen Jugendträumen mit herauf" (II, 338). Eichendorff turns his own distance from the original unity—whose loss he bemoans with such *Wehmut* and such intricacy—to advantage. It is precisely its loss and his attempt to regain it which provide him with a myth for the creative process, and allow him to portray Nature and even to use it as a metaphor for the self. Or, as Leslie Brisman puts it in his *Romantic Origins*, "the imagination is both in search of the origin of things, where natural and literary things come from, and in search of the Nature of originality, what it means to take the self as a source."[49]

There is frequently yet another female presence in Eichendorff's garden: the sphinx.[50] Half monster, half woman, she is the embodiment of the "Rätsel" that we have already found linked to the female. In his preface to *Erlebtes*, Eichendorff depicts his archetypal garden once more. Returning to the ruins of his home, the wanderer comes upon the ominous monster:

Da lag plötzlich, wie in einem Nest von hohem Gras und Unkraut und die Tatzen weit nach mir vorgestreckt, eine riesenhafte Sphinx neben mir, die mich mit ihren steinernen Augen fragend anglotzte. Und in der Tat, das unverhoffte Ungeheuer gab mir ein Rätsel auf, das mich ganz verwirrte."   [II, 1958, 1020]

[Suddenly there lay beside me, as though in a nest of high grass and weeds, with paws outstretched toward me, a gigantic sphinx who stared at me questioningly with her stony eyes. And indeed, the unexpected monster presented me with a riddle (Rätsel) that totally confounded me.]

It is entirely fitting, again, that the "Rätsel" of the garden should be embodied by a female mythological being, a descendent of the sphinx that Oedipus too confronted. The dangerous secret that Eichendorff's sphinx holds is the identity of the muse—the Venus—in the garden. Oedipus destroys the sphinx with his correct solution to her riddle ("Man"). But the hidden meaning of his own answer, that "man" is a sexual being determined by the condition of his limbs, is something that Oedipus may be said to intuit although he is as yet too blind to understand its connection with the riddle of his own life, the final answer to which—that his wife is his mother—destroys him. Similarly, Eichendorff must avoid discovering the solution of the sphinx's "Rätsel," the key to the significance of the garden, which is, in keeping with the ultimate knowledge of Oedipus, that his muse and temptress, the spirit of the childhood garden, is his mother.

And yet Eichendorff must at least intimate the solution, even though it remains forever unexpressed save in the emblem of the sphinx; for it is this intimation that reveals Mother Nature to him in all her sensuality. In one of its aspects, Eichendorff's descent carries him down to the Mothers, or, as Goethe's Mephisto puts it, "Ins Unbetretene / Nicht zu Betretende; ein Weg ans Unerbetene, / Nicht zu Erbittende" (11. 6222–24). But it is also a descent into the grave. In *Oedipus at Colonus*, Oedipus is finally reunited with the Mother in the only natural way: at his death, the ground opens and swallows him up. And so for Eichendorff, the plunge into the lake's "Zauberringe," while it represents a return to the erotic source, also provides the pleasure of a return to the lowest possible form of organization in nothingness.

III

Wird denn nie das Blatt sich wenden
Und das Reich der Alten enden?
—Novalis, *Heinrich von Ofterdingen*

But what of the father in the triangle? It remains to see what part, if any, he plays in Eichendorff's creative myth. One critic suggests that Eichendorff's actual father was the favorite parent of the brothers, that Joseph came into conflict with his mother;[51] and I hasten to point out that in the ensuing discussion the poet's biological father is not the one to which I refer—just as the quintessential mother has been here understood as a transpersonal figure. Owing to his conversion to the orthodox Christian God, a Father who welcomes the son to his eternal home, Eichendorff makes the father prominent everywhere in his work. But references to a paternal figure apart from this religious context are somewhat scarce and indirect. The famous "Mondnacht," in which the soul in the form of a bird "Flog durch die stillen Lande, als flöge sie nach Haus," contains all three members of the Oedipal triangle, albeit in the guise of a pagan fertility myth (I, 306). In the first stanza, Heaven kisses the Earth, who is arrayed in the bridal splendor of her white "Blütenschimmer." The second stanza presents the offspring of this union, the fertile fields in which "die Ahren wogten sacht." Of course this is the description of a moonlit landscape, and its analogical relation to a fertility myth is presented in the realm of metaphor only: "Es war als hätt'." The introduction of the self in the third, concluding stanza of the poem is preceded by the "und" of the first line, which establishes a connection of the naturalized self as a bird with the fertile landscape resulting from the union of paternal sky and maternal earth. What is at stake in this poem is the possibility of the son's—the poet's—transcendence of his origin. This transcendence could be represented by the conversion of the pagan myth into the Christian one, with the replacement of "der Himmel" by the Christian Father, whose heaven is everyone's proper home. But in "Mondnacht" this sort of transcendence does not really take place. The soul's flight over the fertile fields is only compared with, not identified with, the journey to the Christian Heaven—"als flöge sie nach Haus." Half bird, half soul, it lingers halfway between the natural and the spiritual worlds, and its escape from its origin remains hypothetical.

If the reader is tempted to say that what is not clearly escaped in this moon poem is the moonlit landscape of Goethe (see chapter one), there is some confirmation of this notion in a poem we have already glanced at, "Die wunderliche Prinzessin," with its underworld containing both a variant of the mother figure in the princess herself and a father figure resembling Goethe in the form of "der Alte." The relationship between these two is ambiguous, of course, as it must be in order that the "younger poets" may perceive themselves as suitors of the princess, the "bräutlich Ausgeschmückte" (I, 368). The infantilism of the suitors is stressed from the beginning: "An das Tor die Freier kamen / Nun gesprengt, gehüpft, gelaufen" (I, 370), and they soon realize that they have no power over the father figure, that instead they are rendered utterly dependent by him:

> Doch sie fühlen schauernd balde,
> Dass sie ihn nicht können zwingen,
> Selbst zu Spielzeug sind verwandelt,
> Und der Alte spielt mit ihnen.   [I, 370]

> [But soon they feel shudderingly, / That they cannot master him, / They themselves are turned to toys / And the old one plays with them.]

Nor do the "old heroes" of stone acknowledge the brotherhood that the younger poets would like to claim with them; rather the embraces that the poets bestow upon these heroes are the source of their own downfall, crushed beneath the heroes' weight:

> Doch wie diese uralt blicken
> An die Eisenbrust geschlossen,
> Brüderlich die Jungen drücken,
> Fallen die erdrückt zu Boden.   [I, 370]

> [But as these look anciently / Clasped to the breast of iron, / Fraternally embracing the young ones, / These fall to the ground, crushed.]

The younger poets are crushed by the weight of an established literary tradition which they must not embrace wholeheartedly if they are to survive. They are crushed also because they have posed as men of action, as knights and hunters, with the implication that they are themselves heroes; with such assumed identities they have tried to justify their epic descent. In this romance, despite their transgression, Eichendorff allows the poets to withdraw from the underworld, from contention with "der Alte" for the procreative and creative favors of the temptress-mother. He is suggesting, in other words, either that she and her habitat are not the true source of poetic power, or, as is more likely considering his studied characterization of the younger poets, that they are not yet ready for a genuine contest.

The ambivalence that Eichendorff feels toward memory arises in part from what he sometimes presents as a conjunction of childhood innocence, the "unfallen" state, with the threatening figure of the father in the background. Eichendorff often inverts this pattern— without convincingly rejecting it—by appropriating the parable of the prodigal son's return as a secular myth.[52] In the poem "Heimkehr" (1810, I, 129–31), which makes explicit the threat of the fathers in the Oedipal struggle, the prodigal son returns to the family castle only to find it in ruins. Entering the courtyard, he is deeply frightened by figures that appear to be his ancestors returned to life: "Aufrecht sassen meine Ahnen" (I, 130). The most frightening of these is the figure of the father, who stares fixedly at his sword, refusing to speak the word that would release his son from his spell:

Und den Vater unter ihnen
Sah ich sitzen an der Wand,
Streng und steinern seine Mienen,
Doch in tiefster Brust bekannt,
Und in den gefaltnen Händen
Hielt er erst ein blankes Schwert,
Tat die Blicke niemals wenden,
Ewig auf den Stahl gekehrt.

Da rief ich aus tiefsten Schmerzen:
"Vater, sprich ein einzig Wort,
Wälz den Fels von deinem Herzen,
Starre nicht so ewig fort!"
                                                          [I, 131]

[And the father amongst them / I saw sitting against the wall, / Severe and stony his expressions, / But familiar deep in the breast, / And in his folded hands / He held a shining sword, / Never averted his gaze, / Always aimed at the blade. // Then I called with deepest pain: / "Father speak a single word, / Push the boulder from your heart, / Do not stare so steadily!"]

The morning light brings with it the son's realization that what he has seen is merely a collection of broken-down statues: "Steine, wie es lichte worden, / Standen da im Hof zerstreut" (I, 131). But the father's sword symbolically remains upon his grave. In appropriating this sword (" 'Sei denn Hab' und Gut zerstoben / Wenn ich dich, du Schwert, nur hab!' " 131), the son finally finds release from the bondage imposed by the father: "Mir ging hell die Sonne auf" (131).

"Heimkehr" echoes the Venus statue episode of *Das Marmorbild*, but here it is projected guilt and fear of the fathers that animates the stone sculptures. (Ultimately in this poem, though not in "Die wunderliche Prinzessin," their embodiment in stone deprives the ancestors of their power over their descendants.) In "Heimkehr," the authority of the father clearly resides in the phallus, and the son's guilt arises from his knowledge that its possession is what is at issue between them. Expecting on the occasion of his homecoming to be greeted as the prodigal son was greeted, he is at first surprised: "Kommt denn keiner mir entgegen, / Bin ich nicht der Sohn vom Haus?" (I, 129). Because the gate is fastened shut, the son breaks through the lock with his own sword, and the poem indirectly suggests that it is owing to this act of hubris that the castle lies in ruins before him. Discovering the now-broken zither upon which he had played as a child, the son takes it to the place by the window where he had always sat with his mother: "Mutter, bist du auch schon tot?" (I, 130). It is the suggestion of closeness between mother and son—and the connection of mother with muse—that presents the occasion for the son's vision of the threatening fathers from the window.

Like Venus in *Das Marmorbild*, "der Vater ward so bleich" (I, 131); in this Oedipal confrontation, the son has had the upper hand. But another reading of this poem, perpetuating the son's submission, might represent the sword left behind as a mandate on the part of the ancestors that the son take up the sword in order to defend the family on their behalf. Indeed, this interpretation would place "Heimkehr" among the poems in which Eichendorff expresses his nationalistic fervor; it would explain, for instance, why the "Adler" forms a part of the morning landscape (although the eagle, being also a symbol of poetry, does not require this explanation). But nationalism does not adequately account for the atmosphere of terror with which the poem is suffused. If the son is to be seen as the successor to the fathers in this poem, then Eichendorff must be referring to fathers of a different sort. A passage in *Viel Lärmen um*

Nichts, the continuation of *Ahnung und Gegenwart*, sheds light on the nature of such ancestors as these:

> Der Sturm der Zeit, der so viele Sterne verlöscht und neu entzündet, hatte auch den Stammbaum seines alten, berühmten Geschlechtes zerzaust. . . . Aber Unglück gibt einen tiefen Klang in einem tüchtigen Gemüt und hatte ihn frühzeitig durch den tragischen Ernst des Lebens der Poesie zugewendet. *Mit freudigem Schauer fühlte er sich bald einer anderen, wunderbaren Adelskette angehörig*, über welche die Zeit keine Gewalt hat.   [II, 470; italics mine]

> [The storm of the times, which had extinguished and lit so many stars, had also disordered the family tree of his old, well-known race. . . . But misfortune lends deeper tones to a good cast of mind and had early led him through the tragic earnestness of life toward poetry. *With a joyful shudder he soon felt himself to belong to another, wonderful chain of nobility* ("Adelskette"), over which time had no power.]

The appropriation of the sword is also the seizure of the poet's pen, his "Wünschelrute" or "Zauberstab." In *Die Lehrlinge zu Sais*, Novalis connects the process of literary inheritance with the "Zauberstab" of the father as follows: "mir scheinen die Dichter noch bei weitem nicht genug zu übertreiben, nur dunkel den Zauber jener Sprache zu ahnden und mit der Phantasie nur so zu spielen, wie ein Kind mit dem Zauberstabe seines Vaters spielt" (27). Novalis's simile suggests that in his imagination the struggle of the poets with their forefathers has a sexual dimension, anticipating the assertion of Harold Bloom that the precursor is absorbed into the id of his literary descendant. As we shall see, for Eichendorff it is Novalis himself, ultimately displacing Goethe and Schiller, who is foremost among the fathers.

The subterranean ground of the imagination, Eichendorff's *Grund*, combines erotic power with memory and the lure of death. It is also, with all its ambiguous significance, the "hidden region of underground streams"[53] from whence issues "das uralte Lied," or the "Zauberlieder": it is the murmuring "Quellen," or sources—the muse and the literary fathers together—that first draw the poet underground. Also significant is the connection of the "Quellen" with Classical mythology, one that plays a somewhat problematical role in Eichendorff's work. All is untroubled as long as "Die Wunderquelle," so clearly the source of inspiration, is likely to be converted to a safely orthodox "heilige Quelle," as in "Sonette" #4 (ca. 1810, I, 69). Usually, however, the source of inspiration is not redeemed, and we are reminded that a classical source-nymph, Arethusa, at once desirable maiden and underground stream, was a nymph in the train of one of Eichendorff's favorite temptresses, Diana. In the received myth Arethusa forsakes Arcadia in flight from Alpheus, traveling under sea and land to Sicily, thus providing a broad region for various Golden Age locales, all of them belonging to Eichendorff's "schöne, alte Zeiten." The "Quellen" are threatening in part, then, because of their origin in pagan myth and their relation to the pagan literary tradition, of which the epic topos of "descent" into an underworld is, of course, a vestige. In view of Eichendorff's attempt to relegate the pagan gods to their "Göttergrab" in the earth in "Götterdämmerung," the suppression of paganism evidently functions for the poet as an internalization of influence, in this case an attempt to transform the materials of a received tradition. This tradition is not only that of Classical mythology, but also, closer to hand, that of German Classicism as it is reflected in the work of Schiller and Goethe.

In another poem, "Treue" (1837, I, 253), the poet overtly identifies the seat of the emotions and the origin of song with underworld streams and sources; he speaks of "Liederquellen" which course "verwirrend durch die Brust" (253). When we consider that in "Zauberin im Walde" Eichendorff symbolically relegates Novalis's belief (specifically his, as we shall see) in the originary power of the imagination to a garden that is ultimately the place of solipsism and death as well as the home of the threatening "Quellen," we must conclude that Eichendorff's preoccupation with wellsprings definitely touches upon literary sources less remote than pagan myths, however disturbing those in themselves may be. Like his attitude toward the underworld in general, Eichendorff's attitude toward the wellsprings of verse derives from the complexity of the Oedipal triangle.

The wealth of associations that thus accrues to Eichendorff's underworld may help to explain the title of the poem that has long been considered the key to his poetics, "Wünschelrute":

Schläft ein Lied in allen Dingen,
Die da träumen fort und fort,
Und die Welt hebt an zu singen,
Triffst du nur das Zauberwort.   [I, 112]

[There sleeps a song in all things, / That lie dreaming on and on, / And the world begins to sing / If you strike the magic word.]

In German folk tradition the "Wünschelrute," the divining rod, is used by the *Sonntagskind*—in this case the poet—for discovering underground water, sources, or streams. The poet must be inspired, he must have access to Arethusa (the fountain is a maternal symbol in Eichendorff's garden) before he can release Nature into language. In short, he needs "das Zauberwort," and once it is found, the power of verbal magic over the underworld is indeed great; it can name "das Dunkelste" ("An die Dichter," 1815, I, 111), the underworld's and the psyche's darkest depths. In making a case for Eichendorff's "anti-subjectivism," Adorno claims that these darkest depths are those of language itself: "Whether the world sings is determined by the poet's access to blackness, to the darkness of language ["ins Schwarze, ins Sprachdunkel trifft"], as something that already exists for itself"; and again: "Language as the poetic 'means of representation,' as something autonomous, is his divining rod. The self-effacement of the subject serves language."[54] But it seems unlikely that it is language *only* that resides in Eichendorff's underworld or unconscious; language must be sought in order to name the submerged signs that are not themselves linguistic.

The "Wünschelrute," Novalis's poetic "Zauberstab," is presented in the poem of that name as a counterpart of Circe's wand, the token of her sexuality. For Eichendorff the sorceress's exotic spell evokes the spell of the imagination, much as it does in Keats's "La Belle Dame." In Eichendorff's "Der Gefangene" (1812, I, 347–49), to cite another example, the knight is held in thrall by the lady and at the same time by his own interiority, his obsession with his own origin, all of which is represented by the walls of glass that form a crystal palace around him. It is always rhetorically Eichendorff's wish to release Nature and the poet at once from the spell of sexuality and the enchantment of unmediated origination, that is, from the taint of narcissism or incest in inspiration. The voices and the "rushing" of the underworld must be brought into daylight and converted into poetry. The sleeping Neptune, bent over his harp in "Meerestille" (1835, I, 371), and the figure of the sleeping muse in "Der alte Garten" (I, 343), both serve as a reminder that poesy lies dormant in the underworld and, if awakened, must be brought to the surface. Repeatedly the poet aspires to convert the memory of the father and the ambiguous innocence of childhood into images of the divine Father and a renewed innocence guaranteed by the suffering of Christ: in short, he hopes to convert dubious origins into glorious ends. The role of sublimation in this project is the conversion of poetic descent into poetic flight. So too he converts Venus or Mother Nature into the Holy Mother—toward whom, in accordance with literary tradition, the poet's language may remain erotic without implying, any longer, that the maternal muse is also a temptress.[55]

The sublimation of Eichendorff's underworld involves other transformations as well. When, for instance, Eichendorff converts "Waldesrauschen," the rushing forest sounds (and the figurative counterpart of the "Rauschen der Quellen") into "das deutsche Waldesrauschen" ("Rückkehr," 1834, I, 50), or when he converts the tree into the "deutsche Sangesbaum" ("Treue," ca. 1814, I, 94), he is recalling Klopstock.[56] Eichendorff repeatedly rehabilitates the labyrinthine, forested density of his underworld as a symbol of national poetry, which he upholds, together with the Christian Bible, against "die alten Wundergeschichten," the myths of Greece and Italy. In so doing, he recalls Klopstock's "Der Hügel und der Hain," in which the Teutonic bard in his grove is given the last word in his debate with "Poet" and "Dichter."[57] In identifying himself with some definite part of the world, in accepting a national identity, the poet keeps the subjective at bay without undue loss of inspiration; he makes his inner genius become the spirit of the place. It is not surprising, in any case, that one of the "Quellen," one of the voices in the ground that must be transformed, is that of Klopstock, an imitator of Milton who became the vocational model for the religious poet in Germany. It is equally unsurprising, however, that the Catholic Eichendorff would not accept *this* aspect of the Protestant Klopstock's influence, and that he chose to emulate Klopstock only as a national poet, to convert Klopstock's grove (*Hain*) into his own *Wald*.

The voice that is of the greatest significance for Eichendorff, in large part because it anticipates his own conflict with Goethe, is undoubtedly that of Novalis.[58] When Eichendorff began work on his numerous literary-historical essays in the 1830s, he was not only engaging in literary criticism from the standpoint of one whose major literary work was completed, he was also indirectly attempting to place that work in a canon, to describe the tradition in such a way that his own work could be said to be its culmination. Although one of his last works, *Geschichte der poetischen Literatur Deutschlands* (1857) would seem to be encyclopedic in intention, half of it is in fact devoted to what Eichendorff calls "die neuere Romantik."[59] Romanticism is not only the focus of Eichendorff's literary history, it is the goal, as it had been also of "Die geistliche Poesie Deutschlands" (1847) and "Zur Geschichte der neueren romantischen Poesie in Deutschland" (1846–47). As we might expect, first and foremost among the Romantic poets under discussion in the *Geschichte* is Novalis.[60] As one who had attempted the poetic mediation between man and the Roman Catholic Church, Novalis receives the utmost praise from Eichendorff. Indeed, the reader easily perceives the degree to which Eichendorff's literary history is skewed in order to crown Novalis poet laureate. Thus it comes as something of a shock when Eichendorff's high praise of Novalis for the attempt to reunite Christianity and poetry suddenly turns to censure: "Even in this innermost equation lay the danger of error, one that was later recklessly exploited by Novalis's followers, as it is so often the misfortune of the imitators that they only pay heed to the weaknesses of the master and develop these monstrously" (IV, 256–57).

Needless to say, Eichendorff does not include his own work among these monstrous births, or himself, in this instance, among Novalis's literary descendants. Eichendorff ultimately accuses his chosen poet of having transformed Christianity into *mere* poetry, thereby proudly affirming the greater orthodoxy of his own religious imagery. One aspect of the transformation in question, and a further ground of complaint against Novalis, is its pantheism. Eichendorff thinks that Novalis's comments about the natural world and the world of the spirit are contradictory, citing a long series of passages to make his point. Perhaps the most interesting is the following: "'Wem regt sich nicht das Herz in hüpfender Lust . . . wenn . . . er bebend in süsser Angst in den dunkeln, lockenden Schoss der Natur versinkt, die arme Persönlichkeit in den überschlagenen Wogen der Lust sich verzehrt und nichts—als ein verschluckender Wirbel im grossen Ozean übrig bleibt?'" (IV, 259). Eichendorff's descent into his underworld is in fact similarly constituted, and he too is at great pains to redeem it. Clearly, then, Eichendorff's criticism of Novalis carries with it the implication that he himself is the ideal Christian poet of that Romantic movement which he identifies as the endpoint of his teleological literary history. In Eichendorff's schema Goethe, the poet of "visible Nature," and Schiller, whose province is the "invisible world," each represent a half to be made whole by the synthesis of real and ideal that the Romantic poet could be expected to effect. Eichendorff writes of these two luminaries of the German tradition: "Both poets had, each from his direction, brought the great task *nearly to its conclusion*; what was missing was only the voice that dared to speak the magic word ["Zauberwort"], in order to effect the *higher* mediation of both points of view."[61] This mediator should have been Novalis, in Eichendorff's view, but that poet ultimately failed in his attempt at a "neue christliche Mythologie."[62] In a sense, then, Eichendorff wishes to replace Novalis, who in turn has already supplanted Goethe and Schiller in the overt course of his literary history.

Let us approach this matter from another direction. There is little evidence, other than the literary-historical writings themselves, about the course of Eichendorff's attitude toward Novalis, although we can draw indirect conclusions about his feelings from his changing attitude toward Graf Loeben, whom Brentano called "des Novalis zweiten Teeguss.'"[63] The Eichendorff brothers' friendship with Loeben began in Heidelberg in 1807, and it is generally believed that Eichendorff wrote his early poetry under Loeben's influence. Gerhard Möbus takes issue with this assumption, however, insisting upon the direct influence of Novalis even at that stage: "how much he influenced Eichendorff is shown by the extent to which his poetic attempts during the Heidelberg period are determined by Novalis in matters of theme and poetic diction."[64] Actually, Eichendorff had begun to read Novalis even earlier, in Halle. It is ordinarily supposed that in a letter written to Loeben as early as June of 1807, Eichendorff is repudiating the influence of the literarily fashion-conscious Graf; one wonders, however, whether the emotional investment in this repudiation does not indicate that it is intended for the original Novalis rather than for the Novalis imitator. In this letter, Eichendorff speaks of his "Verstummen," which he attributes to having so acutely suffered the oppression of authorial influence as to have deprived himself not only of a personal voice, but nearly of life itself. He bemoans his loss of poetic innocence:.

> I no longer dared to represent what I felt, loved, and thought directly and for its own sake, but rather, unworthy of all original independence, strove to make my independent aspirations into vehicles for particular ideas and to generalize to such an extent that these inspirations became unrecognizable to myself and others, and my being, once detached from actual life, without any substance and nearly ironizing itself dispersed into the four winds. . . . I feel now that this monstrous *poetic suicide* ["*Selbstmord der Poesie*"] must stop or I *will cease to exist.*[65]

Eichendorff regrets the loss of his poetic childhood, in which he imagines himself to have had an original voice, and finds himself in a second, imitative phase of his writing. His terrified phrase, "Selbst-mord der Poesie," suggests that his poetry had become to him a kind of automatic writing that completely bypassed the will of its author. It is no wonder that he intends to begin a third, "original" phase.

Although Eichendorff's poetry is generally thought to have developed its own voice in the course of the Heidelberg sojourn, several critics have noticed his reliance on Novalis at that time.[66] In Oskar Seidlin's work especially, we find interesting turns of phrase concerning Eichendorff's borrowings from Novalis; Seidlin speaks, for instance, of Eichendorff's defense mechanisms ["Abwehrinstinkte"] toward the ethical and religious solutions that Novalis presents in the *Hymnen an die Nacht*, premising what he says on the very interesting prior observation that Eichendorff, who devotes more space to Novalis than to any other poet in his literary-historical writings, never once mentions the *Hymnen*.[67] Correctly, I think, Seidlin calls this silence a "telltale discretion" and feels that it is by no means merely a reflection of Eichendorff's increasing sobriety of judgment in his later years. Furthermore, passing on to discuss several poems in the light of his observation that Eichendorff feared Novalis's "Weg nach Innen," Seidlin notes Eichendorff's "telltale lines," his usurpation of metaphor, together with a certain characteristic "swerve" or "Umschlag." This "swerve" is what I have termed the conversion to orthodoxy—or, as Seidlin puts it, "this abrupt leap out of the danger zone."[68] These phrasings rightly point to Eichendorff's intimate psychic involvement with Novalis; but Seidlin's study draws no further conclusions about Eichendorff's transformations of Novalis, nor does it hint at the psychic mechanisms that stand behind the poet's repressions.

Thus far I have not stressed the obvious connection of Eichendorff's underworld—his unconscious—with night, although I have mentioned it in passing. A number of poems already cited make reference to night or darkness, among them "Nacht," "Nachtzauber," and "Heimkehr." Darkness is appropriate to the descent into the self; it has been pointed out "how natural it is for a Romantic poet to use the word 'darkly' in connection with thought," and that "the word 'dark' is thematically very important in Romanticism, especially in Germany. . . . [I]t usually refers to the seeping of an identity with Nature into the hidden and inner parts of the mind."[69] And when we think of darkness, the texts that come most readily to mind in the setting of the present discussion are, of course, Novalis's *Hymnen an die Nacht*.

Peter Paul Schwarz's study *Aurora: Zur romantischen Zeitstruktur bei Eichendorff* puts Eichendorff's representation of night side by side with Novalis's *Hymnen*.[70] In his preliminary analysis of the *Hymnen* themselves, Schwarz points to several characteristics of Novalis's Night that connect it with the *Grund* or garden complex we have mapped as the place of origin and return, the site of inspiration, for Eichendorff. Not only is Novalis's metaphorical Night suffused with eroticism, but it is also a place of origin, a place where the "Vision der Mutter" takes place.[71] And, naturally, it is the abode of death. But because in the *Hymnen* Night is understood as a mystical space ("zeitlos und raumlos ist der Nacht Herrschaft," I, 55), because in fact it is an inner space that is reached by the "Weg nach Innen," Novalis most often represents the poet's entry into it as a *descent*.

Other features of Novalis's mystical topography are also echoed in Eichendorff's poetry; his typical view from a superior vantage point, the hillside, into the depths strongly recalls a passage from Novalis's fourth *Hymn*: "wer oben stand an dem Grenzgebirge der Welt, und hinüber sah in das neue Land, in der Nacht Wohnsitz—wahrlich der kehrt nicht in das Treiben der Welt zurück, wo das Land in ewiger Unruh hauset" (*Werke in einem Band*, IV, 57).[72] Naturally Eichendorff denies that to enter the region of night, the figurative counterpart of his "Grund," or depths, entails the cessation of process or activity in the stasis of an *unio mystica*. It is his purpose, rather, to redefine the depths as the region of greatest danger—and, of course, of thinly veiled attraction. It is interesting in this regard that, as one critic has written, "The mystical union with God was, a few exceptions aside, a descent, and an experience of the depths in the Middle Ages. According to the mystic's perception, God was experienced as 'ab-grunt' or 'grunt.' "[73] Eichendorff's choice of the term "Grund" for his underworld, and the particular identity with which he invests it, reveal once again his true source of fascination and poetic power. For Novalis the "Brunnen der Quelle" (IV, 57), the "verborgene Gänge" (IV, 57) or underground streams, are the sanctified places of his inner landscape; for Eichendorff they are the home of the voices that will give him no peace.

In order to explain Eichendorff's attempt to replace Novalis more fully, it is advisable briefly to trace yet another line of poetic descent. It has been pointed out that in his fifth *Hymn*, Novalis revises Schiller's "Die Götter Griechenlands," a pivotal poem for the Romantics.[74] And there is justification for saying that in some ways *all* of the *Hymns* take issue with Schiller's poem, which Novalis knew in its earlier, more pessimistic version.[75] It is not only toward Schiller's view of the Greek pantheon that Novalis sets himself. Where Schiller bemoans a disinspirited Nature, the passing of the "holdes Blütenalter der Natur,"[76] Novalis turns his back on the natural world of light and metamorphosis entirely. Where Schiller decries the Christian religion as one which espouses denial as the only form of religious celebration, Novalis is at pains to portray the sensuousness of the Christian mystical union. Schiller expresses the desire to substitute *Phantasie* for *Vernunft* and mimesis, and—with this mandate—Novalis supposes himself to have done so already. In the fifth *Hymn*, finally, Novalis claims that the Greeks achieved their world view by repressing the archaic forces, by imprisoning the Titans—the fathers—under the mountains; this repressed dark world he brings to light, so to speak, redeeming it through Christian belief and the enabling power of the imagination. Thus Novalis purports to move beyond the Greeks and Schiller at one and the same time. It is this twofold triumph that Eichendorff's poetry (and criticism) must reconsider.

Presenting himself as a harsh critic of solipsism, Eichendorff restores God to the upper regions and the realm of light, and looks with fear on the descent into the self; in so doing, he virtually denies the existence of the poetic territory that Novalis has claimed for himself, or in any case redefines it in more orthodox terms. Whereas Novalis abandons the natural world for the mystical inner space which he equates with pure religious experience, for Eichendorff descent into this inner space is a descent into a labyrinth which is imprisoning because Man himself, merely *as* himself without divine mediation, inheritor of Adam and Eve's sin in the Garden, is unregenerate. Because the natural world, which shares this fallen state with Man, provides fitting metaphors for the self and the forces at work within it, Eichendorff can claim that it is far from being the disinspirited world of which Schiller speaks, and in so doing he finds his own way of achieving Novalis's triumph. When Eichendorff personifies these forces in the form of mythological figures, he seems again to be answering Schiller—and at the same time to be expressing his customary ambivalence toward Romantic revisionism.[77] By undermining Novalis in his attempt to revise Schiller, Eichendorff is able to claim a direct line of descent from Schiller to himself, thereby assuming the heroic burden of recovering the Christian world from paganism without prior poetic assistance. Ironically, however, in answering Schiller, Eichendorff perforce falls back upon the very voice he has banished to his unhallowed underworld—the voice of Novalis.

This irony in turn brings us to another twist of poetic revisionism. While Novalis inverts Schiller's value system, equally devaluing light and Classical antiquity, Eichendorff does this also but at the same time reverses Novalis's connection of time of day with historical period and ethos. The Greek gods are no longer associated with light but with darkness and the depths; and light, meanwhile, in the spirit of Herder and Böhme, Aurora or morning light, becomes the sign of Christian redemption.[78] Critics have noticed the exception to this rule in Eichendorff: Fortunato's song in *Das Marmorbild*, published as "Götterdämmerung" in the edition of 1844, begins by maintaining the connection of Classical antiquity with the world of light that one finds in Schiller and Novalis. The obtrusion of this view, to which the novella as a whole does not adhere (the Venus figure appears to Florio at night) has long seemed puzzling. One critic calls it an "error" of oversight, claiming that Eichendorff wrote the poem earlier and simply omitted to adapt it to the novella, but there is no evidence for this.[79] Apparently, in fact, while the first half of the poem was written in 1816, the novella was finished in 1817 and the second half of the poem not written until shortly before the publication of the novella in 1819.[80] It would seem, certainly, that Eichendorff must have had in mind some design to accommodate the presence of both parts of the"Götterdämmerung" poem in *Das Marmorbild*, and I shall assume that he did.

Part I of the poem celebrates the beauty and sensual pleasure of spring ("ich grüsse herzinnig, / Was schön auf der Welt"), making use of Classical mythology, particularly the figure of Bacchus, in order to do so. But this celebration is customary in Eichendorff, and one must remain on the alert for the element of threat that accompanies such moments. Indeed, in this poem we find that the domain of Frau Venus, even in a morning setting, is yet described as being "wie ein Zauberring" (II, 312). In the ninth stanza it becomes clear that the historical period of the poem is the Middle Ages and that the springtime it celebrates belongs to a Christian rather than a Classical context. It is not promising for the knights and their ladies, however, that they are portrayed as lovers: "Und jeglicher hegt sich / Sein Liebchen im Arm" (II, 312).

In the novella, this stanza is followed by a shift in Fortunato's tone ("Hier änderte er plötzlich Weise und Ton und fuhr fort," II, 312). The springtime festivities are revealed to be an "et in Arcadia ego" idyll, threatened from within by the presence of Death, a youth who is a composite of Christ and the torch-bearing Hermes—the latter of whom, according to Lessing in "Wie die Alten den Tod gebildet" and Schiller in "Die Götter Griechenlands," imparts death with a kiss. He is a "Jüngling vom Himmel" (II, 313) who does not take his charge to an underworld but rather, quite conspicuously, "hinauf" to the Heavenly Father. The identity of this syncretistic figure can be precisely inferred from the flowers that enwreath his head: the poppies of oblivion and the lilies of Resurrection. Leaving the world behind, this figure invites the others to do likewise; the flowers he wears, which equally represent—apart from their differing conventional symbolism—the process world of earthly nature, are transformed into the stars of heavenly nature, implying the cessation of time in Eternity.

That the specter of Novalis's fifth *Hymn* and, more indirectly, of Schiller's great poem haunt the whole of "Götterdämmerung" seems undeniable. Certainly Part I is taken from the situation of the fifth *Hymn*: "ein Gott in den Trauben [Bacchus]—eine liebende, mütterliche Göttin. . . .—der Liebe heilger Rausch ein süsser Dienst der schönsten Götterfrau—ein ewig buntes Fest" (59). Also similarly, Novalis's celebration is interrupted by death: "Es war der Tod, der dieses Lustgelag / Mit Angst und Schmerz und Tränen unterbrach" (59). Naturally Christ supplants Hermes in Novalis as in Eichendorff. Yet the reader of Part I of Fortunato's song is actually misled by Eichendorff's withholding of the information that the springtime setting in which Bacchus and Venus reside is to be understood in a medieval context. Hence one temporarily supposes that Eichendorff has turned to Schiller in repudiating Novalis. At the same time, this delay of clarification lends the appearance of a temporal progression in the poem—something both Schiller and Novalis insist upon—where none actually exists. Eichendorff's syncretistic approach to the figuration of death adds to the confusion, or at least to the appearance of ambivalence. What he stands to gain poetically from this anomaly is his having forcibly appropriated the Classical Hermes for the purposes of Christian mythology. But this seemingly radical gesture is not a novel one, as it follows Novalis's revision of "Die Götter Griechenlands."

In *Das Marmorbild*, Fortunato sings Part II of "Götterdämmerung" in the morning, following Florio's "victory" over Venus and the scene of desire. On this occasion the song is intended to explain Florio's encounter as well as to account for the ruined temple that the group of travelers passes by. Venus is transformed into a chthonic deity in this song; she is relegated to her "Göttergrab" during winter and reappears like Persephone in the springtime. In this section of the poem the repudiation of Novalis is more marked, as when Eichendorff causes Venus to emerge from flowers, recalling once again Novalis's "blaue Blume":

Frau Venus hört das Locken,
Der Vögel heitern Chor,
Und richtet froh erschrocken
Aus Blumen sich empor.   [II, 342]

[Dame Venus hears the beckoning, / Of the birds' cheerful choir, / And lifts herself, happily startled / Out of the flowers.]

But the Classical gods—especially Venus—are rendered inanimate by the approach of the Virgin holding the Child. The confrontation between the mother as object of repressed and deadly desire and the pure, idealized Mother holding her infant is nowhere in Eichendorff as explicit as here. Nowhere is the wish for "ein andres Frauenbild" to which "das Menschenkind" can awaken as clearly manifest as it is in this poem. The desired union of mother and child can take an innocent form in this image. In "Götterdämmerung" Venus is not a statue animated by the imagination, as she is elsewhere in the novella; rather she is here literally turned to stone by the superior power of the Virgin.

Eichendorff ascribes the power to arrest the activity of the process world to the representatives of "die ewige Heimat." As the *unio mystica* implies the cessation of movement, so the soul reposes in its *Heimat*, God. Venus remains, however, to be transformed into art. Eichendorff knows very well what Florio has discovered and vehemently repudiated: that for him the source of inspiration is the veiled Venus, the mother concealed, as Novalis puts it, under her "irdischer Schleier." Eichendorff's entire oeuvre may be said to resemble that lady's veil in *Das Marmorbild*, for it too envelopes, "bald enthüllend, bald lose verbergend" (II, 336), the female figure it never quite reveals.

Eichendorff is very much a "lyric" poet: his fiction is musical,[81] his poems are songs and have often been sung. As a poet, Eichendorff believes that his task consists in releasing into poetry the sounds, movements, and colors that characterize the things of Nature, to continue the stories that Nature tells him: "Garten und Bäume erzählen dem jungen Dichter heimlich Geschichten / Die er dann muss weiterdichten."[82] He must also take care to transform the voices in the ground into his own voice. And yet voice itself is not so much one's own as a thing of dubious origin; and the movement of song seems not to rise above the instability of the process world. It is not surprising, then, that in Eichendorff's poetry there is actually a strong current of opposition to voice and song. There is a great difference, after all, between "der irre Spielmann" and the poet. There is an affinity between Eichendorff's desire to transfix, to turn to stone, and the recurrent demythologizing of the threatening figures in his work: the fathers who are revealed to be stone, the Venus figures that are reduced to statuary and thus deprived of their threatening aspect. With his severely limited stock of images, with his recurrent combination of adjectives, nouns, and verbs into various mosaic patterns, Eichendorff effects a kind of iconic fixity in his work even while portraying the turbulence of the process world and of the voices. It is this stylistic feature that has led some critics to trace a connection between Eichendorff and the French Symbolists.[83]

If we understand Eichendorff's religious goal to be the cessation of process, the end of temporality—expressed in the metaphor of "das ewige Meer," for example—we can also understand why he so happily turns to the "Book of Nature" topos when he wishes to present God as Creator, as in the poem "Das Bilderbuch" (1837, I, 64).[84] For Eichendorff, again, voice is to some extent contaminated, and writing, which has the power to fix process, to control and contain voice, is therefore, if only by default, preferred.[85] "Writing" naturally includes writing in images or pictures, in the "natural symbols" that Herder had already called hieroglyphs, the pictures with which God writes in the Book of Nature. The metaphor of the hieroglyph is also central to Novalis, who defined the task of the poet as the decipherment of the "Hieroglyphenschrift der Natur";[86] but for Novalis the aim of this activity was to release such writing—that is, the physical world—into spirit, and his poetic style is meant to effect this aim as much as possible. Eichendorff can therefore be said to turn against Novalis in yet another way: ultimately his poetry insists that the poet must continue the writing of nature *as* writing, as when Nature is the scene of divine inscription: "Da steht im Wald geschrieben, ein stilles ernstes Wort" ("Abschied," 1810, I, 36). In other words, for Eichendorff Nature itself is a system of signs to be read and then re-encoded by the poet because it is best that the "geheime Zeichensprache der Natur" remain precisely that: "Denn mitten in unserer Welt," he says, "liegt eine wunderbare Sphinx, die dem, der unberufen die Lösung ihrer ewigen Rätsel wagt, den Hals bricht" (IV, 1078). Not least among the reasons for her presence is to challenge the presumptuous decipherment of Goethe, Schiller, and Novalis.

Chapter Three
The Poetry of
Regeneration:
Droste-Hülshoff's
Ophelia as Muse

The text functions something like a
neurosis: as the matrix is repressed, the
displacement produces variants all
through the text, just as suppressed
symptoms break out somewhere else in
the body.
—Michael Riffaterre, *Semiotics of*
  Poetry

From the beginning, critics have carefully qualified their praise of Annette von Droste-Hülshoff. The first reviewer of the edition of 1844, Joseph Christian von Zedlitz, found it necessary to temper his positive review of her poetry with the disclaimer "that on the whole we have no great taste for the lyrical outpourings of female rhapsodes."[1] Yet Zedlitz gallantly gives her talent its due, stressing the peculiar originality of her voice, while paying her a dubious tribute as a poetess ("Dichterin") capable even of vying with male poets (I, 750). Even Levin Schücking, who was perhaps closer to her than any other person, makes his assessment of Droste-Hülshoff's poetry in the context of her femaleness:

> This volume of poetry—with such a characteristic imprint, so rich in ideas, in new images and metaphors, so variegated, with new figures of speech to describe all impressions, so prophetic and profound: *no woman in Germany has ever written such poetry.* But often it is so sibylline, so incoherent and incomprehensible in its thoughts and form, turns its back so unconcernedly on customary modes of thought and expression, is so stubbornly closed off to the voices and cries of the time, *as only the poetry of a woman can be.*[2]

Often quite unconsciously, no doubt, Droste-Hülshoff critics tend to give with one hand and take away with the other. Even as prolific and devoted a Droste-Hülshoff scholar as Clemens Heselhaus speaks of her writing as properly belonging to the category of literary dilettantism, claiming that it was the influence of Schücking that made her a "true" writer for a period of six months.[3] To praise the poet means to single out the "masculine strength" of her verse. And on the other hand, as Schücking's pronouncement indicates, the opacity of Droste-Hülshoff's poetry is ascribed to a typically "feminine inability" to think logically. One critic finds himself forced to conclude that Droste-Hülshoff lacked the gift of logical deduction, but happily feels able to affirm that this lack has been turned to advantage in several poems, three to be precise, in which the poetic faculty transcends "its ideational problematic."[4]

Earlier, Emil Staiger had taken a similar view. His condescension toward the poet's observations on literary matters is documented in the oft-quoted passage from his "Meersburger Festrede" for Droste-Hülshoff in 1948, in which he compares her remarks to the "harmless, banal chatter of some tea circle, discussing its reading for the day."[5] In fact she never attempted to write any systematic literary criticism; Staiger refers to casual passages in letters to Schlüter and Sprickmann, where indeed she does often discuss her reading of the moment. It is not ordinarily required of a poet that he be a theoretician or even a particularly astute practical critic (one thinks of Mörike), and Staiger's judgment betrays a more general wish to reduce Droste-Hülshoff to the status of yet another tea-drinking literary lady. In his 1933 study of the poet, Staiger had indicted her for recurrent lack of taste, for the inability to discriminate among her own poems and the tendency—"Where she really said 'I' " ("wo sie wirklich 'Ich' sagte")—to "misinterpret" and "trivialize" herself. It angers him that she appears to have recognized no difference in quality between the poetry commonly thought to be her best, which properly belongs with the greatest German poetry, and a poem like "Mein Beruf"—an error of judgment he describes as "an unprecedented case of self-delusion, of a misinterpreted sense of fate and blundering pride."[6] He bases his opinion on the inclusion of "Mein Beruf" in the edition of 1844; to my mind, though, the fact that Droste-Hülshoff should have chosen to include this programmatic poem, which amounts to a defense of her poetry, is hardly surprising.[7] Having warned his readers from the outset that he will not address the poet's sociological or psychological situation, with which criticism by the "supporters of the women's movement"[8] has supposedly dealt too often, Staiger perhaps finds "Mein Beruf" to raise these issues too inescapably; and indeed—as he might argue—it is true enough that it does not transmute them into anything other than declamation.

Having once accomplished the radical distinction between Droste-

Hülshoff the "literary lady" and Droste-Hülshoff the *Dichter*, the masculine persona of the twenty or so worthy poems, Staiger then expresses the very highest admiration for those poems, all written during the short time when the poet was "ignited to a higher life."[9] Staiger prefers the lyrical poems, the poems of the private voice, to the rhetorical, publicly addressed poems such as "Mein Beruf," in which the poet boldly proclaims her right to be considered apart from her sex:

"Was meinem Kreise mich enttrieb,
Der Kammer friedlichem Gelasse?"
Das fragt ihr mich als sei, ein Dieb,
Ich eingebrochen am Parnasse.
So hört denn, hört, weil ihr gefragt:
Bei der Geburt bin ich geladen,
Mein Recht soweit der Himmel tagt,
Und meine Macht von Gottes Gnaden.   [I, 83]

"What drove me from my circle, / From the chamber's peaceful space?" / You ask me that as though / I had broken into Parnassus, a thief. / So hear now, hear, because you asked: / I was bidden at birth, / My right extends as far as the heavens, / And my power's by the grace of God.

It is not my purpose to urge the aesthetic value of the more declamatory poems; there is certainly an immense difference between their direct manner and the obliqueness of the more hermetic poems— among which I include the ballads. I propose rather to point to the thematic connection between the inward lyrics and poems like "Mein Beruf," and to describe the poetic strategies that allow Droste-Hülshoff to express and overcome her actual uncertainty—so vigorously denied in "Mein Beruf"—as to whether she can achieve an authentic poetic voice. One clear implication of my approach will be, in fact, that the poems "wo sie wirklich 'Ich' sagte" and in which she is most intimately concerned with being a woman writer are not the public poems but the more hermetic lyrics that Staiger prefers.

Everywhere in the criticism here touched upon—this is by no means a complete roll call—there is evident a sense of puzzlement stemming from the reluctance to see in this eccentric and extraordinary woman someone who from childhood had a poet's sensibility and who struggled both to suppress it and to express it. It is widely asserted in the Droste-Hülshoff literature that when she spoke of her poems as "meines Herzens flammendes Blut" ("Herzlich," II, 42), she was merely phrasemaking and did not really identify with the raging storm, as "Am Turme" would suggest.[10] Yet there are some who incline to another point of view. Ricarda Huch, in her introduction to an edition of Droste-Hülshoff's works (1932), speaks of the poet's sense of vocation, and describes the discrepancy between the events of her life and her poetic experiences in a manner that displays an accurate understanding of the biography, the letters, and the works: "Her outer life appears monotonous, but the life within was rich in moving struggles and melancholy victories, in dazzling triumphs and fantastic experiences. Fiery and colorful, the world of her imagination and emotions stood apart from the narrow confines in which she moved."[11] Naturally one might expect Huch, a poet herself, steeped in the Romantic tradition and perhaps looking for a female role model, to take such a view. But from Lore Malechow, writing the introduction to the East German edition of Droste-Hülshoff's selected works in 1955, a similar picture emerges, although Malechow understandably stresses the historical and economic factors that imposed uniformity on Droste-Hülshoff's life.[12] Finally, Renate Böschenstein-Schaefer, in her excellent and suggestive essay "Die Struktur des Idyllischen im Werke der Annette von Droste-Hülshoff" (1974), in large part a Freudian reading based on excerpts from the letters, a novel fragment, and several poems, connects the typical imagery and formulations of the poet's work to her disturbed relationship with her parents.[13] None of these critics question the authenticity of the poet's voice, all of them recognize the constraints arising from the regrettable fact of her femaleness, and none appears to be bothered by those anomalous disparities of taste and talent from work to work that so exercise Staiger.

The portrait of the artist drawn by these last three critics from the evidence of the life and work is that of a woman who was highly imaginative and susceptible to the effects of her imagination, but also forthrightly strong-willed: "Was ich soll, das mag ich nie."[14] We know from Heselhaus that while still a child she was given the task of writing hexameters in an effort to calm her down.[15] As a young woman she writes of her "Glühen und Rasen" in the famous letter of February 8, 1819, to Sprickmann describing the nervous excitement she experienced when she was moved to think of distant places or unfamiliar works of art (*B* I, 34).[16] She suffered long bouts of illness to which doctors were hard put to assign a cause, and which interrupted her writing for weeks, months, perhaps years at a time. One complaint voiced time and again in the letters is unusual indeed: she suffered from "Gesichtschmerzen."[17] These may have been a form of shingles, but they remind one in any case of Simone de Beauvoir's observation that "all her life woman is to find the magic of her mirror a tremendous help in the effort to project herself and then attain self-identification."[18] I would suggest that Droste-Hülshoff's nervous face-pains have to do with the problem of finding a self-image—which was, as the many instances of doubling and mirroring in her work would indicate, a key problem for her, both personal and aesthetic.

Droste-Hülshoff died in the same year as Emily Brontë and shared some features of her life: she remained unmarried, chose to be reclusive, and was sickly yet called upon to nurse the sick and minister to her family whenever need arose. Although she was able to use the proceeds of the 1844 edition of her works to buy a house of her own, the Rebhaus near Meersburg, she was never free from the constraints and demands imposed by her family. In speaking of the urgent need to avoid a scandal concerning her relationship with Levin Schücking, she says she would very much regret "not only the relinquishing of a relationship very dear to me, but also my slowly— and dearly—won freedom (insofar as I may call the passive indulgence that my family displays toward my manner of being in the world and my attitude toward others by that name), a freedom that I would only reattain after a long series of years" (*B* I, 542). Yet this is also the poet who wanted her work to be read a hundred years after her time (*B* II, 191), and who, in her attempt at comedy, "Perdu! oder Dichter, Verleger, und Blaustrümpfe" (1843), displays sufficient self-assurance as a writer—and perhaps defensiveness—to satirize other authoresses.[19] Her self-portrait as Anna, Freiin von Thielen, is unmistakable, as is that of Freiligrath in the character of Sonderrath or Schücking in that of Seybold, who says to Sonderrath of Anna: "die hat mehr Talent als wir beide zusammen genommen" (II, 556). Anna is a remarkably strong and steadfast character who refuses to make the "small changes" in her writing that the publisher requires of her: "Mit ein Paar Worten, mit einer Zeile, könnte sie zuweilen das Ganze klar machen und sie tut's nicht" (II, 564). Rather than clarify her images and ideas and compromise her artistic integrity, Anna von Thielen withdraws her manuscript and goes home.

Another potentially controversial matter, (not wholly unrelated to the first one, as we shall see) requires some initial attention as well, this one concerning the placement of Droste-Hülshoff's poetry among the given periods of literary history. We must ask to what extent the typical movement of her poems corresponds to the Romantic view of lyric, whether the so-called Biedermeier characteristics of her poetry are not better accounted for by her being a woman, and how, finally, the question of Realism should enter into a discussion of her poems. Critics interested in periodization have found Droste-Hülshoff's work difficult to place. In Staiger's view, for example, the works central to her oeuvre "appear to be erratic blocks in the literature of the nineteenth century." He suggests further that the mysterious provenance of her work, its lack of moorings in literary history, might seem less enigmatic if the connections between images and ideas were to be examined from a psychological perspective, an undertaking which he nevertheless then with some perversity condemns, both methodologically and ethically: "An analysis of single motifs and ideas is prohibited where the essential connections are, as it were, subterranean. It would deprive Droste of the solitariness that constituted her greatness and her limitation."[20] What Staiger implies in these last two passages I take to be true—that there is something about Droste-Hülshoff that causes her to swerve from the tradition in an unexpected way, in a way that is quite different, for example, from that of her contemporary Eduard Mörike. And I take the most crucial difference to lie in the fact that she is a woman.

Friedrich Gundolf included Droste-Hülshoff in his *Romantiker, Neue Folge*, calling her, as so many others have done since Schücking, a female Seer, a "Seherfrau."[21] At the same time, however, Gundolf compares her most closely with Mörike, stressing an aspect of her poetry that nearly contradicts what is suggested in the term "Seherfrau": "like Mörike's poetry hers, too, is full of grainy thingness" ("Dinglichkeit"). Although he makes no comment of the kind himself, Gundolf's vivid description of Droste-Hülshoff's imagination— "die gewappnete, Ding-gepanzerte Phantasie"[22]—suggests that the many *things* in her poems constitute a psychic defence against the pressures of the imagination. Indeed, Gundolf's interpretation of Droste-Hülshoff does not finally differ greatly from that of Friedrich Sengle's *Biedermeierzeit*. Sengle quite legitimately places Droste-Hülshoff among the poets of the German *Innerlichkeit*, poets who are usually grouped by comparatists within the Romantic tradition: Droste-Hülshoff's work, he says, manifests "that religiously motivated interiority so much scorned today, out of which, from Klopstock to Rilke, the finest German contribution to world literature has emanated." Sengle does not hesitate to speak of the Romantic Droste-Hülshoff, of her "pact with the demons . . . , her wild muse," and at the same time he too speaks of the *Dinglichkeit* of her poetry, which he calls its "emblematic quality."[23]

The question, clearly, is whether Droste-Hülshoff's *Dinglichkeit* is a sign of her "Realism," as some critics suppose,[24] or whether, as Gundolf and Sengle suggest, it is a dialectical component within her Romanticism. In her letters, Droste-Hülshoff does use the language of Realism when she refers to her fiction; her interest in Regionalism, which is borne out by the emphasized truth to nature of the "Sitten, Charakter, Volksglauben" in her "Westfälische Geschichten," would seem to confirm that at least in her fiction she inclines toward Realism. But even here her intentions are complex. On one occasion, referring to her stories, she claims that she can only write what she has seen (*B* I, 407), but on another occasion, when she begs a friend for a description of a certain church and monastery for one of her epics, she hastens to add that she has no particular interest in detail: "I wish only superficial information" (*B* I, 95). And when we consider that she saw in Washington Irving the most important model for her fiction, the boundaries between "truth" and "imagination" become blurred. The unpredictability of the Socialist attitude toward her work reflects just this confusion: whereas Karl Gutzkow admired Droste-Hülshoff's Realism, Friedrich Engels compared her with Byron and Shelley.[25]

Indeed, it is perhaps through the English and American Romantics that we can most readily establish the connection I wish to emphasize here, her connection with Romanticism. Engels was not the only commentator to recognize Droste-Hülshoff's indebtedness to the English Romantics. Heselhaus mentions Byron and Walter Scott,[26] who frequently appear in the letters alongside Washington Irving and James Fenimore Cooper. Ricarda Huch expresses surprise that Droste-Hülshoff should find English literature so congenial,[27] but that taste seems consistent with her admiration for Shakespeare and Goethe. It has been pointed out that her friend Adele Schopenhauer encouraged her cultivation of the "English tastes of Goethe's Weimar."[28] In 1834 Schlüter sent her Cunningham's *Geschichte der englischen Literatur von Johnson bis Scott*,[29] from which she made numerous excerpts. Perhaps most significant is the fact that Schücking and Freiligrath translated the *Lyrical Ballads*, as this might explain the strikingly Wordsworthian concerns of Droste-Hülshoff's poetry. One might even account for her liking for the German Preromantics (Ewald von Kleist, Gessner, Voss, Klopstock) by pointing to *their* English tastes, which partly contribute to their emphasis on the depiction of nature. What makes Droste-Hülshoff's taste for the English Romantics significant for the periodization of her own work is that it shows how fidelity to nature can be consistent with aspirations that reach beyond nature. The English Romantic "nature poets" rather more than the first group of German Romantics, with their mystical revolt against Goethe's organicism, can be seen on these grounds to have provided Droste-Hülshoff with an important model.

It is often remarked that Droste-Hülshoff expresses contempt for the German Romantics,[30] but in truth her attitude toward them too is a complicated one.[31] Her friend and mentor Schlüter admired them enthusiastically, and Droste-Hülshoff read them at his urging. Apparently she did not like Novalis or Adam Müller and was uncertain about Tieck. But after reading Tieck's *Phantasus* she wrote to Schlüter:

> Tiecks Nervensystem muss gewiss, wo nicht schwach, doch äusserst reizbar sein, weil er alle damit verbundene Zustände von Halbwachen, Schwindel, seltsamen peinlichen fixen Ideen so genau darstellt, ja—als eigentliche Person des Dichters durch das ganze Werk gehn lässt. . . . Glauben Sie nur, das Buch und in minderem Grade alles von Tieck ist höchst aufregend für diejenigen, welche es eigentlich allein ganz verstehen können, und bringt alle alten besiegten Flirren in Aufruhr.
>
> [*B* I, 144]
>
> [Tieck's nervous system must indeed be, if not weak, then highly irritable, because he represents so precisely the conditions of daydreaming, vertigo, and strangely distressing *idées fixes* connected with it, yes— allows it to run through his entire work in the person of the poet. . . . Please believe me, this book and to a lesser degree everything by Tieck is highly agitating for those who can actually alone fully understand it, and brings all the old, conquered instabilities into a state of uproar.]

In this passage Droste-Hülshoff identifies both with Tieck and with his fictional character, and feels threatened by the emotions her reading brings to the surface. The poetic concerns she notices in *Phantasus* are the concerns of the second group of German Romantics—and they are her own as well. As one critic writes, this second group's "primary poetic concern is no longer with the cosmogonic powers of the sovereign spirit, but rather with the subliminal powers of the animated earth and the subconscious depths of the soul of man . . . the primitive, the primordial, the return to sources and earth forces. The basic assumption is that man is a son of the earth and that poetry is a receptive art from the powers of nature, earth, and soul."[32] Droste-Hülshoff's most authentic mode sets out to adapt precisely these concerns to the voice of the female poet.

That this "second group" is indeed a second group is in itself important, because among these poets the belatedness, the alienation from sources that is always present in Romanticism becomes a more prominent, fully conscious issue. The figures Droste-Hülshoff uses to express her myth of poetic origins indeed reveal this problematic, but what inhibits her, and what seems to distance her from Romanticism, has as much to do with her sex as with the feeling of being a latecomer. Staiger speaks rightly of her fear of unmediated feeling,[33] and one consequence of this fear is the introduction of surrogates in her poetry. Many commentaries stress the recurrence of doubling in Droste-Hülshoff's work, and Heselhaus goes so far as to say that "doubleness *is* the characteristically Drostian."[34] He speaks elsewhere of her "dualism," of a distrust of subjectivity that causes her to retreat to a more objective stance, thus generating two voices, lyrical and declamatory.[35] Another critic divides the poems into two groups, depending on whether they reflect an "assertion of self" or "submission of self."[36] But the question remains, why should this division occur? The answer is perhaps not far to seek. When Benno von Wiese claims that Droste-Hülshoff's ballads are not Romantic because they do not display the "sovereign freedom of the self,"[37] we need only remember the restrictions placed upon her writing and publishing by her family. In such circumstances the self is likely to be subdued. It is interesting that the two attributes commonly associated with the Biedermeier sensibility are those that Levin Schücking assigns to women, specifically to Droste-Hülshoff: "the joy in little things . . . which is peculiar to woman," and the "housewifely urge . . . to preserve and to cherish" ("die Freude am Kleinen, . . .-welche der Frau eigen ist," "hausmütterliche Drang . . . zu hegen und zu pflegen").[38] To make sense of the recurrent images in her poetry is also to come to terms with the sense of "doubleness" and discontinuity that pervades it, and it is only by this means that we can arrive at Droste-Hülshoff's self-understanding as a poet. Finally, we must consider how she approaches poetry, the form of writing that most requires a sense of self, and to do this we must describe the myth of imagination she generates to account for her poetic power in the context of those defenses with which, as a second self, she struggles to combat that very myth.

II

Und sollte er auch durch Modergruft
gehen; er findet sicher unsägliche
Schätze.
—Novalis, *Lehrlinge zu Sais*

In "The Queen's Looking Glass," one of the opening theoretical chapters of *The Madwoman in the Attic*, Sandra Gilbert and Susan Gubar present a reading of "Snow White" that stresses "the almost stifling intensity with which this tale concentrates on the conflict in the mirror between mother and daughter, woman and woman, self and self."[39] The Queen and Snow White are represented as two halves of the self, "two-faced," like the apple from which they both eat. While the "pure" Snow White represents the docile, sweetly compliant self, the "wicked" Queen is the witch, schemer, plotmaker—in short, she is a portrait of the female artist.[40] Literary Woman, so continues the argument of Gilbert and Gubar, "frequently finds herself staring with horror at a fearful image of herself that has been mysteriously inscribed on the surface of the glass," and when she examines this image, she sees a monster or a madwoman, an image of the creature "she fears she is rather than the angel she pretended to be."[41] For the nineteenth-century woman writer, the metaphors of Gothic fiction, especially the haunted house, readily offered themselves as projections of an irrational and rebellious self. In the Gothic genre, such figurations could appear naturally, without arousing any suspicion of self-reference. Gilbert and Gubar's study, especially the chapter on Emily Dickinson (whose "The Soul Has Bandaged Moments," for instance, projects a conflict within the self as a confrontation with a goblin) most vividly evokes the situation one finds in a poem of Droste-Hülshoff's called "Das Spiegelbild," but points just as surely to the Gothic encounters with ghosts, madwomen, sisters, and doubles, together with the preoccupation with mirrors and bodies of water, throughout her poetry and prose.

Droste-Hülshoff makes use of the Gothic-tinged ballad, with its expected ghosts and forays into the supernatural, to come to terms with a "demonic" double. In ballads of this kind she confronts a self whose "unnaturalness" is closely related to the "curse" of second sight and of an overwrought imagination—traits that find their spontaneous expression in story-telling and poetry.[42] No one could deny that "Das Spiegelbild" is a highly personal poem that describes a moment of intense self-confrontation and conflict; but it is equally true, albeit less obvious, that "Das Fräulein von Rodenschild," for all its Gothic and folkloric apparatus, is a personal poem of the same kind. Indeed, it may grow out of an actual experience. In his *Lebensbild* of the poet, Schücking writes that this ballad "was originally motivated by an experience that Annette von Droste believed herself to have had, that she recounted with the firm conviction of its truth."[43] Obviously Schücking questions the status of this "Erlebnis," wondering whether the poet may have dreamt or fictionalized it from the beginning, but that is no matter. What remains interesting is that the language in which Schücking goes on to describe the experience, supposedly echoing that in which Droste-Hülshoff related it to him, reinforces the connection between the resultant ballad (1840–41) and the slightly later "Spiegelbild" (1841–42): phrases in his narrative such as "und erkennt sich selbst, ihr eigenes Spiegelbild," and "nähert sich die Doppelgängerin" would establish this connection even if it were not apparent in the language of the poems themselves.[44]

The situation with which "Das Fräulein von Rodenschild" opens is one that occurs more often in the more personal lyrics. "Das Fräulein," unable to sleep, becomes overly sensitive to the sounds and movements of the night. Overcome by tumultuous emotions ("oder ist so siedend jungfräulich Blut?" "[U]nd horcht des Herzens pochender Flut"; I, 225–26), the troubled insomniac crosses to the moonlit window. There she glimpses the servants preparing, in accordance with tradition, to welcome Easter morning with a song. At this witching hour—it is just after midnight—she catches sight of an apparition, her ghostly double: "Hab ich nicht so aus dem Spiegel geblickt? / Das sind meine Glieder—welch ein Geblend'" (I, 227). She is determined to face her double, "dass nicht das Gesicht entrinne!" (I, 228). Significantly, the confrontation between the woman—who suspects herself of psychic powers or of madness—and the ghost who now haunts her house takes place as if in a mirror:

Langsam das Fräulein die Rechte streckt,
Und langsam, wie aus der Spiegelwand,
Sich Linie um Linie entgegenreckt

Mit gleichem Rubine die gleiche Hand[.]   [I, 228]

[Slowly the lady extended her right, / And slowly, as if from a mirror's surface, / Line for line stretches toward her / With the same ruby the same hand.]

When once her phantom double's touch has pierced her hand like a cutting blast of air, it dissolves as though it had accomplished its end: "Der Schemen dämmert—zerrinnt—entschwand" (I, 229). In a final stanza that places this event in an indefinite past, the reader is told that "das Fräulein" became ill for a short time following her experience; it is not indicated, however, that her "madness," her possession by another self, is the direct result of the night's visitation, as some readers have maintained:[45] "sie hiess ja *immer* / Das tolle Fräulein von Rodenschild" (I, 229; italics mine). From that day on, however, as though to mark a new chapter in her madness, she wears a glove on the hand the ghost has touched.

The touch of the ghost does not signify the "touch of death" alone: like the central figure of "Vorgeschichte" (subtitled "Second sight"; I, 210), the lady and, indeed, Droste-Hülshoff herself, are among the "Seher der Nacht, das gequälte Geschlecht." She is marked not only by death but by her own imaginative powers. It is notable that the self-projection that is her ghostly double has appeared, it would seem, in order to consult the family archives. While this deviant self is able to investigate the papers unhindered—"doch einem Rauschen / Der Pergamente glaubt sie zu lauschen" (I, 228)—they are inaccessible to "das Fräulein" ("—Ha! Schloss und Riegel!—sie steht gebannt," I, 228). These documents represent those family secrets that are locked away, but as such they also plainly entail the secrets locked away in the unconscious of the lady, secrets to which only a threatening, ghostly self has access. Furthermore, because the parchments hold the key to the family's past, the ghost is also engaged in a search for an origin, and when it touches the lady's writing hand, the searches for personal and poetic origins become one. Given the premise that the ghost is an emissary from the dead, we can say preliminarily that here as elsewhere for Droste-Hülshoff there is a connection between death and origination. We shall come to see more fully how this connection is constituted.

"Das Spiegelbild" takes the metaphor for second sight, "das zweite Gesicht"—the second face—literally; the confrontation between self and mirror image (minus the narrative elements of the ballad) is an acknowledgement of an inner division as well as a search for poetic identity. Associating the reflected image with duplicity, the speaker heatedly disowns it, perhaps precisely because it remains the personification of narcissistic self-love. In rejecting the double, the speaker alludes both to Faust's discontent with his "zwei Seelen" and also to his exchange with the *Erdgeist* just before the dawning of Easter:

Mit Zügen worin wunderlich
Zwei Seelen wie Spione sich
Umschleichen, ja, dann flüstre ich:
Phantom, du bist nicht meinesgleichen!   {I, 141}

[With features in which wondrously / Two souls like spies sneak / Round, yes, then I whisper: / Phantom, you are not such as I.]

Through this uneasy identification with Faust, Droste-Hülshoff appropriates Goethe to her own end, which is, in this poem, to achieve a poetic voice by disclaiming the demonic origins of poetic power.

The mirror image is called "gespenstig" in "Das Spiegelbild"; and the "Augen Nebelball" echoes the "Nebelgesicht" of the ballad. The lady of the ballad was "kalt . . . wie Eises Flimmer" (I, 229), while here the mirror image is accused of having escaped the land of dreams "zu eisen mir das warme Blut" (I, 141). The speaker's vacillating rhetoric, her alternating rejection and acceptance of what she sees, corresponds to the two-sidedness of the reflection itself, which is both child and demonic present self, and demonstrates that speaker and reflection are indeed "verwandt." These twin alter egos, the child and the wild woman, recur throughout Droste-Hülshoff's oeuvre. The child signifies an earlier self whose relation to the world was unmediated, "naive" in Schiller's sense; it existed harmoniously with Mother Nature because it perceived no difference among its mother, Mother Nature, and itself.[46] Because there is no perceived difference, however, and hence no available standpoint for objectification, the child is always mute, without a voice. This is the "weich und hülflos" self (I, 142) that is threatened by the poetic self. That self, which here, characteristically, appears wild and demonic, has recognized difference and stands in an adversarial relationship with the harmony it has lost and can retrieve only in death.

The speaker recognizes that these two selves have their origin in her imagination, in "the land of dreams"; they are the imagination's attempt at self-genealogy. In general, however, this speaker is understandably reluctant to lay claim to any creative faculty that is so dubiously constituted. In a sense, then, she must fool herself into self-recognition: it is in a moment of denying any connection with the reflection that she is able to speak of it in its entirety, comprising both selves—with revealing complacency:

> Es ist gewiss, du bist nicht ich,
> Ein fremdes Dasein, dem ich mich
> Wie Moses nahe, unbeschuhet,
> Voll Kräfte, die mir nicht bewusst[.]   [I, 142]

> [It is certain, you are not I, / A strange being, whom I / Approach like Moses, without shoes, / Full of unconscious powers.]

It is God whom Moses approaches barefoot, and thus Droste-Hülshoff has here suddenly aligned herself with the Romantic poet who models himself upon God as Creator and feels himself to be "voll Kräfte." To qualify the hubris of this moment of self-revelation, the modest, self-effacing speaker pulls back from her daring religious simile by referring it to the domain of everyday speech: "Gnade mir Gott, wenn in der Brust/ Mir schlummernd deine Seele ruhet!" (I, 142).[47] As we shall see, if the double is to be recovered as a figure of the poetic self for a genteel woman who has no business conjuring with dubious influences, it must appear to have been exorcised while actually being transformed and located in nature.

For Droste-Hülshoff, then, the Romantic double is more than an uncanny opponent or a former or a demonic self, as it would be for any male Romantic writer; it is inseparable in still more intimate ways from the poet's conception of her creative self. We shall learn more about this double as we come to know the topography in which it is most likely to appear. The double is not reflected in an actual mirror only, but also in bodies of water—again in accordance with folklore and Gothic convention. Whereas Eichendorff finds a suspiciously maternal muse in the "Weiher," Droste-Hülshoff finds a floating corpse, a mad Ophelia whose ravings have ended and who has become one with pond or stream. I shall call this apparition an Ophelia figure, following Gaston Bachelard, who has seen in Ophelia the most highly generalized symbol of female suicide: drowning is "la mort bien féminine," because water is the element of "la mort jeune et belle, de la mort fleurie."[48] Once we recognize it as an existing archetype, the Ophelia figure may be seen to occasion the ghosts in Droste-Hülshoff's ballads, and begins to explain the way in which the double is located in nature.

In Droste-Hülshoff the double, which in much other literature is a means of self-punishment or harbinger of death, has already become a corpse. Ophelia singing her mad-song is also closely tied to the imagination, and provides the woman poet with an indirect means (necessarily indirect, given her social and psychological circumstances) of confirming her identity as a poet. The image of the drowning woman forges the firmest link between Droste-Hülshoff and another literary woman of the Romantic period, Karoline von Günderode. Günderode, whose poetry is saturated with death and has a distinct charnel-house mood, committed suicide under weeping willow trees on the banks of the Rhine (1806).[49] As the medium of birth, water represents the mother, but for the woman writer in search of wellsprings, the return to the mother must remain, in the absence of sexual fantasy, an imagined submersion. A variant of the descent into water, and which occurs just as frequently in Droste-Hülshoff, is the descent into the earth; but these forms of descent are more closely related even than may appear. As Freud declares in his essay on "The Uncanny," the fantasy of being buried alive, which "to many people is the most uncanny thing of all," is a variant of the fantasy of "intra-uterine existence."[50]

Droste-Hülshoff characteristically approaches the Ophelia figure in the following manner: she projects a second self into nature in the form of a disintegrating corpse, which is either not the living self or at most a discarded former self, a corpse joining its organic matter to the surrounding elements, especially the vegetation, while its spirit lingers on to haunt—and inspire—the surrounding region. Purging the self of the demonic other by projecting it into nature, and thus conveniently disowning it, the poet at the same time gains the advantage of having invested nature with her own imagination as its immanent genius. In effect she can then say, "Nature has no voice but mine." Yet further, the double as the spirit of the place allows her to be her own muse, an originary self animated without mediation by Nature: "jedes wilden Geiers Schrei / In mir die wilde Muse weckt" ("Lebt wohl," I, 433–34). The merger effected among Nature, femaleness, and poetic election by the Ophelia figure can be further outlined: the flowers and garlands with which Shakespeare's Ophelia is bedecked ("la mort fleurie") not only serve to trope women themselves as vegetation (as Goethe does in "Heidenröslein," for instance) but are also traditional tropes for poems, for collections of poems (like Mörike's *Klassische Blumenlese*), and also for rhetoric, the flowers of poetic language (Shakespeare's Ophelia speaks "the language of flowers").

The Ophelia figure has furthermore to do, in what amounts to a mild paradox, with those literary sources that cannot quite disappear into the natural landscape. As a woman writer, Droste-Hülshoff found the task of situating herself in the literary tradition at once simpler and more difficult than it is for her male counterparts, in part because she lived in a literary culture in which there were few female poets to emulate. Her relation to the poet who can be said most clearly to have influenced her, Goethe, is necessarily not as tortured as that of a male poet would be because she had no share in the psychic energies the male writer harbors for the denial of the father. And yet her "mouldering corpses," which in part comprise her enabling fiction and are thus far originary in intent, are also a way of ensuring that nature remain vital, and thus belatedly capitulate to Goethe's organicism. It is interesting in this regard that she modeled her muse, the figure by means of which she worked out her self-image as a poet, on a female literary character (with what degree of conscious intention we cannot say) which exists at only two removes from the poet to whose work she was most indebted. The Ophelia figure not only aligns Droste-Hülshoff with Goethe by way of his admiration for Shakespeare, but more specifically evokes his Gretchen—and thus stands as a sly reminder, typical of the way latecomers call their predecessors to account, that on at least one occasion Goethe's imagination was not sui generis. Thus it is just when the poet turns to the theme that sacrifices her to nature, winning freedom from self-consciousness in death, that she has in fact yielded herself not to nature but to the conventions of art, but with the consolation of knowing at least that Goethe's artless heroine is in turn one of his most literary inventions.

The proximity of flowers is perhaps the most important feature shared by Ophelia and Gretchen. In the scene tellingly called "Garten," Faust finds Gretchen (herself a "Margarete") tearing apart a daisy-like aster in order to determine, according to custom, whether he loves her or not, and urges: "Lass dieses Blumenwort / Dir Götterausspruch sein!" (I, 3184–85) Here the flower is a language, the language of nature, as it will be for Droste-Hülshoff when the environment of the corpse, sometimes flower-strewn, becomes inspirational. And although the theme of drowning is deflected in Gretchen's case onto the drowning of her child, her symbolic self-dismemberment in "Garten" finds its parallel in Droste-Hülshoff's disintegrating corpses. Later, finally, in the dungeon scene, Gretchen, who has now joined Ophelia in madness, has a vision of her drowning child, now long since dead, and urges Faust to save it:

Fort! immer den Weg
Am Bach hinauf,
über den Steg
In den Wald hinein,
Links, wo die Planke steht
Im Teich!   [I, 4553–58]

[Quick, follow the trail / Up the river dale, / Cross on the trunk / Into the copse / Left, where the planking stops, / Into the lake.]

This hurriedly-evoked genre scene—woodland with pond—resembles many similar landscapes in Droste-Hülshoff that are also places where children have drowned or are threatened with drowning. Gretchen and her child anticipate the paired doubles already encountered in Droste-Hülshoff: the "abandoned" woman and the mute child. Below I shall show in detail how this pattern reveals itself in Droste-Hülshoff's work.

In March of 1813, fresh from a reperusal of Shakespeare, the sixteen-year-old Droste-Hülshoff began work on her play *Berta*, which she was never to finish.[51] The opening scene serves mainly to develop a contrast between the heroine, Berta, and her sister Cordelia, a name suggesting that in some sense Berta is wicked, a Goneril or Regan. The conventionally feminine Cordelia contrasts with the relatively unfeminine Berta, who resembles Droste-Hülshoff in some ways.[52] When Cordelia describes herself as one whose heart "nur im Kreise holder Häuslichkeit / Für sich und seine stillen Pflichten lebt" (II, 382), she describes what she takes to be an ideal feminine nature. Berta in contrast describes her state of mind in violent, stormy images: "Mein Geist ist unstet und hinwegezogen / Wird er gewaltsam, wie von Meereswogen" (II, 384). Cordelia offers the suffering Berta the sort of insight into her problems that she might be expected to offer: "Zu männlich ist dein Geist; strebt viel zu hoch / Hinauf, wo dir kein Weiberauge folgt" (II, 384). But the contrast is a little more complex than this: Berta's conception of her *Geist* as something forcefully torn away must be qualified by Cordelia's presumably accurate depiction of her sister as timorous and pale-cheeked. Evidently Berta is herself divided, with the wildness and passion hidden within. Thus the potential conflict between the two sisters preexists in Berta herself, who admits that she wants to conform to conventional models of womanhood but is unable to do so: "[Ich] möchte gerne / Dir gleich tun, aber, ach, ich kann es nimmer!" (II, 384).

The difference between the sisters is reflected in the art that each practices. Engaged in the feminine art of the needle, Cordelia embroiders screens, at once art-objects and useful objects. Cordelia's screen depicts a fitting scene: a reverential young priestess kneels at an altar in a posture of submission to its powerful flame. She is only the keeper of the flame, neither oracle nor hierophantic sibyl. Berta, on the other hand, is a musician and poet, and it is in her song, conventional and uninspired in most respects, that Droste-Hülshoff for the first time begins to sketch in the lineaments of the Ophelia figure. This song, with which *Berta* opens, has for its subject a young girl in a pastoral setting who weaves a garland of flowers— "Massliebchen und Veilchen und Blümelein mehr" (II, 381)—which she tosses into the "kristallene Helle" of the water. In her yearning, an "unbegreifliches Sehnen," she gazes into the blue distance "und dann in die silberne Welle" (II, 381). The miniature catalog of flowers, the weaving of the garland, and the flowers floating on the water, all already evoke the images surrounding Shakespeare's Ophelia. Although as yet there is no connection of *Sehnsucht* with madness and death, the young girl of Berta's song does suffer from depression, and the presence of illness is suggested by her pallor; she can no longer identify, as she once did, with the blooming rose of May.

The Ophelia motif in *Berta*, where it is the subject matter of an "unfeminine" art practiced by a soul with "masculine" aspirations, takes more definite shape in the autobiographical novel-fragment *Ledwina* (1819–24). The sisters Ledwina and Therese closely resemble Berta and Cordelia; and, like the young girl of Berta's song, Ledwina has a "krankes, überreiztes Gemüt" (II, 228). Once again the opening scene portrays a pale young girl at the edge of a body of water, and once again the girl is compared to flowers—and a tree. The first sentence of the novel makes the stream a mirror, a trope that is later several times repeated: "Der Strom zog still seinen Weg und konnte keine der Blumen und Zweige aus seinem Spiegel mitnehmen. Nur eine Gestalt, wie die einer jungen Silberlinde, schwamm langsam seine Fluten hinauf; es war das schöne, bleiche Bild Ledwinens, die von einem weiten Spaziergange an seinem Ufer heimging" (II, 267). Ledwina's doubling reflection, which seems to be carried along by the stream, is prefigured by Berta's *Geist*, which is said to have been carried off by turbulent waters. Later, when Ledwina approaches the river and gazes into it—"träumend"—she becomes aware of her reflection and, as her image is dispersed, she perceives herself in a graphic description as a disintegrating corpse: "Ledwinens Augen aber ruhten aus auf ihrer eignen Gestalt, wie die Locken von ihrem Haupte fielen und fortrieben, ihr Gewand zerriss und die weissen Finger sich ablösten und verschwammen, . . . da wurde ihr, als ob sie wie tot sei und wie die Verwesung lösend durch ihre Glieder fresse und jedes Element das Seinige mit sich fortreisse" (II, 267–68). Ledwina draws back for the moment from this object of her reverie, but it recurs later in the novel, when she awakens from a dream to see the moonlight undulating on the white covers of her bed.

The link between covers and shroud—and by extension bed and coffin—is unmistakable, but what Ledwina notices especially is the undulating movement of the light, and thus she evokes the Ophelia image once more: "Die Idee einer Ondine ward zu einer im Fluss versunkenen Leiche, die das Wasser langsam zerfrisst" (II, 291). Typically in Droste-Hülshoff, the Ophelia figure which dissolves into Nature, and which in later formulations lingers as spirit or ghost, replaces the living nature spirit, the nymph called Undine. But this substitution is not as radical as it seems to be, because Undine, an invention of the late Middle Ages, herself has no spirit or "soul," being pagan, but only body.[53] But in her visions of herself as an Ophelia, Ledwina seems less concerned about reunion with nature than with escape from parental authority; the above-quoted passage continues: "während die trostlosen Eltern vergebens ihre Netze in das unzugängliche Reich des Elements senden" (II, 291). Ledwina is preoccupied with death in general, to be sure, but it is the dissolution of her image on the water's mirror that she watches with the greatest fascination; here she finds the death of that self which her parents pursue with nets as if it were a fish—the wild, yearning self for which Cordelia had also rebuked Berta. Like Berta, Ledwina has a split personality: "diese süsse, überteure Seele lebte ein doppeltes Leben, eins für sich, eins für andre" (II, 288). In her daydreams, then, Ledwina kills off, and in so doing liberates into a more safely concealed sphere, the artistic self that her family has wished to suppress.

After lying for some time in her underwater bed, Ledwina

wrenches herself away from the experience of her own corpsehood. Ironically, however, shortly after she has crossed from her moonlit window—like "das Fräulein" in the ballad—she witnesses a death by drowning. Because she is at a distance, it is nighttime, and a storm has come up, the event remains indistinct. Like the man in "Vorgeschichte" who watches the preparations for his own funeral (I, 210–14), Ledwina can be said to watch her own drowning; the victim is later revealed to be her nurse's son, with whom Ledwina was nursed in infancy and who is thus in a sense nearly her twin. She returns obsessively to the riverbank, where she imagines the fate of the drowned man as vividly as she has imagined her own corpse in the water, stimulating her always-feverish imagination with unusual intensity: "Es zog sie gewaltsam zu dem Ufer des Flusses, und tausend wunderbare Möglichkeiten, die nur für sie so heissen konnten, tanzten in greulichen Bildern um ihr brennendes Haupt" (II, 304). This is just the language Droste-Hülshoff uses in her letters when she speaks of the content of her own imagination: "summen und gaukeln die Bilder vor mir wie Mückenschwärme" (*B*I, 154), she writes, or again: "das Zuströmen ungeborener Ideen, die mir um den Kopf summen wie Bienenschwärme" (*B*II, 411).

We can now turn to her lyrics in order to draw the body of Ophelia in the water closer to Droste-Hülshoff's conception of the imagination and of poetry. In the ballad "Die Schwestern" (1841–42), the Ophelia motif again reinforces the theme of sisters and doubles. This ballad is composed of four temporally disconnected episodes that tell the story of one sister, Gertrude, who wears out her life searching for the other, the fair Helene. Weighed down by the guilt she feels at having allowed her sister to go to the city, there to become a fallen woman, Gertrude eventually goes mad. It is unwise, however, to distinguish between these two as neatly as this summary has done. As one critic has pointed out, "[a]t no point in the story can we detach these two figures from each other: Helene's 'separateness' resulted from Gertrude's act of acquiescence, and the purpose of the sister's existence thereafter is centered in the reunion."[54]

In the first episode, Gertrude searches for her sister in woods and fields, where all her senses deceive her: what she imagines to be Helene's lantern is a shepherd's fire, and what she thinks is Helene—"ein schlanker Hals, / Zwei glänzende Augen" (I, 235)—is revealed to be a deer ("eine Hinde nur"); likewise the sounds she hears are made by Echo, which is to say, they are her own. Although it is

Helene who has vanished, it is Gertrude who is already called "das irre Gespenst im Tanne" (I, 236).[55] In this figure, Droste-Hülshoff has brought together the madwoman and the ghost, recalling "Das Fräulein von Rodenschild" and her ghostly double. When Gertrude is discovered asleep in the grass the next morning, her body is still twitching in response to a nightmare; in other words, like the other figures discussed, she haunts herself.

The second vignette presents a threatening scene of city turmoil, "Babels würdige Klänge" (I, 236). Danger materializes in a pair of wild horses which pass precariously close to Gertrude on several occasions ("schon dampfen die Nüstern ihr am Gesicht," I, 237) and are revealed to be pulling her sister's carriage. As the poem makes abundantly clear, the horses' wildness represents that of Helene, who is now a purple-clad whore of Babylon. When Helene kicks Gertrude's dog, Fidel, she is symbolically kicking the faithful Gertrude herself. Gertrude is ready to declare herself insane rather than admit that the harlot in purple is really her sister: "Ich bin eine Irre leider!" (I, 237). Ten years later, in the third episode, Gertrude has become a madwoman in fact, with gray tresses and burning, sunken cheeks. In this condition she finds her sister floating to the shore, "eine triefende Leich' im Kies" (I, 239). Helene's Ophelia-like, flowing hair is bedecked not with flowers but with shells and seaweed.

In the last section Gertrude's complete breakdown is suggested when she identifies her own reflection on the surface of the water as that of Helene:

Doch schlief die Welle, dann sah ihr Gesicht
Man über den Spiegel sich beugen,
Und zeigte es ihr das eigene Bild,
Dann flüsterte sie beklommen:
"Wie alt sie sieht, wie irre und wild,
Und wie entsetzlich verkommen."   [I, 240]

[But when the wave slept, then one / Saw her face bending over the mirror, / And if it showed her own image, / Then she whispered anxiously: / "How old she looks, how mad and wild, / And how horrifyingly ruined."]

Ostensibly, Gertrude's madness in itself accounts for this case of mistaken identities; what stands revealed, however, is the extent to which Gertrude not only identifies but identifies with the guilty sister. Hence when Gertrude hurls herself into the waves during a storm, her suicide is as much a hopeful effort to reconcile herself with a self-image, at once to acknowledge and to punish her own suppressed desires, as it is an attempt to be reunited with Helene. So it is that the two sisters, the madwoman and the whore, repression and fulfillment, wildness of spirit and wildness of body, are finally united in the figure of Ophelia, the suicide in the water.

Gertrude's madness accords her a special relationship with nature; when the lake is calm, she is calm, but when "der Sturm die Woge gerührt" (I, 240), she is like one possessed. (Here one recalls Berta's lament that her spirit is carried away by turbulent waves.) Gertrude becomes a *Naturgeist*, and the woodland site of her grave—as a "lost soul" she cannot be buried in sanctified ground[56]—is an uncanny place across which animals will not venture. An image with which the poem opens and closes, "Sacht pochet der Käfer im morschen Schrein," emphasizes the role of process in nature even as it follows the bug's progress through Gertrude's disintegrating coffin. In the last section the corpse of Helene meanwhile ("ihr Haar voll Muscheln und Tange," I, 239) has already begun to return to nature. Wild grasses and flowers spring from Gertrude's grave, but even as Gertrude becomes one with the ground, her spirit lingers to haunt it. Here she resembles Droste-Hülshoff's lost souls who haunt the moor in "Der Knabe im Moor" (I, 60–61): "die unselige Spinnerin, . . . die gebannte Spinnlenor," "die verdammte Margret," and "der Geigenmann ungetreu." All three of these Romantic figures are converted, like Gertrude, into ghosts that do not rest in peace. In all their moral ambiguity as nature-spirits, they and they alone animate an otherwise disinspirited landscape. This is the crucial function of drowned bodies and bodies that lie mouldering in the earth in Droste-Hülshoff's work; in them, mediated by her appropriation of Ophelia, Droste-Hülshoff finds figures that afford a renewed access to Nature. It is her stratagem, again, to project a "wild" or "damned" self into the landscape by killing it off and burying or submerging it there, so that its body may return to the elements and its spirit linger. In either case, safely distinct from the rational or merely eccentric feminine self that is socially acceptable, this self becomes her muse; and the poetry which the submerged muse inspires is generally a poetry of descent rather than flight.

In the last episode of "Die Schwestern," what appeared to be an impersonal omniscient narrator is revealed to be a speaker in the first person, a hunter, and we are taken back to the wooded setting of the first episode. It is well to ask why the poet should want to distance herself from a situation that is so important in her writing by adopting the persona of the hunter. For one thing, the idea of the hunt is prefigured in the opening section of the poem, when Gertrude mistakes "eine Hinde" for Helene. "Whoso list to hunt," wrote Sir Thomas Wyatt, "I know where is an hind." The metaphor of the hunt is also central to Eichendorff, for whom, as for Wyatt and for many other writers, it indicates sexual pursuit. The connection between woman and deer, as also between Gertrude and the fallen Helene, is effected once more when the hunter speaks of Gertrude as an "armes gehetztes Wild der Pein" (I, 241). Perhaps we can understand the hunter, then, as one who is able to control or dominate his world by purging its wildness. Having hunted the hind, he has figuratively killed both sisters, just as the poet has destroyed these wild selves in order to provide another, more stable and less guilt-ridden self with material for poetry. This is precisely the implication of the hunter's gesture when he picks a flower—flower of rhetoric or poetic "posy"—from Gertrude's grave. (A poem discussed later, "Meine Sträusse," will shed more light on this image.) But to break off a flower is also to deprive a woman like Helene of her virtue. Thus the hunter also remains merely a man, and by means of this complication Droste-Hülshoff reveals an ambivalence toward the persona she has chosen to adopt. Evidently her sympathy remains as much with the two sisters as with the calm and reflective hunter with his deadly gun.

A passage from "Der Spiritus Familiaris des Rosstäuschers" (1842) will serve to show how the imagery connected with the drowning Ophelia can be expanded and made to open outward, figuring forth a modest poetics. Droste-Hülshoff's darkest and rankest image of the mouldering corpse is to be found in this long poem, from which the entire section devoted to the pond in the middle of the forest is quoted:

Da seitwärts durch Geröhres Speer erglänzt des Kolkes Dintenbecken,
Ein wüster Kübel, wie getränkt mit schweflichen Asphaltes Jauche,
Langbeinig füsselnd Larvenvolk regt sich in Fadenschlamm und Lauche,
Und faule Spiegel, blau und grün,
Wie Regenbogen drüber ziehn.

Inmitten starrt ein dunkler Fleck, vom Riesenauge die Pupille,
Dort steigt die Wasserlilj' empor, dem Fusstritt lauschend durch die Stille;
Wen sie verlockt mit ihrem Schein, der hat sein letztes Lied gesungen;

Drei Tage suchte man das Kind umsonst in Kraut und Wasserbungen,
Wo Egel sich und Kanker jetzt
An seinen bleichen Gliedchen letzt.   [I, 277–78]

[There sideways through spears of reeds gleams the pool's inky basin, / A
filthy vat, as though saturated with sulphurous noxious liquid, / Long-
legged, shuffling larvae move about in water plants and mud, / And foul
mirrors, blue and green, / Pass over it like rainbows. // In the middle
there stares a dark spot, the pupil of a giant's eye, / There the water lily
ascends, listening for footsteps in the stillness; / He whom she entices
with her appearance, he has sung his last song; / Three days they
searched in vain for the child in the grasses and water plants, / Where
now leech and canker / Refresh themselves on his small, pale limbs.]

Before discussing this passage, I wish to place it alongside a
related one from another unfinished novel of Droste-Hülshoff's, *Bei
uns zu Lande auf dem Lande*, written at about the same time as
"Spiritus Familiaris," 1841–42. It is commonly acknowledged that
in this novel the author portrays herself as Sophie, who serves as
muse for the male poet Wilhelm. Significantly, Wilhelm's poems are
called "Das Mädchen am Bache" and "Der Knabe im Rohr," the
original title of "Der Knabe im Moor"[57]—Wilhelm being, as these
titles would suggest, simply the vessel into which Droste-Hülshoff
projects her poetic self. The narrator, a cousin of Sophie's and perhaps another self, makes this judgment of the poet: "bleib in deiner
Heide, lass deine Phantasie ihre Fasern tief in deine Weiher senken,
und wie eine geheime Wasserlilie darüber schaukeln" (II, 354). The
passage from the novel and the passage from the poem share the
image of a pool or pond with a waterlily (belonging to the genus
Nymphaea) emerging from its center. In the poem, the beauty of the
waterlily lures the unwitting to their deaths; the child's dissolving
body, feasted on by spiders and worms, bears witness to its lethal
powers. In the novel, "die geheime Wasserlilie," the seed of which is
in the mysterious depths of the pond, represents the poetic imagination. In the poem, the swampy pool, the "Kolk," is described as
having "faule Spiegel" floating on it, and later the wanderer and
sinner is said to have his moment of conversion when "[e]r sieht sein
faltiges Gesicht im Wasserspiegel widerscheinen / Wie er sich selber
nicht erkannt, und kindisch dann begann zu weinen" (I, 284).[58] Like
Gertrude and Ledwina, he is estranged from his own reflection. But
here the pattern is varied somewhat, for instead of committing

suicide or imagining himself as a corpse, he redeems himself by remaining alive, wandering from land to land in expiation of his sin. There is already a corpse at the bottom of the pool, however, that of a child; and thus the wanderer, whose weeping was "kindisch," has left a self behind.

At this point we can venture upon a typology of the images that surround the drowning Ophelia. A childish version of the self (in some ways resembling the child in Goethe's "Erlkönig") is lured to its death and decay in the water by an appeal to its imagination. And the imagination figured as a waterlily has its beginnings in turn in the secret depths of the pond. The circle of these images seems to return upon itself, and with good reason: the insight sustaining and configuring the cluster, anticipating Freud and Otto Rank, is that death and the imagination are motivating projections—doubles—of one another. The awareness of mortality begets the counterassertion of poetic power, which turns its attention, fatally and inevitably, back toward its own "wellsprings," and is pulled down into the watery place from which it has arisen. Thus when the heroines of Droste-Hülshoff see their own faces rising to meet them in the water, what attracts them, as it attracted Narcissus, is the enabling power of what they see, the sense that what gazes back at them makes their own vision possible. Thus in addition to keeping one's "wild muse" at a safe distance, the projection of a demonic self into Nature is an escape from mere inwardness, albeit an illusory one: turned inside out, the imagination finds itself in the world.

The poem "Der Weiher," one of the *Heidebilder* (1841–42), shares in the Ophelia imagery. The figure of the pond as mirror lingers in each part of this five-part poem; it is explicitly mentioned in the first two parts, it is evoked by the figure of "Kristall" in the third and fourth, and in the fifth it is implied in the image of the face at the bottom of the pond. The lily—the woman-flower—that inspirits the pond is also present, carried over, once more, from regional folklore and linked to the world of flowers by simile: "die Wasserfäden" claim "Uns nur traut die holde Wasserfei / Sie, die Schöne, lieblicher als Rosen" (I, 41). In addition, the last poem in this miniature cycle evokes the companion images of the corpse and the flower in a variant of the "Spiritus Familiaris" passage quoted above: "O sieh doch! siehst du nicht die Blumenwolke / Da drüben in dem tiefsten Weiherkolke?" (I, 41). Once this question has been uttered, the poem quickly moves from flowers on the surface of the pond to a frog and a fish, to the "Wassermann" who haunts the foliage at the pond's edge, and to the ominous image of the face at the bottom: "Mich dünkt, ich sah am Grunde ein Gesicht—" (I, 41). The significance of these images is hardly exhausted by saying that the poet makes use of regional folklore to give her poetry a Gothic tone or an uncanny quality. She does this, to be sure, but when the complex of images around the Ophelia figure returns so persistently and takes on such force, we must realize that for Droste-Hülshoff poetically and—we assume—personally, something more is at stake. In "Der Weiher," Ophelia becomes the face at the bottom of the pond, the wild muse that haunts the Droste-Hülshoff landscape together with the toads, frogs, newts, and bats that might have escaped from the witches' cauldron in *Macbeth*.

"Am Bodensee" (1841–42, still the same period) is a ruminative poem that to some extent naturalizes the uncanny, balladesque moments we have passed in review thus far; in an image that anticipates characteristic images of C. F. Meyer,[59] the lake is seen as a repository of all images that have been gathered on its surface. The lake harbors the past, but it does so uncompromisingly in the form of those who peopled the past, "[u]nd nur ihr flüchtiger Spiegelschein / Liegt zerflossen auf deinem Grund" (I, 73). The poet personifies the lake as "alte Wasserfei" and apostrophizes it in a moment of despair about her own death: "o, schau mich an! ich zergeh wie Schaum" (I, 74). This passage recalls Ledwina's image as it dissolves on the waves, and also recalls various decomposing bodies in the depths. But the thinly veiled wish *for* death in other poems is here reversed and becomes anguish about its likelihood—a more conventional stance that brings with it the compensatory possibility of *literary* immortality. This is just the kind of turn we would expect a publicly proclaimed "personal" poem—in contrast with a poem that is personal because it stumbles across personal matters—to take.

The characterization Droste-Hülshoff bestows upon the lake has certain traits in common with herself. She suspects it of suffering from insomnia, ascribes dreams to it, and endows it with restlessness. The "alte Wasserfei" in this poem is somewhat staid; but one does not miss the demonic in her altogether. The face at the bottom of the pond appears even in "Am Bodensee" as a partly visualized voice: "Eine Stimme klaget im hohlen Grund, / Gedämpft, mit halbgeschlossenen Mund" (I, 73). Possibly the subdued voice of the muse, engulfed at the bottom of the immense lake, is complaining precisely because it *has* been subdued and suppressed, deprived in great measure of its power just as the natural world is here smothered by a blanket of fog.

As I have suggested, the drowning Ophelia may stand for poems themselves as well as for the imagination; she is the flower of which posies are made in another poem of this period, "Meine Sträusse" (1841–42). This poem presents a catalog of dried flowers and bouquets that seem to symbolize poems. Associated in memory with a person or place, each recalls one or another of Droste-Hülshoff's own poems to mind. Even if we take into account the poet's documented penchant for collecting natural objects, it still seems certain that these flowers more specifically refer to poems, if only because in the first stanza garlands and bouquets are fashioned as "Zeichen," signs, in this case elaborate souvenirs. Over these the poet's soul then "undulates" or flows: "Liess' drüber die Seele wallen" (I, 131). More convincing still is the fact that "Meine Sträusse" scatters verbal signs of past Droste-Hülshoff poems along its path. For instance, "Und dies' Tange entfischt ich der See / Aus Muschelgescherbe und Kiese" (I, 132) vividly recalls the body of Helene, washed up on shore in "Die Schwestern"; here the seaweed synecdochically represents the drowned woman, but it also now represents the poem which is contructed around this figure. There is also an indirect reference to the situation of being "Im Moose," a place of reverie in the poem of that name where the poet envisions her own death as a dissolution into nature. Here is the entire stanza:

> Und wenn ich grüble an meinem Teich,
> Im duftigen Moose gestrecket,
> Wenn aus dem Spiegel mein Antlitz bleich
> Mit rieselndem Schauer mich necket,
> Dann lang' ich sachte, sachte hinab,
> Und fische die träufelnden Schmelen;
> Dort hängen sie, drüben am Fensterstab,
> Wie arme vertrocknete Seelen.   [I, 132]

[And when I lie musing near my pond, / Stretched out in the fragrant moss, / When out of the mirror my visage pale / Teases me with a shiver running down my back, / Then I reach slowly, slowly down into it, / And fish out the dripping water plants, / There they hang, over there at the window, / Like old, dried-up souls.]

A flower is plucked from the pond in response to a startling vision of a ghostly double that is mirrored there. The verb *fischen* reminds one of Ledwina's vision of herself as a floating Ophelia escaping the parents who want to capture her in their net. The act of picking a flower in this poem—the act of making a poem—is rather conventionally presented as a defense against death. What is implied, however, is that the poem comes into being as a result of the poet's projection of a dead self into the elements; the metaphor of the "arme, vertrocknete Seelen" begins to make sense if we recall the uncanny place of Gertrude's grave, haunted by her alienated soul, where the hunter picked the "Schmele" that becomes the narrative of her story.

Another passage in "Meine Sträusse" echoes yet another poem: "Und wie Blutes Adern umschlingen mich / Meine Wasserfäden und Moose" (I, 133) repeats imagery to be found in the "Wasserfäden" section of "Der Weiher"; in that place the "Wasserfäden" describe their interaction with the pond:

> des Teiches Blutsverwandte, fest
> Hält er uns an die Brust gepresst,
> Und wir bohren unsre feinen Ranken
> In das Herz ihm, wie ein liebend Weib,
> Dringen Adern gleich durch seinen Leib.　　　　　[I, 41]

[the pond's blood relations, tightly / He holds us pressed to his breast, / And we bore our fine vines / Into his heart, like a loving wife, / Penetrate his heart like arteries.]

All these passages from "Meine Sträusse" suggest the identification of self with pond through the mediation of poems as waterplants; the "Wasserfäden" however stand for poems even more definitely than the other flora. They are poems which remain so much a part of the poet that they can be called blood vessels. But precisely because they are inseparable, they can be burdensome as well as satisfying; like the downward pull of the imagination, they both embrace and entrap the poet ("umschlingen mich"). This sensation is described in another, more conventional way in the poem "Herzlich," where Droste-Hülshoff calls her poems "Meines Herzens flammendes Blut" (II, 43; *Erstdruck der Letzten Gaben*, 1860). The figures used to describe the relationship of "Wasserfäden" to "Weiher" likewise consistently have to do with blood vessels that pierce the heart. In such patterns one can again see the outline of the corpse in the pond.[60]

"Der Dichter. Dichters Glück"[61] gathers together the images of water, corpse, flower, and poem once again, this time explicitly in connection with its title subject. Here are the pertinent lines from

Part II:

Locke nicht, du Strahl aus der Höh;
Noch lebt des Prometheus Geier.
Stille, stille du buhlender See;
Noch wachen die Ungeheuer
über deines Hortes kristallnem Schrein,
Senk die Hand, mein fürstlicher Zecher,
Dort drunten bleicht das morsche Gebein,
Des, der getaucht nach dem Becher.

Und du, flatternder Fadenstrauss,
Du der Distel mystische Rose,
Strecke nicht deine Fäden aus
Mich umschlingend so lind und lose!   [p. 255]

[Do not beckon, you ray from above; / Prometheus' vulture still lives. /
Quiet, quiet you wooing lake; / The monsters still lie awake / In watch
over your hoard's crystal coffer, / Lower your hand, my royal tippler, /
Down below the crumbling skeleton is bleaching, / of him, who dove for
the goblet. // And you, fluttering water plant bouquet, / You, the this-
tle's mystical rose, / Do not stretch out your filaments / Entwining me
so gently and loosely!]

This poem ostensibly warns against the dangerous lure of the natural
world for the imagination, recalling the attraction of the child to the
waterlily. But in fact the movement of descent into nature is here
sanctioned in more than one way. Because Droste-Hülshoff's imagination does not as a rule strive upward to "die Höh," she does not
linger over the myth of Prometheus. Instead, she uses motifs from
medieval romance—and Goethe's "König in Thule"—to reformulate
her central metaphor of watery descent, which is presented in this
poem, with some straining, as a safer route than flight aloft for an
orthodox religious quest. The figure who has drowned in the lake has
done so in order to retrieve a Grail, and, in thus giving himself to
Christ, himself becomes the sacrificed "morsche Gebein" reposed
beneath the glassy surface of the lake, which subtly acquires the
appearance of a reliquary. But the "buhlender See," the "fürstlicher
Zecher," and, most tellingly, the "Becher," when read in the context
of the poem's title—"Der Dichter. Dichter's Glück"—all point beyond this reading to "Der König in Thule," a song sung by Gretchen
in *Faust*. Droste-Hülshoff's title seems to insist on an allegory apart
from the religious one. At this level, the "Becher" is not a Grail but

an emblem of Goethe's poem, and to descend back through tradition to retrieve it as one's own is to lose consciousness of one's personal identity as a poet.[62] Having become another—both Goethe and nature itself—in death, one then becomes, as we have seen before, one's own tradition, just as by diving for the Grail the quester is merged with the sacrificed body of Christ. In this case the "fürstlicher Zecher" no longer has prior possession of the "Becher"; the poet can openly appropriate it because it is now neither given nor loaned but shared between equals, both sovereigns.

The surviving speaker in Droste-Hülshoff's poem then repeats with impunity the movement of diving performed by the sacrificed self: "Senk die Hand" recalls the way in which poems are made by fishing or dredging in "Meine Sträusse": "Dann lang' ich sachte, sachte hinab, / Und fische die träufelnden Schmelen" (I, 132). (Sarah Kirsch, a woman poet of our time, seems fully to understand this metaphor when she says in her poem, "Der Droste würde ich gern Wasser reichen": "wir verstehen / Uns jetzt gründlich auf das Handwerk Fischen.")[63] Indeed, in Part I of "Der Dichter. Dichters Glück," Droste-Hülshoff seems to recall a supposed death by drowning in *The Tempest* when she writes of the poet: "Ja, Perlen fischt er und Juwele / Die kosten nichts als seine Seele" (p. 254). But what the poet as pearl-fisher removes from the pond with its corpse is always, again, the poem, appearing as a jewel or flower. That which survives the poet becomes permanent through metamorphosis, as Ariel may secondarily suggest in the passage to which Droste-Hülshoff alludes above:

> Full fathom five thy father lies;
>   Of his bones are coral made;
> Those are pearls that were his eyes;
>   Nothing of him that doth fade
> But doth suffer a sea-change.   [*The Tempest*, I, ii, 401–05]

So it is for poets when they go, in the words of another recent female poet, Adrienne Rich, "Diving into the Wreck."

The lure of the shimmering deep is, of course, an almost universal Romantic theme, as is the figure of the double. As a late Romantic poet struggling to revitalize a disinspirited world and an increasingly dispirited outlook for the imagination, Annette von Droste-Hülshoff modulates these themes to reflect that struggle. In his later, "Post-Romantic" poetry, Mörike solves the problem posed by his alienation from Nature by seeing the objects of Nature as though they were objects of art. The Ophelia figure, the corpse resurfaced as a flower, is Droste-Hülshoff's stratagem for coming to terms at once with the sense of belatedness she shares with Mörike and also with the problems unique to women poets: she must exorcize a "demonic" self, socially unacceptable precisely because it is natural, and yet somehow retain this self, which is the origin of her art. In creating her "wild Muse," she accomplishes just that, providing an unusually cogent, naturally grounded explanation for the muse's femaleness as well. Ophelia, the maiden weaving garlands by the river, furthermore provides a metaphor for the gathering of poetry from nature. She is a female Narcissus, contemplating her own image—not in delight, however, but in terror as it dissolves upon the water. The deviancy of all these images must be rationalized, however, and so Droste-Hülshoff indicts herself as a madwoman who seeks union with her double in suicide. She then becomes a corpse lingering in the water, remaining to haunt it as a skeleton, a face, or else, simply and most pertinently, as a voice. She is the wild self who is sacrificed to Nature, where she becomes a fitting muse. As Hamlet's mother says, Ophelia's last moments were spent in singing: "she chanted snatches of old lauds" until she sank, pulled down "from her melodious lay to muddy death" (*Hamlet*, II, vii, 177, 183–84).

III

Deswegen kömmt es mir aber vor, als
sähe ich mich im Sarg liegen und
meine beiden Ichs starren sich ganz
verwundert an.
—Bettina von Arnim, *Die*
  Günderode: Ein Briefwechsel

What are we to make of a poet who creates a corpse for a muse but whose images of decay differ markedly from those of the English graveyard school, for instance, which generally contribute to a mood of accepting melancholy? Neither is there any of the textbook-sublime rhetoric of Young's *Night Thoughts* in Droste-Hülshoff's evocations of death. Droste-Hülshoff's poetry is most genuine, at its most disturbingly original, when it renders a negative landscape not unlike the one Keats savors—only to reject—in the first stanza of the "Ode on Melancholy."[64] Yewberries, the death-moth, the downy owl—Keats rejects this landscape of suicide because he perceives images of this kind to be signs of failure, of diminished poetic energy, as though the poet had numbed his imagination with a drink from Lethe's waters. These situations spell poetic death for Keats. His rejected first stanza decries the thought of building "a bark of dead men's bones" as a means of poetically discovering melancholy, which for Keats resides in the very fruitfulness and vitality of Nature; but Keats's rejected stratagem is precisely the one Droste-Hülshoff chooses. As Heselhaus points out, "it is from her dead that Droste's poetry derives its heavy, serious tone and from her submersion ("Hineinversenktsein") in the soul of the homeland it derives its consecrating and healing power."[65] The expression "Hineinversenktsein" points to one of Droste-Hülshoff's most important poetic self-orientations: to locate herself, in many of the poems, in a grave-like place, and to descend into the earth with its many dead.[66] Whether her involvement with the dead has a salutary effect on the poet, and what the precise nature of that involvement may be, remain to be considered.

Ledwina's daydream, in which she imagines herself to be a corpse submerged under the waves of moonlight on her bed, is preceded in that highly autobiographical novel by a dream, a complete narrative sequence that sheds considerable light on the lyrics that I have been discussing. In her dream, Ledwina is accompanied by a group of friends and relatives to what is supposedly a theatrical performance. On the way, the leader of the group, who becomes Ledwina's guide, informs her that they have entered a cemetery and warns her to walk with care, as there are several freshly dug and open graves. Ledwina surveys the scene and laughs aloud when it occurs to her:

> dass hier ihr Liebstes auf der Welt begraben liege. Sie wusste keinen Namen und hatte keine genauere Form dafür als überhaupt die menschliche, aber es war gewiss ihr Liebstes, und sie riss sich mit einem furchtbar zerrissnen Angstgewimmer los und begann zwischen den Gräbern zu suchen und mit einem kleinen Spaden die Erde hier und dort aufzugraben. Nun war sie plötzlich die Zuschauende und sah ihre eigene Gestalt totenbleich mit wild im Wind flatternden Haaren an den Gräbern wühlen, mit einem Ausdrucke in den verstörten Zügen, der sie mit Entsetzen füllte. Nun war sie wieder die Suchende selber.   [II, 290]

> [that here her dearest one on earth lay buried. She knew no name for it and had no more precise form for it than the human one after all, but it was certainly her dearest, and she pulled herself loose with a terrible broken whimper of fear and began to look among the graves and to dig up the earth here and there with a small spade. Now she was suddenly the spectator and saw her own form burrowing among the graves,

deathly pale, with hair fluttering wildly in the wind and with an expression on her disturbed features that filled with her with dread.]

When Ledwina attempts to read the gravestones, she cannot decipher them, although she knows instinctively that none of them is "der rechte"—presumably that of "ihr Liebstes." The danger of sinking into one of the graves becomes clear to her, and she tries to avoid the mounds, but the "Zwang des Traumes" pulls her toward one of them (II, 290).

As she falls into the grave, Ledwina hears the boards of the wooden coffin breaking and finds herself lying next to a skeleton. She immediately recognizes "ihr Liebstes," embraces it, and only later examines its features, "für die sie selbst keine Norm hatte" (II, 290). Snow begins to cover the scene, obscuring her vision, even though it is now morning. Still unperturbed, Ledwina grasps the skeleton's hand—which detaches itself from the frame—and presses it to her lips. Finally she buries her face in "den modrigen Staub" (II, 291). When she looks up again, she sees that night has fallen once more; at her command the guide leaves her his lantern, and by its light she begins to caress the skeleton with heartrending tenderness. Suddenly a child carrying a basket of fruit and flowers appears at the grave, and Ledwina buys the basket and then adorns the skeleton with its flowers: "Da sie den Korb umschüttete, wurden der Blumen so viele, dass sie das ganze Grab füllten. Des freute sie sich sehr, und wie ihr Blut milder floss, formte sich die Idee, als könne sie den verwesten Leib wieder aus Blumen zusammensetzen, dass er lebe und mit ihr gehe" (II, 291).

Ledwina's highly suggestive dream points to a connection between death and poetic inspiration. Instead of entering the theater of life, she chooses the abode of death. The torches held by the company, recalling the one held by Lessing's smiling youth, grow brighter when the cemetery with its fresh graves is entered, suggesting that this stylized charnel scene is itself the theater—the theater, we shall see, of the imagination. The white markers and black grave mounds form a backdrop for the drama that Ledwina herself enacts. She is warned by the "Führer," whose function may be likened to that of the superego, not to fall into the open graves. But Ledwina still searches for "ihr Liebstes auf der Welt," whom she instinctively knows to be buried there. The sense of doubleness so often experienced in dreaming, the feeling of being one moment the spectator, the next the actor, significantly occurs here when the emotional sense of trespass strikes Ledwina most forceably; that is, when she perceives the wild abandon and desperation of her search. She sees herself "totenbleich mit wild im Winde flatternden Haaren an den Gräbern wühlen." It is the wild poetic self that digs with such frenzy. The other self, meanwhile, the spectator, perceives but cannot avoid the danger of "einsinken."

The desire for descent, for being pulled downward by the "Zwang des Traumes"—here disguised as a fall—is the same desire that is revealed in so many of Droste-Hülshoff's most central poems. The suggestion of an erotic past in the happy *re*union with "das Liebste," despite its being a skeleton to which she can attach no specific identity, together with Ledwina's attempt to press her face into the mouldering earth, all this reinforces a desire for death that is openly acknowledged by the dreamer. The "Führer," again the bringer of light, does his best to fulfill the function of the superego, bidding her leave the grave, but Ledwina vows to remain until she too is dead. (The lantern left with Ledwina at the gravesite, with its resemblance to Death's torch, is the same lantern that burns so ambiguously in many of Droste-Hülshoff's poems.) It seems apparent that what the wild self is searching for in the earth is an understanding of its own beginnings. "Beyond the pleasures of poetry," writes Harold Bloom, "lies the maternal womb of language out of which poems arise, the literal meaning that poems both evade and desperately seek."[67] The proximity of death to the imagination arouses anxiety. The dreamer's wish to turn to "dust," the wish for complete annihilation or at least for reduction to the simplest of organic forms, is transformed—sublimated—in the wish to "revive" the skeleton by covering it up with flowers; that is, to make the corpse the site of poetry. Again the pattern is circular: if death is the source of inspiration, then the wild self is the very skeleton it is searching for. The child bringing the fruit and flowers is a mute, regressive self with the power nonetheless to provoke the creative process, which in turn constantly reformulates this drama of the selves in the hope that a lost unity of being—whether in death or in infancy—may be regained. To the childish self, nature implies generation and fruitfulness, but for Ledwina, who rejects the child's fruit while keeping its flowers—surely poetic language itself—the earth is more notable for harboring the dead than for creating life. Whereas Keats rejects his deadly landscape as implying poetic suicide, choosing instead the plentiful moment that "fills all fruit with ripeness to the core,"

Droste-Hülshoff lingers apart from the vitality of nature. In Ledwina's dream, the sole image from the natural world is the falling snow, which suggests gentle burial, until she accepts the flowers— the "Sträusse"—which are in turn expressive of death rather than life.

In *Women Writers and Poetic Identity*, Margaret Homans argues that for the woman poet writing within a tradition in which nature is mythologized as Mother Nature, hence threatens to engulf her, her relationship with nature remains fragmented, ambiguous, or even openly hostile. Homans suggests that the best strategy for the female poet writing in the Romantic tradition would consist in "turning Mother Nature back into nature."[68] This is a radical strategy, but one that can take many forms. One might be the curtailing of Mother Nature's powers of generation by focusing upon a decaying landscape such as the swamp and its inhabitants, the toads and fungus, in *Rosstäuscher*. The contents of the witches' cauldron in *Macbeth* shows how persistently natural ingredients of this kind have been associated with the arts of women. Another tactic to which Droste-Hülshoff has recourse for delimiting the abundance of nature is to invest even seemingly tranquil scenes with threatening forces. Böschenstein-Schaefer points out that more often than not "that landscape that for her is alone capable of being considered idyllic is revealed to be a landscape of death."[69] When Benno von Wiese describes the uncanny—"das Unheimliche"—in Droste-Hülshoff's ballads, he means not only the ghosts that populate them but in general the threatening force of which we are speaking: "that magical something that emerges from the darkness formless and incapable of being named and that sometimes reveals itself in hazy forms."[70] This is the equivalent of Ledwina's "Liebstes"; the death wish pervades the wild self and forms poems that undermine the germinal energies of nature. Because Nature is a rival Creatrix, her powers are made to seem inimical, and her threat to the poet is rendered as a threatening landscape.

Another antidote to Nature is, as we have seen, the killing off of the wild self, whose body returns to the elements and whose spirit malingers to become the genius of the place. Droste-Hülshoff's intention is here similar; in becoming herself the inspiration of nature through the negation of death, she doubly undermines the notion of nature as a creative source. Since woman is traditionally symbolized as "Nature," literary woman can scarcely avoid conceiving of nature as a woman poet who precedes and overshadows her. Thus when in the poem "An die Schriftstellerinnen in Deutschland und Frankreich"—written in her public voice—Droste-Hülshoff calls upon female poets to awaken "der Natur geheimnisreichste Laute" (I, 20), she suppresses the subversiveness of her own poetics. And when she reminds these women that "Ihr höret sie die unterdrückten Klagen / Der heiligen Natur geprägt zur Dirne" (I, 20), acknowledging the identification of women with nature and calling upon them to restore "her" to her dignity, she speaks with conviction but perhaps without poetic self-knowledge.

In a rather conventional poem called "Die Sterne, Frage" (*Umkreis der Gesammelten Werke*), Droste-Hülshoff addresses the stars as emblems of the sublime mysteries guiding the spirit upwards:

> Er sieht
> Von Lichtglanz umglüht
> Euren mystischen Lauf,
> O hinauf, hinauf,
> Aus der Wirklichkeit finstern Schranken hinauf!   [II, 89]

[He sees / Illumined by aureoles of light / Your mystical course, / O upward, upward, / Beyond reality's dark boundaries, upward!]

The echoes of Goethe in this poem's rhythm and subject matter never attain the magical, bewitching quality of his "Ganymed," and it not surprisingly remained unpublished. However, in the second stanza of an otherwise unswerving argument, there is an unexpected turn. Here the derivative plea for illumination from above is reversed:

> Doch schweigen
> Die Bleichen
> Gestirn wie das Grab,
> O hinab, hinab,
> Zu des Geheimnisses Urquell hinab!   [II, 89]

[Yet the pale stars / Are silent / As the grave, / O downward, downward, / To the mystery's primal source, downward!]

This is an instance of what Bloom calls "daemonization," a powerful poetic moment in which repression is not working properly. That this image has its source in the colloquial expression "schweigen wie das Grab" is likely, but the downward pull of this grave is still remarkable; for all its silence, the grave is still thought with some urgency to be "des Geheimnisses Urquell."

That the source of sublimity and poetic ecstasy for Droste-Hülshoff is death is still more abundantly clear in the following passage from "Die Unbesungenen" (I, 140–41):

O, wenn dich Zweifel drückt herab,
Und möchtest atmen Ätherluft,
Und möchtest schauen Seraphsflügel
Dann tritt an deines Vaters Grab!
Dann tritt an deines Bruders Gruft!
Dann tritt an deines Kindes Hügel!

[O when doubt depresses you, / And you wish to breathe aethereal air, / And you wish to see seraphs' wings / Then come to your father's grave! / Then come to your brother's tomb! / Then come to your child's burial mound!]

The experience of the sublime described here does not derive from the contemplation of the eternal soul or from the promise of everlasting life, as it does in the poetry of Klopstock, for whom the mouldering body can be safely spurned in quest of the immortal soul. By contrast Droste-Hülshoff, who is also much concerned with the contrast of body and soul in the religious poetry of the *Geistliches Jahr*, seems inescapably to find the body more fascinating. It is her imagination's privileged subject:

Wie tiefberauschend ist dein Odem,
O Phantasie! was kommt ihm gleich
Wenn über Mauerzinnen bleich
Du gleiten lässt den Grabesbrodem!   [Canto II, *Die Schlacht im Loener Bruch*, I, 387]

[How deeply intoxicating is your breath, / O imagination! What can compare / When over pale castle battlements / You let glide the breath of the grave!]

In "Meine Toten," the poet approaches the dead before setting out on an important, unspecified mission—which may be the poetic venture itself. Subverting the Wordsworthian recollection of having come to consciousness on the breast of Mother Nature, the poet claims to have been awakened by the dead: "Ich bin erwacht an eurer Gruft" (I, 85). When the elements speak to her, they do so with the voice of the dead: "Aus Wasser, Feuer, Erde, Luft / Hat eure Stimme mir geboten" (I, 85). She reads the presence of death in the natural world, as when the withered leaf is recorded as a memento mori. Recalling Ophelia once more, the dead smile at her "aus der Welle

Kreis" and out of an icy winter landscape: "Habt aus des Angers starrem Eis / Die Blumenaugen aufgeschlagen." Here the dead have nearly usurped nature. In this moment of poetic timidity their meaningful presence in nature seems more powerful than poetic speech: "So spricht kein Wort wie Grabesbrodem." The poet requests that she be vouchsafed "truth" through the direct agency of the dead, and lowers her forehead to the grass in the manner of Ledwina burying her face in the grave. In "Meine Toten" the poet listens for the voice of the dead in the "Gräserhauch" as another poet might wait for inspiration from above.

In Ledwina's dream the descent into the grave implies a descent into the psyche for material that can be made into poetry. The connection of writing with the sensation of burial or enclosure in the womb (with death and gestation) is even discernable in the figures with which she describes the tower room at Meersburg where much of her poetry was written. In a letter to Levin Schücking (Dec. 14, 1843; *B*II, 246), she exclaims, "I feel as though I were buried in my tower"; and later she says, "Oh, it is a splendid thing, my tower; I sit in it like a bird in its egg and with even less desire to come out" (*B*II, 290).[71] In one of her last letters she calls the tower "meine Spiegelei" (*B*II, 527; a hall of mirrors, but jokingly entailing an allusion to the egg), gently mocking the state of health that confines her not only to the room but to the pleasures of the imagination for amusement, but also connecting the room with psychological inwardness. In the more vertiginous and daring poems of descent, by contrast, the poet's alarmed conscience increases the pressure to abandon interiority to so great an extent that she retreats back to reality, relativizing her reveries. She shies away both from the imagination and from her awareness of what informs it.

This contrast between descent and retreat to the surface is fully visible in "Die Vogelhütte." This poem records the poet's progress toward the writing of a poem, and here too the predicament that provokes the imagination—humorously presented in this case—is her confinement in a space that feels coffin-like. The poem passes through stages during which the poet is gradually freed from constraints imposed by ordinary life, in this instance the norms evoked by the circle of salon "critics" whom she knows to be discussing her poetry. Her anger is registered not so much in her rather petty protests as in the powerful image of herself as a fish: "Bohrend wie ein Schwertfisch möcht ich schiessen in den Wassergischt" (I, 35).

She then enters a less outward-turning state in which she fancifully transforms the space of the "coffin," the "Vogelhütte," into a literary setting, an idyllic hermitage with blowing thyme, in which solitude and confinement make writing possible: "Hier möcht ich Heide-bilder schreiben," she proclaims. The third section of the poem is indeed a *Heidebild*.

The gradual increase of subjectivity and imaginative involvement are reflected in the verse form chosen for each section of the poem. The third section, which is incantatory in tone, culminates in a solid line separating this section from the next and last, this being the only such mark of division in the poem.[72] It marks an access of interiority so profound that it is not to be expressed in language. The last section documents the poet's return to the ordinary world and her resumption of its values, indicating that a time of absence has elapsed between the previous section and this one. Already the imaginative period belongs to a distant past time, a "damals." Here then is the escape from reality to the imagination followed by a retreat back to reality of which we have been speaking. The pattern holds even though "Die Vogelhütte" is only superficially, again, a poem of descent. Never, even at its most magical, does it reach beyond the description of nature to an actual intimation of the psyche. Indeed, its most personal and revealing figure presents the poet as a fish. What *might* have been written is indicated solely by the line of division.

The *Heidebild* section of this poem is also an interesting instance of another recurrent tendency in Droste-Hülshoff's work. She frequently personifies nature, with the effect of subordinating it to human experience, as in the following passage, which makes nature speci-fically a domestic female:

In den feinen Dunst die Fichte
Ihre grünen Dornen streckt,
Wie ein schönes Weib die Nadel
In den Spitzenschleier steckt . . .   [I, 38]

[Into the fine haze the spruce / Stretches its green spikes, / Like a beau-tiful woman / Sticks the needle into the veil of lace . . .]

This is yet another means whereby the poet seeks to get the better of her powerful rival, Mother Nature, and her minute descriptions of nature have the same purpose. This section is written in the manner of an appreciative and sensitive observer of nature who is female but in her outlook could be Goethe as naturalist. A geologist who has been caught in the rain, as a scientist she implicitly has the power of reason and knows how to harness nature for human ends. As I have already maintained, Droste-Hülshoff's penchant for close and accurate observation is not a sign of her "Realism" but still another form of defense, rather, whereby she can dominate and demystify a natural world that would otherwise overwhelm her and keep her from writing. The result may be Realism, but it is motivated by an almost opposite impulse. It is the same with the adoption of Goethe's approach to nature: the result may be Goethean, but it is motivated by the urge to harness nature rather than to embrace it.

"Der Hünenstein," a poem with strong Gothic overtones, ventures to describe the descent into a grave. The poet's imagination is unleashed here, sanctioned in part by the eerie moonlit setting. The description of the moor in this poem resembles that of the wild self elsewhere; it is a place where "[k]rankhafte Funken im verwirrten Haar / Elektrisch blitzen" (I, 42). The preoccupations of the wanderer on the moor are those of a poet for whom "Entwürfe wurden aus Entwürfen reif" (I, 42). The wanderer is startled to find himself lying in the grass as though submerged, significantly, in water: "ich schreckte auf und lag / Am Grund, um mich des Heidekrautes Welle" (I, 42). The wanderer-poet discovers himself to be in a "Hünengrab," and what follows will be familiar to us from Ledwina's dream: "Und fester drückt ich meine Stirn hinab / Wollüstig saugend an des Grauens Süsse (I, 43). As in "Meine Toten," the poet receives inspiration from the presence of the dead. The landscape is feminized, with the moonlight lying "wie ein Witwe an des Gatten Grabe" (I, 43), and is everywhere marked by death (ashes are "leichenbrandig," for instance).

The wind, a divine breath, brings "Kunde aus dem Geisterland" (I, 43), and this time when the poet returns to the image of a woman mourning her dead, the image is not just a passing metaphor, yet another glimpse of the wild self (with blond, flowing hair like her own), this time expressly with the lineaments of a poetess, one whose incantations are magical. It is the central image of the poem. Yet the speaker of this poem is a man who obliquely identifies with the poetess when he sees an apparition and thinks he has conjured up a ghost: "Wie? Sprach ich Zauberformel?" (I, 43). Droste-Hülshoff withholds any clue that the speaker is male until the end of the poem, when she rejects imagination and turns to the safety of humor and the quotidian; and because the identification of this speaker with "die Drude" is so carefully effected, the assumption of the male persona is unconvincing. It is "die Drude" who has the power to make the place magical. "Umwandeln" is not far from "verwandeln" in this context, and this is the image of female power Droste-Hülshoff has evoked, not the object the speaker supposes to be a "Riesenleib" but which turns out to be an umbrella. The trivialization of the speaker and the humorous deflation of his vision is an example of Droste-Hülshoff's pulling back from the impassioned voice that responds to the presence of death. At the end of the poem, the speaker is reduced to a Spitzweg figure, bourgeois to the core. In repudiating the imagination almost entirely, the last lines would deny that the grave has any bearing on inspiration: "Ach Gott, es war doch nur ein rohes Grab, / Das armen, ausgedorrten Staub bedeckte!" (I, 44).

Withholding the sexual identity of the speaker until late in the poem—which we have already observed in "Die Schwestern"—is what Droste-Hülshoff does again in "Die Mergelgrube." Here too the speaker's imaginative "descent" is finally subjected to mild ridicule, and here too the turn to humor decoys the reader's attention from the poet's most heartfelt concerns. The distance effected by the conclusion contrasts sharply with the masculine, assertive strength of the opening: "Stoss deinen Scheit drei Spannen in den Sand, / Gesteine siehst du aus dem Schnitte ragen" (I, 45). The geologist robs the earth of its treasure; for his invasion he uses not only the "Scheit"—of which more in a moment—but also his hands and feet: "bröckelt bei dem Griff / Der Hand, dem Scharren mit des Fusses Spitze" (I, 45).[73] In bringing the stones to the surface, the geologist performs an "Eingriff" that exposes his "Findlinge" to view; he dislodges the stones as they had once been dislodged by the Deluge: "Findlinge nennt man sie, weil von der Brust, / Der mütterlichen sie gerissen sind" (I, 45–46). The poet is clearly thinking of traditional myths of origin in the first stanza of "Die Mergelgrube." The stones are displaced orphans, the part of nature that has survived the Flood—which brought death to all else: "Und eine *fremde*, üppige Natur, / Ein neues Leben quoll aus neuen Stoffen" (I, 45; italics mine). In this first section, the speaker is barely present, but the concerns of Ledwina's dream are already present and will become clearer. Writing is again animated by death when the poet claims that she can reverse the natural process and bring life (living art) out of death.

The narrative of "Die Mergelgrube" begins with the second stanza.

As in so many other poems, the speaker, once more a geologist, descends into the earth: "Tief ins Gebröckel, in die Mergelgrube / War ich gestiegen" (I, 46). He enters a cave-like "Höhlenstube" where the mysterious and presumably creative forces of nature surround and enchant him; he hears "ein Zischen," "ein Rispeln und ein Schaffen." But instead of encountering the life-bringing forces that Goethe in this place might have experienced, this speaker now envisions nature as a site of devastation:

> doch die Natur
> Schien mir verödet, und ein Bild erstand
> Von einer Erde, mürbe, ausgebrannt[.]   [I, 46]

[but Nature / Seemed desolate to me, and an image emerged / Of a brittle, burned-out earth.]

Once again Mother Nature is deprived of her procreative and creative powers, just as when, earlier, the stones are declared to be the "children" of an antediluvian nature which is no more. The speaker identifies with the stones in calling himself "[e]in Findling im zerfallnen Weltenbau" (I, 46), and he associates his own origin with the accounts of creation myths. In asking "War ich der erste Mensch oder der letzte?" (I, 46) he once again insists upon the obverse inseparability of creation and destruction, birth and death.

While the speaker's reverie itself takes place in a timeless visionary moment, the epic-influenced association between descent and submersion in the past—the descent into memory—continues to obtain. In harboring the skeletons of the dead alongside its antediluvian stones, the earth is a repository of the past in all its sweep, whether it be the quasi-mythical past of "Der Hünenstein" or the overtly historical past of *Die Schlacht im Loener Bruch*.[74] But it is death that is always emphasized as the condition, the medium, of the past; and the descent into the past is typically once more, therefore, a descent into the grave. This part of the speaker's reverie in "Die Mergelgrube" is dominated by images of death, which color his self-perception as well: he is a "Petrefakt," a remnant of the same "old Nature" which produced the stones. When he hears the sound of the "Totenkäfer," Droste-Hülshoff's favorite negative sign of the process world, the speaker sets geological concerns aside and calls up images of death in general. Through the agency of the imagination he simply *becomes* the buried, mouldering corpse in various historical guises: "eine Leiche im Katakombenbau" (I, 47), or "eine Mumie" (I, 47). As the "Mergelgrube" becomes more and more clearly a grave in the mind of the speaker, we recall that the opening line of the poem features a "Scheit," a tool for digging that may be a "Grabscheit"; all along, evidently, the geological treasure has been the equivalent of Ledwina's "Liebstes."

In the case of this poem once again, a facetious conclusion reintroducing everyday existence backs away from a prior visionary insight. The speaker is roused when he is hit on the head by a ball of yarn dropped by a shepherd knitting socks. This figure out of pastoral stands in such a harmonious relation with nature that he can barely be distinguished from his sheep, and in a poem written by one whose view of nature is both severe and distant, we should be alert to the suggestion of something silly as well as enviable in the shepherd's merger with his maternal surroundings: "Er schaut so seelengleich die Herde an, / Dass man nicht weiss, ob Schaf er oder Mann." This shepherd is a Fundamentalist, and rejects the scientific explanations of the geologist-speaker's bible, Bertuch's *Naturgeschichte*. At the same time, however, the shepherd is a Romantic poet. His song opens with an enigmatic image that is not apparently connected with what follows, an image of a fish deep in the waters of a lake: "Es stehet ein Fischlein in einem tiefen See, / Danach tu ich wohl schauen, ob es kommt in die Höh" (I, 48). Scholars differ as to whether the shepherd's song was traditional or was written by Droste-Hülshoff.[75] Regardless of its authorship, however, in the fish in the lake the song contains the key to the complex of images that comprises the poem as a whole. The submerged fish is the submerged poetic self. Although the poem appears to contrast the shepherd and the geologist, the naive Romantic and the scientist, they are not really opposed at all; we have not come to know the speaker as a scientist, after all, but as a seeker with an obsessed imagination. Droste-Hülshoff does project her self-conception into this geologist, not only because of her own interest in rocks and fossils, not only because she favors accurate and detailed descriptions of nature, but also because a persona of this kind, again resembling Goethe as scientist, can be relied upon to dominate and subdue nature with the power of knowledge. For the shepherd she reserves a role customarily given to the female by male poets; he is wholly at one with nature—and he even knits socks. It may have been in the interest of thus intricately undermining the potential dichotomy between these two figures that the poet chose to belittle the imagination of the geologist by causing him, as in "Der Hünenstein," to misinterpret the prosaic as the exotic and uncanny. This tactic is perhaps deliberately misleading, as it seems to privilege by negation an intuitive sympathy with nature that the poet can neither share nor praise.

"Im Grase," "Im Moose," and, to some extent, "Durchwachte Nacht" are also poems of descent. "Im Grase" presents a reverie that describes nature in its particularity (in this respect resembling Gessner's "Im Grase"), but this description is not the focus of the poem. The aroma of the grasses engulfs the poet as though it were water—"Tiefe Flut, tief, tief trunkne Flut" (I, 436)—and thus she is submerged in her own imagination, which, as always, dwells upon death and the past: "Tote Liebe, tote Lust, tote Zeit, / All die Schätze, im Schutte verwühlt" (I, 436). To be buried in the grass is like being buried "im Busen," itself the abode of the dead—"Wenn im Busen die Toten dann, / Jede Leiche sich streckt und regt" (I, 436)—and reminds one of the imagery of Ledwina's dream, with which it is also connected by the sweet laughter that helps initiate the poet's reverie:

Süsses Lächeln gaukelt herab,
Liebe Stimme säuselt und träuft
Wie die Lindenblüt' auf ein Grab.   [I, 436]

[Sweet laughter drifts downwards, / Dear voice sweetly dripping / Like lindenblossoms on a grave.]

In "Durchwachte Nacht," this is the sound that heralds the approach of the blond, blue-eyed child—as in "Doppelgänger" (II, 11), an earlier fragment from which portions of "Durchwachte Nacht" are taken. The regressive alter ego is teasingly inaccessible in "Durchwachte Nacht," and thus comes to obsess the speaker at the most vulnerable hour of the night, just before dawn.[76] In "Im Grase," however, the imagined laughter of the child has the further function of raising the dead in the breast of the poet, thus recalling the child who helped bring Ledwina's "Liebstes" back to life.

Although the imagery evoked in "Im Grase" is central in Droste-Hülshoff's imagination, the message of the poem remains rather conventional, affirming as it does the pleasures of the imagination and of human feeling. "Im Moose," by contrast, which begins with a strikingly similar situation, ends in fear and dissolution. Again the speaker is lying amid moss and grasses and is attuned to nearly disembodied sensations—fragrances, sounds, and light. Once again she imagines herself a corpse: "Fast war es mir als sei ich schon entschlafen" (I, 71). In this condition reverie and poetry appear to come most easily. The passing of thoughts from one time to another—into the past, into the future—is itself motivated by the death instinct, the repression of which displaces into the future the desire to restore the past. In "Im Moose," even the projected future is dominated by things of the past, by "Löckchen vermorscht, zu Staub zerfallen schier" (I, 72). The speaker envisions an aging self, kneeling on the graves of her loved ones in prayer, and finally, in the strongest image of all, she projects her own death: "Und noch zuletzt sah ich, gleich einem Rauch, / Mich leise in der Erde Poren ziehen." This astonishing final image of a disintegrating, disembodied self is continuous with the disembodiment of nature at the present moment of twilight. But this in itself is frightening to the female poet, who in declaring her own disembodiment has identified herself with the filmy appearance of nature at twilight. And when Mother Nature—personified as such in this poem—absorbs her through her pores, the poem is in danger of ending, the speaker's vision having been wholly subsumed by her Mother. It is not death as such but this particular death that is terrifying.

The poet's shock at what she has imagined rouses her forceably from her daydream—"Ich fuhr empor, und schüttelte mich dann" (I, 72)—reestablishing a sense of self and of difference. It is only at this point in the poem that she is willing to acknowledge the full ambivalence with which she views the vaguely threatening light. Earlier she called it "der Heimat Lampe," but now she compares it with a "Traumgesicht." She is now uncertain whether the star she sees "sei wirklich meiner Schlummerlampe Schein, / Oder das ew'ge Licht am Sarkophage" (I, 72). Since the death she imagines is the death of her poetic self being absorbed, speechless, into Mother Nature, it is that threat, arguably, that transforms the "Heimatlampe" into the light on a tomb. At the same time, however, this light, which takes many forms in Droste-Hülshoff's work, remains the light of imaginative thought, the Romantic "lamp" documented by M. H. Abrams.[77] In thus transforming the lantern into "das ew'ge Licht am Sarkophage," Droste-Hülshoff registers the ambivalence of her feelings—as woman, woman poet, and compulsive topologist of descent—toward the characteristic movement of her own imagination, but at the same time she finds a suitable emblem for the darkest insight of her work, which is that the light of poetic life arises from death.

Rather than summarize the pattern of Droste-Hülshoff's poetic descent once more in concluding, I have thought it best to append here a biographical note concerning Droste-Hülshoff's relationship with her mother, given that that relationship may afford some further explanation of the poet's surprising ambivalence toward the natural world. It has long been understood that Droste-Hülshoff was in most things subservient to her mother throughout her lifetime. Levin Schücking's *Lebensbild* presents a negative picture of this personage even where it attempts praise:

> She suppressed and removed all traces of passion and eccentricity that were able to develop in such a talented and imaginative personality and applied to all youthful urges the standard of noble femininity. But she also hampered a certain sense of independence which is essential to the genius; only in her last years was the poet able to emancipate herself from outside influences, influences which, in the form of advice, remonstrances, and wishes of those closest to her, adversely affected her free creative powers.[78]

Ricarda Huch speaks of the mother's "strength of will," while of the father she says, "Autorität übte er nur durch seine Güte aus."[79] Renate Böschenstein-Schaefer makes much of the effect that this reversal of roles had on Droste-Hülshoff, daughter of a "mother with masculine energy."[80] One can lean too heavily on "evidence" of this kind, and in any case at least some of the typology outlined here will be found in most women writers, or least in most women writers at this stage in the history of the poetic treatment of nature; nevertheless, in Droste-Hülshoff's letters especially confirmation of specific traits in her work are found.

A tone of apology and guilt pervades this daughter's letters to her mother. They are full of long explanations and excuses for her behavior—and above all, from the beginning, for her poetry. They are always much more veiled concerning her intellectual and artistic concerns than are the letters to Schlüter and Sprickmann, and more evasive concerning personal matters than those to Elise Rüdiger and to her sister.[81] The poet's protestations of affection for her mother are frequent, and she is purportedly willing to defer to her opinion in all matters, even in the matter of her writing. In a letter to Sprickmann (Mar. 23, 1837) she explains: "The opinion of my mother has such great value for me, even when it is not my own; you understand!" (*BI*, 202); or again: "Any word which I had written against her will would weigh upon me like a stone" (*BI*, 547). It is easy to wonder, though, whether this exaggerated concern—exaggerated even for the times—is not a reaction formation, the result of the perhaps internalized guilt she feels about her writing and about the unusual life she chooses to live whenever she can. There is no doubt about the mother's attitude toward her daughter's work; the story is well known that Droste-Hülshoff presented an early version of the *Geistliches Jahr* to her mother, who put it in a drawer and refused to read it, so much did she disapprove. And this attitude never changed. In 1838 the poet wistfully writes, "I do wish that you would derive some pleasure from my scribblings, my dear, dearest Mama" (*BI*, 306); and there is a tendency in general to mention writing and knitting in the same breath as forming "a good pile of work" (*BI*, 561). All this is interesting, then, but again, one scarcely needs a disapproving mother if there is a well-socialized self within the self that censors and polices all wilder selves whenever possible.

Perhaps more profound and specifically relevant to the dynamics of Droste-Hülshoff's work are the hints one detects in her correspondence and other writings of a struggle back and forth between mother and daughter quite simply for available energy, for priority and initiative in commanding the will to live. Böschenstein-Schaefer mentions a passage in one of the Westphalian stories in which it is said of a mother that she will outlive her entire clan save one grandchild; she is " 'eine steinalte Frau. . . . [M]an hat fast denken sollen, sie werde nimmer sterben.' " Böschenstein-Schaefer quotes this passage, rightly commenting on its expression of "Estrangement . . . toward such an aggressive vitality."[82] In one of her letters Droste-Hülshoff writes in this vein that "Mama is markedly healthy" (*BI*, 522). The hale and hearty mother did indeed outlive her sickly and nervous daughter, who must have resented her elder's rude health at times. Her tellingly exaggerated response to the fear that her mother may be dangerously ill in a letter to Elise Rüdiger possibly expresses guilt at such occasional resentment (see *BI*, 569).

Be this as it may, it is a resentment that does seem to surface in the poet's work whenever nature threatens to oppress, eclipse, or engulf her with its immemorial, inimitable power. I have not stressed here, as I did in the case of Eichendorff, the question of authorial influence and its attendant intimidations. For Droste-

Hülshoff and women writers resembling her, the relationship with the literary father is for the most part benign; nature itself is the oppressive influence, and at the last one is oneself the only muse available to embrace.

Chapter Four
The Poetry of
Transformation:
Rilke's Orpheus and
the Fruit of Death

> *Death, in the human perspective, is*
> *not a given, it must be achieved. It*
> *is a task, one which we take up*
> *actively, one which becomes the*
> *source of our activity and our mastery.*
> —Maurice Blanchot, *The Space*
> *of Literature*

The aim of Rilke's poetic life is the mastery of death. Although "authentic" death is nearly everywhere affirmed in Rilke's work, and although it is clearly an animating presence, there remains a perceptible resistance to its lure. The theme of death permeates everything Rilke wrote—the poetry, the fictional prose, the letters, and the diaries. In her book on Rilke, written after his death and long after her involvement with Freud and his work, Lou Andreas-Salomé asserts that from the beginning there had been something remarkable in the poet's attitude toward death.[1] The analyst Erich Simenauer likewise insists upon Rilke's preoccupation with death, and in her eccentric way, E. M. Butler expresses fascination with the topic as well, arguing that the fear of death lies at the heart of Rilke's work. She traces the power of this theme to an incident recorded in the Tuscan diaries; during his stay in Viareggio Rilke associated a silent, masked mendicant friar with the mysterious death of a dog: "As for the complex of emotions and thoughts in which a black brother of mercy and a dead dachshund are fortuitously involved, whoever or whatever was the origin opened up a trail in the poet's mind which blazed its way through the whole of his subsequent work, achieving its final goal in the *Sonette an Orpheus*."[2] Butler's conviction that Rilke's affirmation of death concealed a secret loathing and horror is certainly plausible when we consider his extreme fastidiousness; it helps to lessen the incongruity one feels at Rilke's reveling in the most earthbound stage of biological process, and explains why he subjected that process to a thoroughgoing mythological transformation. As Butler writes: "His conviction of the greater glory of death was founded upon a rock. Yet this was embedded in dark, submerged hatred and abhorrence, loathing and fear of dying."[3] Presumably for this reason, Rilke appears superstitiously to have avoided anticipating his own death. He refused to learn the name of his fatal disease, and whenever the word "death" was about to be mentioned in conversation with his doctor, he quickly changed the subject.[4]

For these reasons, then, death becomes an aesthetic object in Rilke's work. Maurice Blanchot believes, in fact, that the proper level on which to read Rilke's achieved view of death is a metaphysical one: "he did not want to put between himself and his end the mediation of any general knowledge."[5] Rilke himself ascribed his emphasis on death to the Danish writer Jens Peter Jacobsen, whose stories and novels, with their decadent aestheticization of death, he began to read as early as 1896. It is widely agreed that Rilke derived his theme of "personal death" from Jacobsen, together with the atmosphere of apparition and inwardness that would later inform *Malte Laurids Brigge*.[6] Rilke's early poems treat death with a preciosity that is typical of the fin-de-siècle, and it is not until the *Stunden-Buch*, in particular the section called *Das Buch von der Armut und vom Tode* (written in Viareggio in 1903), that the theme of death begins to emerge in an individual way. When Rilke subsequently developed the idea of a "personal death" in *Malte*, he meant a death which was a fitting, natural culmination of a particular life, contrasting—for example—the properly eccentric death of old Brigge with the impersonal death experienced by the masses in Paris's Hôtel de Dieu. Blanchot argues that even this early conception of a personal death was still primarily an aesthetic one: "In this terror before mass-produced death there is the sadness of the artist who honors well-wrought things, who wants to make a work, and make his death his work. Death is from the start linked to the movement, so difficult to bring to light, of the artistic experience."[7] Similarly, Geoffrey Hartman has linked the notion of death in Rilke with "the experiencing of an original, creative force."[8] It is in the later poetry, in the *Duineser Elegien* and the *Sonette an Orpheus*, that Rilke's preoccupation with death takes its most abstract form. In the late work Rilke leaves behind the notion of "personal death." Vastly expanded conceptually, death now becomes "the other relation," "der andre Bezug." It is as limitless as being, having become what Beda Allemann aptly calls "death's form of Being" ("die Daseinsform des Tot-seins").[9]

The poet's task then becomes the affirmation of *both* ontological dimensions, being and nothingness, once they are brought closer together by metaphor. Rilke conceives of this new unity as a merger of origins and ends reminiscent of Freud's *Beyond the Pleasure Principle*. Not only would memory extend into the past, but, as Allemann contends, one's future death would also constitute the realm of the past.[10]

Several metaphors in Rilke's poetry effect the unification of past with future, childhood with death. One of the most prominent involves vertical movement, ascent and descent, an axis along which Jacob Steiner discovers Rilke's most deep-seated poetic impulses.[11] Of these two directions it is the descendental movement that is especially affirmed. The Tenth Elegy ends with a message that the "forever dead" would wish to impart to the living if they could only point to the rain falling on the dark earth on a spring day; if, that is, they could underscore the promise of regeneration embodied in that image, they would then be able to convince us, the living, of their positive contribution to "Dasein":

> Und wir, die an *steigendes* Glück
> denken, empfänden die Rührung,
> die uns beinah bestürzt,
> wenn ein Glückliches *fällt.*[12]

> [And we, who think of *ascending* / happiness, then would feel / the emotion that almost startles / when happiness *falls.*[13]]

In the *Sonette*, movement along a vertical axis is embodied in Orpheus himself. Like a tree, he is rooted in the chthonic underworld with its many dead but also reaches up, branch-like, into the sublimity of the starry sky. Dependent upon the tree, as it were, is the metaphor of fruit, which is nourished by the earth harboring the dead and thus becomes another figure reconciling life with death. In the *Stunden-Buch* and in *Malte*, the fruit is the death we contain within our bodies as though it were an unborn child, a procreative symbol being here usurped, as is typical in Rilke, by a thanatological one; and the fruit of death continues prominent in the *Sonette*, the poetic aim of which is to build a bridge between life and death.

Another aspect of Rilke's "vertical" thinking appears in his attitude toward dreaming and the psychoanalytic process. Although he had frequent and vivid dreams and attributed great power to them, associating them with nervous attacks and other health problems, not to mention difficulties in writing, Rilke rarely related his dreams either in conversation or in writing. He had been made acquainted with psychoanalysis by Lou Andreas-Salomé and other friends; he was familiar with Freud's writings and read the psychoanalytic journal *Imago*.[14] Although he several times considered undergoing psychoanalysis, he shied away from it, fearing that it would prove too effective. In a letter of December 28, 1911, he writes to Andreas-Salomé: "I think a lot less than before about seeing a doctor. Psychoanalysis is a too thorough treatment for me, it helps once and for all, it tidies up, and to find myself all tidied up one of these days would perhaps be even more hopeless than this disorder."[15] As another letter indicates, Rilke accepted the Freudian idea that his neurosis sustained his writing, and therefore resisted digging too deeply into his childhood: "I know now, that analysis would only be meaningful for me, if I were really serious about the peculiar idea in the back of my mind *not to write any more*."[16]

One of the few dreams divulged by Rilke was related to the Princess von Thurn-und-Taxis in Vienna during the war and recorded in her memoirs. Apparently Rilke dreamt that he was holding a lump of damp, foul earth in his hand and that he was ordered to create a form, an image, from this lump—a task which disgusted him. Then, while he was carving at the earth with a knife, a lovely butterfly emerged from it and flew away.[17] What interests one here is Rilke's altogether predictable interpretation of this dream as a poetic mandate to transform the base into the beautiful and transcendent. He read the dream as an artist would naturally read it; and what he read, of course, was only a secondary elaboration tailored for a friend by one who was always reluctant to reveal any glimpse of his inner life. But even this version of the dream accords priority to descent— to *digging*—in the creative process, and even if it is a deliberate allegory, we can still take it as a significant comment on Rilke's creativity.

We also possess the narrative of another Rilke dream, a recurrent dream that is still more central to the theme I wish to pursue here. He frequently dreamt that he was lying between an open grave and a tall gravestone. Trembling with fear, he struggled to remain motionless because, were he to move, he would be in danger of being pushed into the grave. Lou Andreas-Salomé and Erich Simenauer have both thought that this dream expresses the fear of bisexuality,[18] but other associations also come to mind. Both male and female are present here, to be sure, but even if one were to read the dream solely from this standpoint, one would still have to point out that the dreamer feels the danger of being pushed into a female symbol by a male symbol and chooses to evade that fate by remaining motionless—or asexual. Be this as it may, another kind of a reading, this one along the lines of Rilke's allegorization of his butterfly dream, while doubtless superficial clinically, yields the reassuring maxim that poetry survives the grave. In supplying this particular redaction of his dream, Rilke may well have read his fear of the grave and gravestone as something to be resisted and overcome; to this end he could affirm the—inscribed—gravestone as a commemorative tablet testifying to the "thingness" of poetry (a Rilkean concept to which we shall return) while at the same time representing, both by metonymy and directly, the engraving stylus or pen. In this perspective the phallic symbol noted by Andreas-Salomé and Simenauer is retained, but it now serves mainly to reinforce, with sexual emphasis, the importance of verticality and descent in Rilke's imagination. The inscriptive writing, a phallic assertion that nullifies the grave, is performed by the very act of penetration that constitutes falling into the grave. To confirm this habit of association, there is a line playing on "Fallen" and "Phallen" that Rilke wrote in connection with the *Sonette* but never used: "That is the silent climbing of the *phalloi*" ("Phallen") (II, 473).[19] In Rilke's work as a whole, libidinal impulses seem very much to be submerged and dominated by an attraction to something beyond the pleasure principle, the death drive. In examining this tendency, which never amounts to complete repression or yields a proclamation of clear alternatives, I shall focus on the figure of Orpheus, whose descent for Eurydice in Rilke's work always becomes a quest for something darker and more profound.

II

Gegen alles Ererbte muss ich
feindselig sein.
—Rilke, *Letter to Lou*
 Andreas-Salomé, 1903

The description Ovid gives of the power of Orpheus's song in the *Metamorphoses* occurs when the singer is already in the underworld, accompanying his plea for the release of Eurydice with the music of his lyre (Book X). The song of Orpheus is elegiac; it laments the absence of the loved one and describes the pain her absence occasions. It concludes with the assertion that if the Fates will not grant Eurydice a reprieve, Orpheus is willing to remain in the underworld with her. Ovid stresses that Orpheus experiences the death of Eurydice as a problem of separation, not as a tragedy of mortality. The conclusion of Orpheus's song finds Tantalus forgetful of his thirst, Sisyphus sitting on his rock, the Furies moved to tears, and Proserpine and Pluto willing to grant the singer's request. But it is only later, after Orpheus has ascended from the depths, looked back, and lost Eurydice once more, that Ovid describes the power of the poet's song over the animals, birds, and trees. One implication of beginning the Orpheus story with an account of his loss is that it is precisely the fact of loss that strengthens his song and extends its power to move to the whole natural world. Eurydice's absence, which inspires his descent, is also twice over the inspiration of his song. In that she remains in the realm of the dead, Ovid's version of the myth can be said to allegorize the (re)union of poetry's origins, its inspiration, with death. In Blanchot's words, "Eurydice is the limit of what art can contain; concealed behind a name and covered with a veil, she is the profoundly dark point towards which art, desire, death and the night all seem to lead."[20] The failure to renew Eurydice renews the song of Orpheus, and her demise ensures the survival of his imaginative powers. In Ovid's narrative, Eurydice's metamorphosis into a "bloodless ghost"[21] animates the songs of metamorphosis that Orpheus will sing henceforth. Blanchot explains the importance of Eurydice in this allegory of renewal grounded in loss by insisting that the poet's descent must not be disinterested, a merely gratuitous exercise in dialectic: "one cannot create a work unless the enormous experience of the depths . . . is not pursued for its own sake."[22]

Years before the *Sonnets to Orpheus* (1922), in which he was to elaborate the Orphic principle of pure song, Rilke presented his version of the singer's descent in one of the *Neue Gedichte*, "Orpheus. Eurydike. Hermes" (1904). In this well-known poem Rilke pauses to theorize the problem of poetic descent as he understands it and, in so doing, justifies the repudiation of his Romantic forerunners, a turning away that has the same strengthening effect as Orpheus's looking back at and then relinquishing Eurydice: separation from the "ground" revises a traditional way of singing. To this end, Rilke begins his song at a point further along in the middle of things than

Ovid's beginning, after the song of Orpheus has won Eurydice's release. Although this poem purports not to be concerned with Orpheus's descent, it is nevertheless a critique of his *as*cent as a failed mission, thus tacitly suggesting that downward may have been a better direction.

The opening of the poem, which sets the scene, is strongly affirmative: "Das war der Seelen wunderliches Bergwerk" (I, 542). Rilke and we his readers are the uninvolved but delightedly appreciative connoisseurs of a drama in the depths. The kind of spectacle we witness is indicated by the Romantic metaphor of the "Bergwerk," or mine, which is a longstanding trope for the unconscious.[23] The use of the word "Seelen," souls, rather than "Schatten," shades, confirms the inward-turning of this Classical scenario. But in the course of the poem's first stanza, the metaphor of the mine, despite its established connection to mind, is surprisingly and forcefully associated with the body instead:

Wie stille Silbererze gingen sie
als Adern durch sein Dunkel. Zwischen Wurzeln
entsprang das Blut, das fortgeht zu den Menschen,
und schwer wie Porphyr sah es aus im Dunkel.
Sonst war nichts Rotes.   [I, 542]

[And they, like silent veins of silver ore, / were winding through its darkness. Between roots / welled up the blood that flows on to mankind, / like blocks of heavy porphyry in the darkness. / Else there was nothing red.]   [II, 188]

"Ader," or vein, is commonly enough used for mineral deposits not to call attention as yet to Rilke's slide away from his initial emphasis. Not until the underworld appears suffused with blood do we realize that this is neither the land of "bloodless shades" nor a Romantic metaphor for the unconscious, but a place of burial for bodies where the bodies already seem to have the renewed vigor attendant on their entry into the organic cycle. (This revision of the underworld of Romanticism will be developed in greater detail in the *Sonnets*.) The burial ground of this first stanza is also the place of "Wurzeln," roots, perhaps betokening the beginnings and submerged support of poetic expression; these are filled with regenerative, recycled blood passing upward by osmosis to be transfused, as the poem surfaces, into the living. Far from suggesting absence, this underworld sustains presence.

It comes as a new surprise to the reader, then, when the second

stanza of "Orpheus. Eurydike. Hermes" abandons this assertive reformulation and returns to poetic tradition—but this time to the
underworld of Virgil's *Aeneid*. Now the underworld is a negative
region, a place of absence after all, a place of "wesenlose Wälder" (I,
542) with a gray, blind pond (Cocytus), "Brücken über Leeres" (I,
542), and a path "wie eine lange Bleiche hingelegt" (I, 542). It is as
though Rilke were omitting—bracketing—Romantic internaliza-
tions of the underworld in order to claim direct descent from an
earlier, hence more authentic poetry.

In presenting the Classical underworld as he does, however, Rilke
drains it of all color; he vitiates it, empties out its imagery, and even
blinds it. "Das Rote" is nowhere to be seen. Just as the landscape is
thus deprived of vigor, Orpheus is deprived of his poethood. He is a
slender man in a blue coat, unnamed (like the other two characters,
to be sure) and struck dumb, "stumm" (I, 543). When he does
speak, his utterance is not divine song but an empty formula to
assure himself that Eurydice and Hermes are behind him. His voice
is weak and soon dissipated: "Und hörte sich verhallen" (I, 543).
This powerlessness is the more surprising in contrast with the preter-
natural strength Rilke accords to the song of Orpheus later in the
same poem:

> Die So-geliebte, dass aus einer Leier
> mehr Klage kam als je aus Klagefrauen;
> dass eine Welt aus Klage ward, in der
> alles noch einmal da war: Wald und Tal
> und Weg und Ortschaft, Feld und Fluss und Tier;
> und dass um diese Klage-Welt, ganz so
> wie um die andre Erde, eine Sonne
> und ein gestirnter stiller Himmel ging,
> ein Klage-Himmel mit entstellten Sternen—:
> Diese So-geliebte.   [I, 544]

> [She, so belov'd, that from a single lyre / more mourning rose than from
> all women-mourners,— / that a whole world of mourning rose,
> wherein / all things were once more present: wood and vale / and road
> and hamlet, field and stream and beast;— / and that around this world
> of mourning turned, / even as around the other earth, a sun / and a
> whole silent heaven full of stars, / a heaven of mourning with disfigured
> stars: / she, so beloved.]   [II, 189]

This stanza, framed by the absence of Eurydice, "die So-geliebte,"
suggests that Orpheus's song has the constitutive power of poetic

naming. It creates a second world made of language whose relation
to an "actual" world is no longer mimetic. This second world,
bounded by the horizon of elegy, is a separate realm entirely; language is now originary for Orpheus because in an empty world it can
no longer designate anything.

As a character, the poet Orpheus does not understand what has
happened, but it is something that the poet Rilke emphatically
insists upon, placing himself in a situation analogous to that of
Orpheus; although Orpheus does not perceive the advantages of loss
or absence for his song, Rilke implies, he himself can compensate for
his lack of priority by understanding the loss of primal unity (symbolized by the marriage of Orpheus and Eurydice) as a necessary
precondition for elegy—and for song in general. The description of
Orpheus's song, which occupies its own stanza, rather abruptly inter-
rupts Rilke's narrative poem. It seems out of place because it is not
really suited for this much diminished, imperceptive Orpheus and
stands forth rather as an instance of the kind of lyric evocation that
Rilke himself will increasingly affirm in and as his own unprecedented voice. Thus Rilke gains priority not only over the Romantics
but over the originary poet Orpheus himself. The attempt by
Orpheus to retrieve the dead from the underworld is made out to be
a futile enterprise because self-presence, waiving the unattainable
presence of the other, can only reside either in language or in the
indivisibility of death itself.

In this poem Rilke returns to the metaphor of the fruit of death
that he had introduced in the *Stunden-Buch*, where he proclaimed:
"Der grosse Tod, den jeder in sich hat, / das ist die Frucht, um die
sich alles dreht" (I, 347). In "Orpheus. Eurydike. Hermes," the fruit
of death is represented, typically for Rilke, as the fruit of Eurydice's
womb. Eurydice is imperturbably self-contained, pregnant with her
own death:

Sie war in sich, wie Eine hoher Hoffnung,

. . . .
Sie war in sich. Und ihr Gestorbensein
erfüllte sie wie Fülle.
Wie eine Frucht von Süssigkeit und Dunkel[.]   [I, 544]

[Wrapt in herself, like one whose time is near, / . . . / Wrapt in herself
she wandered. And her deadness / was filling her like fullness. / Full as a
fruit with sweetness and with darkness.]   [II, 190]

Making death a birth, a generative event, is one of Rilke's strongest poetic gestures. Eurydice belongs to his initial underworld of blood and roots: "Sie war schon Wurzel" (I, 545). Rilke's gesture can be read as an attempt to transform what he considers to be the sublimity of Romanticism, which Paul de Man calls "the poetry of the sky," back into a chthonic "poetry of earth." Rilke wishes in general to reverse the transcendental tendency of Romantic poetry as he sees it, in which, as de Man writes, "the poet's word has become an off-spring of the sky. The ontological priority, housed at first in the earthly and pastoral "flower," has been transposed to an entity that could still, if one wishes, be called "nature," but could no longer be equated with matter, objects, earth, stones or flowers."[24] What Rilke attempts to do in the *Neue Gedichte* and even in the later *Sonette an Orpheus* is to write a poetry that is *itself* in various senses material and substantial. Many of the *Neue Gedichte* have rightly been called *Ding-gedichte*;[25] and one critic has said of Rilke's poems in this period, "he puts his poems down like carvings, tombstones, memorials, and statues."[26] As the "Klage-Welt" passage intimates and as Rilke fully realizes later in his career, however, poetry cannot become material and substantial until it gives up its attempt to refer to and embody material and substance other than itself; it does not cease to be secondary until it banishes the reality it had never been able to bring to light.

The Orpheus myth with its abandonment of the dead lends itself especially well to Rilke's poetic effort to undermine German Romantic poetry.[27] Orpheus's forbidden glance back at Eurydice ensures that he must leave her and the rest of the dead behind. For Rilke it is the idea that the dead are not in themselves inspirational that provides inspiration. But this independence requires acclimatization; at first it is only a source of insecurity. It is precisely because Eurydice and Hermes are silent, uninspirational, that Orpheus anxiously glances back. Temporarily he is left without sound, the medium of his singing voice. As I shall argue later, the instability of this medium is what causes Rilke to reject the privilege poetics normally accords to sound in favor of the greater permanence of poetic objecthood. But there is also a more specific significance, perhaps less consciously present for Rilke, in Orpheus's turning first toward and then irreversibly away from the dead. The myth is an allegory of apprenticeship followed by the illusory rejection of poetic sources—"illusory" because the dead become for the first time truly inspirational when they cease to be present, which is to say, present to consciousness.[28]

A parenthetical passage in the poem supposedly expresses Orpheus's thoughts as he makes his way toward his goal:

> Dürfte er
> sich einmal wenden (wäre das Zurückschaun
> nicht die Zersetzung dieses ganzen Werkes,
> das erst vollbracht wird), müsste er sie sehen[.]   [I, 543]

> [If he durst / but once look back (if only looking back / were not undo-
> ing of this whole enterprise / still to be done) he could not fail to see
> them.]   [II, 189]

This passage and the few lines that precede it are not written in the simple past tense of narration but in the subjunctive, and constitute the only moment in the poem when the reader does not stand outside the characters, a detached witness of their movements. For this reason these lines (beginning at "Er aber sagte sich"; I, 543) seem as fully set apart from the main course of the text as the "Klage-Welt" passage. I would suggest that this parenthesis refers to the poem in which it appears as much as to the quest being narrated; in this case it would express a fleeting awareness of the poet's debt to the past—to his own childhood but also to the literary past—an awareness that he cannot allow to surface without bringing about the destruction of his work in progress, without "die Zersetzung dieses ganzen Werkes, / das erst vollbracht wird." As when he explains his avoidance of psychoanalysis, here for a moment Rilke recognizes repression to be a source of his poetic strength. Ironically, however, just when the poem seems to speak most openly of the need to evade poetic indebtedness, for the first time the hitherto successful resistance of Romantic tropes breaks down, and the underworld becomes the unconscious after all.

Toward the end of this poem the figure of Orpheus grows ever more indistinct. Eurydice, when informed that he has turned, asks "who?"—and through her eyes we see Orpheus from a distance, an unrecognizable figure:

> Fern aber, dunkel vor dem klaren Ausgang,
> stand irgend jemand, dessen Angesicht
> nicht zu erkennen war.   [I, 545]

> [But in the distance, dark in the bright exit, someone or other stood,
> whose countenance / was indistinguishable.]   [II, 190]

In the full context of Rilke's poem, Orpheus has failed, and it would seem that his defeat is presented as a triumph for the dead. Eurydice remains self-sufficient, content to be self-absorbed, while at the same time she is depersonalized, faceless and broken down into her constituent parts,

> aufgelöst wie langes Haar
> und hingegeben wie gefallner Regen
> und ausgeteilt wie hundertfacher Vorrat.   [I, 545]

[loosened like long hair, / and given far and wide like fallen rain, / and dealt out like a manifold supply.]   [II, 190]

But although the poem presents Eurydice's loss of human presence as a triumph for the dead—and, therefore, for those who precede us—it is just as much a triumph of the poet himself. He has reduced the individuality of the predecessor to a state of impersonal generality which can be called upon solely as an abstraction, a state of being, by virtue of this effacement. If Eurydice then abstractly represents the pastness of the past, Orpheus in this poem is more specifically a past poet whose priority must be undermined, hence *his* ultimate facelessness. Later, in the Seventh Elegy, Rilke will claim in confirmation of this reading that his own poetic powers exceed those of Orpheus:

> Siehe, da rief ich die Liebende. Aber nicht *sie* nur
> käme . . . Es kämen aus schwächlichen Gräbern
> Mädchen und ständen. . . Denn, wie beschränk ich,
> wie, den gerufenen Ruf?   [I, 710]

[Look, I've been calling the lover. But not only she / would come . . . Out of unwithholding graves / girls would come and gather . . . For how could I limit / the call I had called?]   [II, 239]

But what is the role of Hermes in this allegory? Paul de Man calls the turning of Hermes the "genuine reversal" of the poem: "The genuine reversal takes place at the end of the poem, when Hermes turns away from the ascending movement that leads Orpheus back to the world of the living and instead follows Eurydice into a world of privation and nonbeing. On the level of poetic language, this renunciation corresponds to the loss of a primacy of meaning located within the referent."[29]

In this reading, de Man relies upon the connection between Hermes and interpretive language ("hermeneutics") that was first made in writing by Socrates in the *Cratylus*: "I should imagine that the name Hermes has to do with speech, and signifies that he is the interpreter, or messenger, or thief, or liar, or bargainer; all that sort of thing has a great deal to do with language."[30] The whole structure of "Orpheus. Eurydike. Hermes" anticipates the loss of referential meaning, which is recorded in conclusion by the narrative. But from Rilke's point of view, I have been arguing, the underworld is nevertheless not a world of "privation and non-being"; in this poem the decision of Hermes to remain below aligns language with death and repressed inspiration in the region that Rilke at the outset has described as life-giving. The commitment of Hermes to earth aligns him, as a predecessor, with the poetic tradition that persists in seeking reality as an organic entity, while Orpheus remains the predecessor who rightly rejects this false faith in the symbol, thinking all along however that he has made a terrible mistake in doing so.

One can certainly suspect that one of the precursors from whom Rilke turns away in "Orpheus. Eurydike. Hermes" is Novalis, whose episode of Heinrich von Ofterdingen and the miner (see above, chapter 1) anticipates the "Bergwerk" of Rilke. On the authority of Herder, Orpheus was the model of the visionary poet for the visionaries of German Romanticism. Novalis translated the Orpheus episode from Book IV of Virgil's *Georgics*; he began an epic in hexameters on the subject of Orpheus; and the singer from Hellas in the fifth of the *Hymnen an die Nacht* is an Orpheus figure.[31] In addition, the Orpheus myth clearly leaves its mark on the relationship of the poet with his beloved in the *Hymnen*; he descends into her grave—which is also the night—and is reunited with her in imagination. Having said this, however, and having remarked the influence of Novalis in the *Duino Elegies* and elsewhere, one should add that the mystical poetics of Novalis corresponds neither to the organic poetics of Hermes nor the reluctantly self-referential poetics of Orpheus in the poem under consideration; again, Rilke uses the myth of Orpheus to proclaim a separation from the beloved, not the achievement of unity with her.[32]

A poet who is not so easy to leave behind, however, is Hölderlin. Rilke's description of the underworld in the second stanza of the present poem—the underworld seen through the eyes of an enervated literary tradition—contains the expression "Brücken über Leeres," which echoes lines from the opening of Hölderlin's "Patmos":

> und furchtlos gehn
> Die Söhne der Alpen über den Abgrund weg
> Auf leichtgebaueten Brücken.[33]

[and fearless over / The chasm walk the sons of the Alps / On bridges lightly built.]   [Hamburger, 463]

In Rilke's reformulation, the abyss is emptied of its danger and poetic energy alike, leaving only neutral vacancy. Here is a revisionary swerve of sorts, then, but certain aspects in the later development of "Patmos" Rilke is unable to transform. For Hölderlin, "der Stab des Gesanges" ("the wand of song"—Hamburger, p. 473) has the power to awaken the dead—those among them, that is, who have not yet been captured "vom Rohen" ("whom coarseness has not / made Captive yet," "die noch gefangen nicht / Vom Rohen sind," I, 181). Hölderlin's "das Rohe," by means of which the dead are swallowed up or absorbed in such a way as to make them inaccessible to poetic song, appears to have some bearing on Rilke's turn toward an affirmative view of death's life-giving blood, which he calls "das Rote" (I, 542). Somewhat more effectively transformed by Rilke is Hölderlin's staff or wand. Rilke's Hermes Psychopompos, who follows tradition in carrying "den schlanken Stab" (I, 543), derives from Hölderlin's "Stab des Gesanges," as well as from the "Zauberstab" of Novalis and the "Wünschelrute" of Eichendorff, but whereas for these poets the magic staff is the means whereby the treasures of the underworld are brought to light, in Rilke the quest for the referential synthesis of reality is the project of Hermes alone, whose poetics are left behind with his staff and person.

There is a great deal more to say about Rilke's response to the influence of Hölderlin, but for the moment it remains only to stress the most important of Rilke's revisions of Hölderlin in "Orpheus. Eurydike. Hermes." The key passage in this poem is the "Klage-Welt" passage, which points toward the next phase of Rilke's poetics, with its claim that poetic language which successfully abandons reference can attain the ontological status of an object. The Romantics, and among them Hölderlin most profoundly, had acknowledged the desirability of such language but had everywhere conceded their failure to attain it. In "Brot und Wein," Hölderlin looks back nostalgically to a time when "Worte wie Blumen entstehn," a time when language and the things of nature are alike generated organically and with equal immediacy.[34] And Novalis, praising Christ—but not himself—says that he speaks words "wie vom Baum des Lebens gebrochen."[35] Rilke on the other hand, beginning with the "Klage-Welt" passage in the poem we have been examining, turns away from these poets in hubristically claiming that the generation of poetic language as an object in the world is within his power. This is perhaps the ultimate sense in which Rilke at every stage in his career leaves the dead behind.

In summary, Rilke stations his poetry over against essentially two Romantic ideas, both of which he imagines vertically, as model figures of descent. The first of these, that poetic language can embody nature referentially—that nature can "live" in poetry—is the easily rejected organic idea which Rilke, like Droste-Hülshoff, can scarcely have escaped associating with Goethe. From the organic point of view, language must condescend to take nature up into itself, as in the "reifende Frucht" of Goethe's "Auf dem See." According to the second idea, on the contrary, poetic language must acknowledge its separation from nature in order to come into its own, to be its own nature. On this view language must descend in order to discover both its referential inadequacy and its consequent expressive independence. This idea, with which Rilke agrees, he imagines himself to have inherited from Hölderlin, but he makes it his own by treating it as a poetic project rather than as a regrettable impossibility. These two descendental conceptions of poetry are both imitations of death's decline: the first is the yielding of language to process and simulates burial and decay, while the second is what de Man calls allegory, the release of language from the illusion that it designates the living world into the continuity of self-reference from which existence is always absent. Each form of death has its consolation. Organic descent offers the consolation of what Paul Ricoeur calls the symbol, a demystified return to earth which entails intimations, seeds (Rilke's "Frucht") of an eschatological meaning. Orphic descent as it is treated in "Orpheus. Eurydike. Hermes" makes death the achievement of indifference to mortal dissolution, a rejection in advance of the vitality of the process world, and a yielding even of selfhood to the self-presence of the other that is language.

III

Da dich das geflügelte Entzücken
über manchen frühen Abgrund trug,
baue jetzt der unerhörten Brücken
kühn berechenbaren Bug.
—Rilke, *"Irrlichter"* (February, 1924)

It is commonly accepted that Rilke's handling of language in the later poems owes much to Hölderlin. Jost Hermand can find Hölderlin's influence even as early as "Orpheus. Eurydike. Hermes," in such expressions as "Klage–Himmel" and "So-geliebte."[36] But there is no concrete evidence that Rilke read Hölderlin before 1911.[37] (For that matter, scholars are uncertain whether he knew Novalis at all.[38]) It is quite possible, however, that Rilke, among whose correspondents was Friedrich Huch—who was close to the Stefan George circle and himself a Hölderlin enthusiast—began reading the great "Sänger" of German poetry as early as 1902.[39] But the possibility that Rilke had not read Hölderlin in 1904 is unimportant. It is enough to say that even this early in Rilke's career the Orpheus figure had acquired a special resonance and was available to play out an important allegory of poetic descent.

It has often been noted that Rilke's completion of *Malte Laurids Brigge* in 1910 was a kind of watershed for him, the end of one epoch of writing and the beginning of a long crisis of inspiration. From 1910 until the publication of the *Elegien* and the *Sonette* in 1923, Rilke published only one small volume of poetry, the *Marien-Leben* of 1913. He came to feel during this inactive period that Auguste Rodin's principles of "sehen-lernen" and "le modelé" were no longer sufficient to stimulate his imagination and had to be discarded—in favor of principles that were however as yet unformed. During these twelve years Rilke voiced his anxiety about "the work" time and again in his letters. It must be remembered, though, that much poetry was actually written at least during the first five years of this interval, notably the first and second Elegies early in 1912, the third Elegy, completed the next year, and the beginnings of the sixth and ninth, followed by minor flurries of poetic activity, in 1914 and 1915. Then came the great breakthrough of February 1922, when all ten Elegies were completed together with all fifty-five of the *Sonnets to Orpheus*. It is notable that the onset of Rilke's poetic crisis came at the same time as his intensive reading of

Klopstock, Goethe, and Hölderlin—the great practitioners of the German elegiac-hymnic tradition. Before that time, he had for the most part resisted reading poetry.[40] Eudo C. Mason has pointed out that until he began reading his predecessors in earnest Rilke had been inclined to forget that anyone other than himself had written great poetry in German, and that he chose his acknowledged masters from among sculptors and painters, together with Scandinavian and Russian writers.[41]

Rilke's greatest enthusiasm for Hölderlin came in 1914–15, when he frequently declaimed "Brot und Wein" and "Der Rhein" aloud. A friend's diary states, "He sets Hölderlin above all lyric poets."[42] Evidently Rilke owed this phase of his admiration for Hölderlin to his growing friendship with Norbert von Hellingrath and to Hellingrath's edition of Hölderlin, three volumes of which Rilke had received by the end of July, 1914.[43] In the same month Rilke wrote to Hellingrath concerning Hölderlin: "His influence on me is great and magnanimous, as only the influence of the richest and inwardly most powerful can be."[44] Herbert Singer claims in his study of Rilke and Hölderlin that this is the only time, presumably since 1900, that Rilke admits to having been influenced by another poet.[45] But admissions of indebtedness should be read as carefully as denials. Rilke's magnanimity toward Hölderlin's work and the modesty of his own posture as humble beneficiary of its largesse seem somewhat implausible, and may in part be an attempt to please and flatter Hellingrath, who was not apparently overjoyed with Rilke's poetry. Perhaps, too, Rilke's fulsome acknowledgement is an attempt to ward off an inner suspicion of Hölderlin's influence by exaggerating an open indebtedness out of all probability.

In the one poem which Rilke dedicated to the earlier poet, "An Hölderlin" (written in September and October of 1914), Rilke at first overtly allies himself and his poetic enterprise with that of Hölderlin. Beneath the surface, though, and increasingly as the poem progresses, Rilke's ambivalence toward Hölderlin emerges in a series of maneuvers. This complex poem is quoted here in full:

Verweilung, auch am Vertrautesten nicht,
ist uns gegeben; aus den erfüllten
Bildern stürzt der Geist zu plötzlich zu füllenden; Seen
sind erst im Ewigen. Hier ist Fallen
das Tüchtigste. Aus dem gekonnten Gefühl
überfallen hinab ins geahndete, weiter.

Dir, du Herrlicher, war, dir war, du Beschwörer, ein ganzes

Leben das dringende Bild, wenn du es aussprachst,
die Zeile schloss sich wie Schicksal, ein Tod war
selbst in der lindesten, und du betratest ihn; aber
der vorgehende Gott führte dich drüben hervor.
O du wandelnder Geist, du wandelndster! Wie sie doch alle
wohnen im warmen Gedicht, häuslich, und lang
bleiben im schmalen Vergleich. Teilnehmende. Du nur
ziehst wie der Mond. Und unten hellt und verdunkelt
deine nächtliche sich, die heilig erschrockene Landschaft,
die du in Abschieden fühlst. Keiner
gab sie erhabener hin, gab sie ans Ganze
heiler zurück, unbedürftiger. So auch
spieltest du heilig durch nicht mehr gerechnete Jahre
mit dem unendlichen Glück, als wär es nicht innen, läge
keinem gehörend im sanften
Rasen der Erde umher, von göttlichen Kindern verlassen.
Ach, was die Höchsten begehren, du legtest es wunschlos
Baustein auf Baustein: es stand. Doch selber sein Umsturz
irrte dich nicht.
Was, da ein solcher, Ewiger, war, misstraun wir
immer dem Irdischen noch? Statt am Vorläufigen ernst
die Gefühle zu lernen für welche
Neigung, künftig im Raum?   [II, 93–94]

[Lingering, even with intimate things, / is not vouchsafed us; the spirit
plunges / from filled to suddenly fillable images; lakes / exist in eternity.
Falling is here / fittest. Cascading down out of compassed feeling / into
surmised beyond. // You, though, glorious invoker, for you a whole life
was that / importunate image; when you expressed it, / a line locked up
like destiny, even in the gentlest / there lurked a death, which you
lighted upon, but the god / going before you guided forth and afar. //
Oh, you ranging spirit, you rangingest! Look how they all / dwell as at
home in cozy poems and make / long stays in narrow comparisons.
Participators. You only / move like the moon. And below there brightens
and darkens / your own nocturnal, sacredly startled landscape, / the one
you feel in partings. No one / surrendered it more sublimely, gave it
more wholly, / dispensably, back to the whole. Such, too, / was your
holy play, through the now uncounted years, / with happiness, as though
it were not internal, / but lay about unclaimed / on Earth's soft turf, left
by celestial children. / Oh, what the loftiest long for, you laid, with
never a wish, / stone upon stone: it stood. And when it collapsed, it left
you / unbewildered. // Why, after such an eternal life, do we still /
mistrust the terrestrial? Instead of earnestly learning / from fleeting
Appearance the feelings / for, oh, what affections, in space?]   [II,313]

Ironically, the poem's powerful beginning humbly bows to Goethe's *Faust* with its first word, "Verweilung," the referent of which Rilke temporarily withholds by using obviously Hölderlinian periodic syntax. Indeed, this syntax somewhat belies its theme: evoking a mountain stream rushing downward, Rilke denies the possibility of "Verweilung"—lingering—for the poet, whose imagination must leap forward and down from image to image, poem to poem. This metaphor recalls the well-known questions of Faust in "Wald und Höhle":

"Bin ich der Flüchtling nicht? der Unbehauste?
Der Unmensch ohne Zweck und Ruh',
Der wie ein Wassersturz von Fels zu Felsen brauste
Begierig wütend nach dem Abgrund zu?   [I, 3348-51]

[Am I not fugitive, the homeless rover, / The man-beast void of goal or bliss, / Who roars in cataracts from cliff to boulder / In avid frenzy for the precipice?]   [Arndt, 82]

And in this context, the mountain stream may perhaps also suggest the stream Faust apostrophizes when he awakens at the beginning of Part Two, a complexly imagined stream intercepted by a rainbow representing the imaginative reflection that constitutes its own flimsy bridge as a stay against constant gravitational motion. If at this point in the poem it seems that Rilke subverts Goethe's themes by using Hölderlin's language, it soon turns out that this process is reversed.

From fulfilled, completed reflection resembling Goethe's rainbow the imagination moves down and away quickly, Rilke complains, toward reflections that are always in the process of formulation. The stasis, the fulfillment, represented by the lake is only to be found beyond time, he says, in eternity. Here and now, in the mortal dispensation, "Fallen," a downward movement—a descent, indeed—is "das Tüchtigste," a term Rilke is probably using here to mean "most proficient" ("viel könnend") and linking with the "gekonnte[s] Gefühl," the poetically mastered feeling. The movement from achieved experience and, implicitly, from emotion poetically embodied in an image, toward an emotion as yet only intimated, is presented as the downward movement of water from its source. "Seen," with its play on seeing ("sehen") connects the poetic images ("Bildern") with water. The word "überfallen" similarly points to "Überfall," the point at which water flows over a dam or dike, suggesting the watershed or entry into a new phase of a poem or poetic career. But who is "der Vertrauteste," the one in whom one places the greatest confidence and trust but with whom one cannot linger, if it is not Hölderlin himself, the poet whose influence upon himself Rilke had characterized a few months earlier as "grossmütig," magnanimous? If this is so, then in the first stanza of this poem Rilke appears to be describing the headlong force of his own imagination as it rushes down and away from its source; and although this movement is couched in the language of regret ("*zu* plötzlich"), the reader will entertain some suspicion when any poet *complains* that his imagination is a forceful one.

It has been suggested that the third stanza of Hölderlin's "Hyperions Schicksalslied" is a source for the opening movement of Rilke's poem:[46]

Doch uns ist gegeben,
   Auf keiner Stätte zu ruhn,
     Es schwinden, es fallen
      Die leidenden Menschen
       Blindlings von einer
        Stunde zu andern,
         Wie Wasser von Klippe
         Zu Klippe geworfen,
          Jahr lang ins Ungewisse hinab. [*Werke und Briefe* I, 45]

[But we are fated / To find no foothold, no rest, / And suffering mortals / Dwindle and fall / Headlong from one / Hour to the next / Hurled like water / From ledge to ledge / Downward for years to this vague abyss.]   [Hamburger, 79]

But whereas this passage evokes the existential plight of all humanity (echoing Goethe's "Gesang der Geister über den Wassern" and Faust's complaint in "Wald und Höhle"), Rilke speaks explicitly of the poet and his work. From the standpoint of the poet, then, in the course of "An Hölderlin" Rilke redeems the sense of "fallen," which always means more in his poetry than simply the yielding of the self to imagination or the poetic process. As we have seen, the movement away from the source (the spring or "Quelle" of a mountain stream) is presented here as a descending movement, and the fall into the confinement of an underworld (a subterranean stream or ocean floor) is paradoxically imagined as a liberation from influence. As if in celebration of this release, Rilke relaxes and does not fully subvert the stanza from "Hyperions Schicksalslied" (having simply narrowed its focus), but rather merges it, diluting its force, with other streams in Hölderlin's poetry: the river as culture-bearer signaling the Progress of Poesy in "Der Rhein" and the metaphor of "das strömende Wort"—the inspired word—in "Brot und Wein."

If the shadow of Hölderlin does not fall across the figure of Orpheus in "Orpheus. Eurydike. Hermes," the Orpheus of that poem does contribute, however, to an understanding of Hölderlin as Rilke presents him in "An Hölderlin." The second stanza addresses the earlier poet directly in a sustained imitation of Hölderlin's syntax:

> Dir, du Herrlicher, war, dir war, du Beschwörer, ein ganzes
> Leben das dringende Bild, wenn du es aussprachst,
> die Zeile schloss sich wie Schicksal, ein Tod war
> selbst in der lindesten, und du betratest ihn; aber
> der vorgehende Gott führte dich drüben hervor.

In now explicitly addressing Hölderlin, Rilke carries over and transforms several images from the first stanza. Etymologically, "das dringende Bild" suggests *pathbreaking* as well as penetration and force. From Rilke's point of view, what is especially pathbreaking about the images produced by Hölderlin's poetic language ("wenn du es aussprachst") is their configuration of death. Rilke says that a Hölderlinian line ends as though by a decree of Fate; its closure is as inevitable as death. But Rilke's praise extends beyond Hölderlin's facility with language; he is also fascinated by the way Hölderlin enters the place of death within each line, which is thereby rendered, in an apparent paradox, "ein ganzes / Leben."

Herbert Singer locates the source of Rilke's association of Hölderlin's language with death in Hölderlin's note to his translation of *Antigone*, which Rilke would have found in Hellingrath's fifth volume: "that the word from an enraptured mouth is terrible, and kills."[47] But this sentiment does not support the sense of Rilke's lines. More apropos, perhaps, is the fact—to which the same critic calls our attention—that on the night before he completed "An Hölderlin" Rilke read Wilhelm Michel's book about Hölderlin containing the essay called "Hölderlin und die Sprache."[48] One of Michel's remarks in particular concerning Hölderlin's idea of language would have appealed to Rilke: "Speaking is a revaluation of the deathly into nourishment for life ("Sprechen ist eine Umwertung des Tödlichen in Nahrung des Lebens").[49] And in Michel's second essay, "Hölderlin und die Götter," there appears the quotation from Hölderlin's "Stimme des Volks" over which we have hitherto paused and which may have provided another source for Rilke's first stanza, tying it more closely, indeed, to the second:

Ins All zurück die kürzeste Bahn, so stürzt
    Der Strom hinab, er suchet die Ruh, es reisst,
        Es ziehet wider Willen ihn von
            Klippe zu Klippe, den Steuerlosen,
                Das wunderbare Sehnen dem Abgrund zu[.] [*Werke und Briefe*, I, 85]

[Speed back into the All by the shortest way; / So rivers plunge—not movement, but rest they seek— / Drawn on, pulled down against their will from / Boulder to boulder—abandoned, helmless— // By that mysterious yearning toward the chasm.]   [Hamburger, p. 179]

Later in the poem this yearning is expressly called "Todeslust."

Using "aber" in the manner of Hölderlin—not necessarily to indicate qualification—Rilke concludes his second stanza by introducing Hermes, "der vorgehende Gott" who leads Hölderlin "drüben hervor." With this indirect reference to the Styx in the presence of Hermes, the image of the stream as figurative language reenters the poem, having already been connoted, as suggested above by "das dringende Bild." As conjuror or magician ("Beschwörer"), the visionary poet Hölderlin led into the underworld by Hermes begins to resemble Orpheus. The substitution of a horizontal crossing for a more vertical entry into the realm of Hades is a common one in literature, but in Rilke's ode it has the special function of retrospectively flinging a bridge across the hurtling stream of the first stanza. There, the inspired course of a poem—its "strömende Wort"—or, by extension, the course of a poetic career, is like a river flowing onward, "weiter," and the poet feels encouraged to ignore the self-critical faculty and succumb to the flow of inspiration ("Hier ist Fallen das Tüchtigste.") When Hermes leads Orpheus "drüben hervor," however, Rilke is insisting upon the crossing or intersection of this flow, implying that the course of inspiration must be subject to self-consciousness, the checking of inspiration against some logic of reference.

Above, Hermes was connected with referential language, and in the present ode "der vorgehende Gott" has the same function. Reference, or interpretation by an external standard, must cut across the onrush of inspiration, drawing the Hölderlin-Orpheus figure behind it. It is ironic but not surprising that Rilke would address Hölderlin thus didactically when we realize that he is indebted to Hölderlin himself for the trope of the steadying bridge. The poem "Heidelberg" constructs the city around just such a bridge, a moment of insight that spans the distance between the natural and cultural worlds. This insight is itself understood to be the bridge of language that unites the poet with the community. Even more telling in this regard is the bridge in "Patmos":

Nah ist
Und schwer zu fassen der Gott.
Wo aber Gefahr ist, wächst
Das Rettende auch.
Im Finstern wohnen
Die Adler und furchtlos gehn
Die Söhne der Alpen über den Abgrund weg
Auf leichtgebaueten Brücken.   [*Werke und Briefe* I, 176]

[Near is / And difficult to grasp, the God. / But where danger threatens / That which saves from it also grows. / In gloomy places dwell / The eagles, and fearless over / The chasm walk the sons of the Alps / On bridges lightly built.]   [Hamburger, 463]

Here again, the bridges which allow the abyss to be crossed are not gusts of inspiration solely, but inspiration steadied within a communicable code; just so, later in the poem, the Word of St. John must leave the island of Patmos, bridging the water, in order to be disseminated throughout the biblical world—and, ultimately, Germany.

Here a short digression is in order. "Pont du Carrousel," a poem earlier than "Orpheus. Eurydike. Hermes," anticipates the Orpheus-Hölderlin figure in Rilke's later work. Another of the *Neue Gedichte*, "Pont du Carrousel" was probably written in Paris in 1902–03. The blind man in this poem is a Tiresias figure, a seer whose blindness produces visionary insight. More specifically, he embodies the course of Orpheus, "der dunkle Eingang in die Unterwelt," in the act of standing on a bridge:

Der blinde Mann, der auf der Brücke steht,
grau wie ein Markstein namenloser Reiche,
er ist vielleicht das Ding, das immer gleiche,
um das von fern die Sternenstunde geht,
und der Gestirne stiller Mittelpunkt.
Denn alles um ihn irrt und rinnt und prunkt.

Er ist der unbewegliche Gerechte,
in viele wirre Wege hingestellt;
der dunkle Eingang in die Unterwelt
bei einem oberflächlichen Geschlechte.   [I, 393]

[That blind man standing by the parapet, / grey as some nameless empire's boundary stone, / he is perhaps that something unbeknown / to which the planetary clock is set, / the silent centre of the starry ways; / for all around him strives and struts and strays.// He keeps his movelessly inerrant station / where manifold perplexing crossways go; / the sombre entrance to the world below / among a superficial generation.]   [II, 115]

The blind man anticipates the Orpheus of the Sonnets who constitutes a bridge between the underworld and a region of transcendence. Merged with the figure of the poet at cross-purposes with the gamboling flood in this poem is the figure of Hermes, in whose honor the Ancients erected stone-heaps at crossroads.[50] His is the fixed point of reference in a chaos of movement, "denn alles um ihn irrt und rinnt und prunkt." Although these verbs refer to the water that passes under the bridge, each also refers to one of the tropes with which Rilke has tried to evoke the blind man, and all of them refer finally to the eddying of tropes themselves—as I have argued elsewhere[51]—that must be regulated by the cross-section of hermeneutic or referential language.

As we have declared, the unification of life and death by means of poetic language is a project especially of Rilke's later years. He was then to speak of his *own* poetry in terms that remind one of his characterization of Hölderlin's language in "An Hölderlin": "Das Tötliche [*not* "das Tödliche," the death-bringing, but the thing of death] hat immer mitgedichtet: / nur darum war der Sang so unerhört" (II, 315). Hölderlin's use of poetic language was repeatedly and effusively praised by Hellingrath and also by Michel, who wrote: "Never has the German language so trembled inwardly to the pulsebeat of the Divine as here."[52] However, although it is Hölderlin who is portrayed in Rilke's ode as Orpheus preceded by Hermes to the land of the dead, these figures can be identified in another way. In a sense it is Hölderlin himself who is the "vorgehende Gott"—the precursor god—leading Rilke into the underworld: the self-consciousness of Hölderlin's language, the standard of reference that makes it communicable, in some measure guides and determines these same qualities in the language of Rilke. The indistinctness of the human figures in "An Hölderlin" calls to mind Rilke's substitution of himself (that is, of his own developing poetics) for Orpheus in the "Klage-Welt" passage of "Orpheus. Eurydike. Hermes." When we reread "der vorgehende Gott führte dich drüben hervor" in the context of the first stanza, where poetry tries to rush down and away from its source, we discover in this line an artfully hidden acknowledgment of the debt Rilke owes to the earlier poet. Although it is easy for Rilke to speak in general terms of Hölderlin's influence, as he did in the letter to Hellingrath, when he touches upon the issues that he has most at heart and naturally supposes to be most authentically his own, he will be less eager to present himself as a disciple.

The third stanza of "An Hölderlin" can be called a Progress of Orpheus. In beginning this stanza with the apostrophe "O du wandelnder Geist, du wandelndster!"—which refers both to movement through the landscape and to its transformation—Rilke again forges a link between Hölderlin, who is still directly addressed, and Orpheus, who will quite simply *become* the process of metamorphosis in the *Sonette*. In granting both poets the power of *Verwandlung*, transformation, Rilke acknowledges their prior possession of what he characteristically identifies as his own special genius. Praising Hölderlin as the poet who most radically transforms, Rilke at the same time scorns other poets who remain confined "im schmalen Vergleich," within the compass of a narrow comparison. In this regard, Beda Allemann has interestingly pointed out that " 'der einsame Gang über die Landschaft' is an unmediated poetic formula for that which we have poetilogically understood as the metaphor."[53] What Rilke praises, then, is the power and scope of Hölderlin's metaphors; but their scope especially gives him cause for concern. In comparing Hölderlin with the moon—"Du nur ziehst wie der Mond"—he imagines him to be a determinate influence over himself as well as the landscape. But in the very moment of revealed anxiety Rilke undermines Hölderlin by implying that his light is borrowed, reflected from the sun, which is the genius of language itself if not that of a prior poet. Rilke suggests furthermore that Hölderlin's magnetic *Verwandlung* is also distortion, that in tidally altering things like the songs of Orpheus, his poetry misleadingly silvers over reality. And what he is saying finally, of course, is that Hölderlin was a lunatic.

In the main, however, Rilke's apostrophe to Hölderlin remains very high praise indeed. By 1923 the moon has become for Rilke a figure for the implicit oneness of life and death: "Like the moon, life too certainly has a side, always turned away from us, that is not its opposite, but a complement toward perfection, toward completion."[54] In "An Hölderlin," Rilke develops the notion of Hölderlin as moon into a powerfully affirmative evocation of the nighttime landscape of *Brot und Wein*: "die heilig erschrockene Landschaft" in Rilke's ode very probably refers to the holy night which in Hölderlin deserves to be praised in song "weil den Irrenden sie geheiliget ist und den Toten" (*Werke und Briefe*, I, 115), the night from which "das Heiligtrunkene" and "das strömende Wort" emerge. When Rilke declares that no other poet has been able to restore the unity of night and day as Hölderlin did—

> Keiner
> gab sie erhabener hin, gab sie ans Ganze
> heiler zurück, unbedürftiger.

—he also refers, as the metaphor of the moon indicates, to the unity of life and death.

It would seem, then, that Rilke could not praise Hölderlin more highly, but tacit qualifications of the kind we have already remarked can be enumerated further. Not only the presence of the moon but the epithet "heilig" evokes Hölderlin's madness. (Rilke borrows this sense of "heilig" from Hölderlin himself, who could have adopted it from several traditions but appears to have derived it specifically from the *Phaedrus* and the *Ion*, where to be divinely inspired is to be literally out of one's mind.) In the unself-consciousness of his madness, Hölderlin is no different from a naive child:

> So auch
> spieltest du heilig durch nicht mehr gerechnete Jahre
> mit dem unendlichen Glück, als wär es nicht innen, läge
> keinem gehörend im sanften
> Rasen der Erde umher, von göttlichen Kindern verlassen.

The mad poet is Schiller's Naive Poet.[55] No longer estranged from nature, the mad poet experiences no difference between inner and outer; "das unendliche Glück" has nothing about it of what Rilke so deplores, the "Gegenüber." But here too there is an underlying note of condescension: "als wär es nicht innen." Because in his madness Hölderlin appears to have restored language to its originary unity with nature, he has in a sense become a more threatening and enviable precursor than ever, one whose absolute priority can be neither questioned nor challenged. Rilke's defense against this state of things entails the suggestion that Hölderlin's "unendliches Glück" *must* be "innen" and is thus only illusorily a union of self and other. By implication, then, Rilke's own "Weltinnenraum," to which we shall return, is for all its belatedness the preferable, more self-aware, and more authentically difficult mode of unification.

The figure of the child at play—now with its "Bausteine"—continues:

Ach, was die Höchsten begehren, du legtest es wunschlos
Baustein auf Baustein: es stand. Doch selber sein Umsturz
irrte dich nicht.

There is probably a deliberate ambiguity about the identity of "die
Höchsten" in this passage; in Hölderlin's vocabulary the expression
would certainly refer to the gods, but in Rilke's ode it could easily
refer to the great poets who lack the advantage of Hölderlin's madness, the self-consciously estranged poets whom Schiller calls "sentimental" and who can write only with the greatest difficulty the kind
of poem that comes spontaneously and without reflection or desire to
a Hölderlin who is "wunschlos." Their estrangement is obviously a
disadvantage for these great poets, being the ineradicable sign of
their belatedness; but—as in Schiller—it brings with it the compensatory honor, even superiority, that the greater difficulty of a task
entails. Could it be that it is Hölderlin's poetry, not that of others,
that is merely "häuslich" and "warm" because it is so easy, its
"Bausteine" the building blocks of language thoughtlessly put together? Probably not, but there is still paradox in the suggestion that
these "Bausteine" are monumental yet still vulnerable—despite being or perhaps because of being monumental—to an "Umsturz."
And if Hölderlin is nobly indifferent to the likelihood that his poetry
will undergo a radical revision (one meaning of "Umsturz" is
"grundsätzliche Veränderung"), this worthy quality in turn can be
ascribed to the facile carelessness of genius. We are meant to understand in any case that the "Umsturz" of Hölderlin is primarily
reserved to be accomplished by Rilke himself, who will later claim
the unique status of an enduring stone monument for his *Sonette*,
which ascribe the power of visionary song to Orpheus alone.

The concluding movement of Rilke's ode keeps up the appearance
of celebration:

Was, da ein solcher, Ewiger, war, misstraun wir
immer dem Irdischen noch? Statt am Vorläufigen ernst
die Gefühle zu lernen für welche
Neigung, künftig im Raum?

Rilke here assumes the posture of a student toward a much-revered
teacher, but undermines his reverence somewhat with his rhetorical
question. What sort of teacher is it whose lesson "we"—all of
mankind, but especially the poets—have universally and persistently
failed to learn? Hölderlin's lesson is that from transitory things,
which we must not mistrust, we must acquire the sense of a leaning,

an orientation—"Neigung"—within a future, timeless space. Temporality is redeemed when we understand its timelessness, and is no more part of a duality than the two sides of the moon or life and death. Similarly, no contrast remains between "das Irdische" and "das Fallen," or "die Neigung," into death. This is not really Hölderlin's lesson, however, since no one has learned it, but rather Rilke's saving interpretation of Hölderlin's *attempted* lesson. As a lesson as yet unlearned, however great the poetic example of Hölderlin may have been, it is held in reserve to become the original teaching of the *Duineser Elegien* and the *Sonette an Orpheus*. In associating Hölderlin with "das Irdische," Rilke says in effect that Hölderlin is "only" another Goethe—an inference that is supported by the fact that Rilke bases this last stanza on a quatrain he had written in August:

> So lernen wir am Hiesigen Gefühle
> für welche Neigungen im Raum?
> Und gehen fühlend durch die Abendkühle
> und schauen fühlend in den nächsten Baum.   [II, 421]

Thus we learn from the earthly feeling / for which inclinations in space? / And go feeling through the evening coolness / And gaze feeling into the next tree. (Translation mine)

So programmatically that we can understand why they have been altered, these lines clearly reflect Goethe's conception of nature, a nature with no need of the poet, who loves it nevertheless. That love is the poet's referentiality, from which it is Rilke's project to release poetic language.

The element of critique and self-promotion in the conclusion of Rilke's ode to Hölderlin can be further understood by looking at the poem he wrote just before it, the oft-quoted "Weltinnenraum" poem called "Es winkt zu Fühlung" (Sept. 1914), together with "Wendung," written a few months earlier (June 1914). These poems delineate the new poetic program with which Rilke hoped to turn away from the *Neue Gedichte*. In "Wendung" he writes:

> Denn des Anschauens, siehe, ist eine Grenze.
> Und die geschautere Welt
> Will in der Liebe gedeihn.
>
> Werk des Gesichts ist getan,
> tue nun Herz-Werk
> an den Bildern in dir. . . .   [II, 83–84]

[For gazing, look, has a limit. / And the on-gazeder world / wants to mature in love. // Work of sight is achieved, / now for some heart-work / on all those images . . . within you. . . .]   [II, 306]

And in "Es winkt zu Fühlung":

Durch alle Wesen reicht der eine Raum:
Weltinnenraum. Die Vögel fliegen still
durch uns hindurch. O, der ich wachsen will,
ich seh hinaus, und *in* mir wächst der Baum.   [II, 93]

[*One* space spreads through all creatures equally— / inner-world space.
Birds quietly flying go / flying through us. Oh, I that want to grow, /
the tree I look outside at grows *in* me!]   [II, 312]

"Herz-Werk," as Rilke understands it, is the affinity not for nature but for a world made out of words that is manifest both in "Orpheus. Eurydike. Hermes" and in "An Hölderlin." Orpheus must seek Eurydice and then partially succeed in drawing her toward him magnetically in order to know through experience that he can only constitute her in her absence; if it were not for his preliminary effort to embody her directly in words, he would not know that it is for her that his poem must substitute itself, not by naming her nostalgically but by "Herz-Werk," recreating her in the heart. So in "An Hölderlin," one's feeling for the images and spaces one loses and leaves behind must be affectionate; one must almost have captured the startled landscape to know intimately what it is that one must reconstruct in verse.

Seen in the context of the self-consciously programmatic lines from "Wendung" and "Es winkt zu Fühlung," then, the conclusion of the ode to Hölderlin acquires a new dimension of meaning. It is significant that these decisive, independent pronouncements about the being and function of poetry should emerge just at the time of Rilke's deepest involvement with the poetry of Hölderlin.[56] The poems discussed thus far are not in any sense elegies for lost inspiration betraying Rilke's sense of belatedness; rather, they provide him with a way of turning his lack of unity with "das Irdische," or "das Hiesige," to advantage. The period of Hölderlin's madness can be seen as the fulfillment of what Hölderlin himself understood to be his regressive longing for a past time when language was still originary;[57] and Rilke's preoccupation with the poems written during this period has at least two implications. First, by representing Hölderlin as one whom madness has made a Naive Poet, Rilke can affirm his own status as a Sentimental Poet the more unequivocally as a condition of clear-sightedness. And second, he can assure himself that in any case even Hölderlin could only avoid estrangement, the condition of being "gegenüber," by virtue of his madness. With this access of confidence, Rilke can set forth his own agenda. "Es winkt zu Fühlung" hypothesizes an "interior-world-space," a place where the poet can locate inner equivalents of those things of the world that he has most intensely gazed upon: "ich seh hinaus und *in* mir wächst der Baum." And as "Wendung" declares, this translation of the seen requires a Goethean act of love, "Herz-Werk," that subserves ends wholly other than those of Goethe.

Rilke seems to station his paradoxical images of Hölderlin, an elegist who is not estranged, and of Goethe, a poet of celebration for whom beyond the unitary being of nature there is nothing to praise, so that they will undermine each other. "Klage," also written during the period of Rilke's enthusiasm for Hölderlin (July 1914), is a negative counterpart to the affirmative "Wendung" and to the "Weltinnenraum" poem that epitomizes the cross-purposes of these images. The group formed by this poem together with the others from which it differs reflects Rilke's typical vacillation between immodest stances and the modesty of this one:

Früher. Klagtest? Was wars? Eine gefallene
Beere des Jubels, unreife.
Jetzt aber bricht mir mein Jubel-Baum,
bricht mir im Sturme mein langsamer
Jubel-Baum.
Schönster in meiner unsichtbaren
Landschaft . . .   [II, 84]

[Once. You lamented? What was it? A fallen / berry of triumph, unripe! / Now, though, my triumph-tree is breaking, / breaking in the storm is my gradual / triumph tree. / Loveliest in my invisible / landscape . . .]   [II, 306]

Through the metaphor of the invisible world of language, this poem is linked with the "Klage-Welt" passage in "Orpheus. Eurydike. Hermes." Its title, "Klage" or elegy, connects it also with "An Hölderlin," in which Hölderlin at the outset is presented as a great elegist taking leave of one landscape after another. And further, "Klage" points ahead to the *Elegies* and to the *Sonnets* that comprise their context. As Sonnet I, viii will assert: "Nur im Raum der Rühmung darf die Klage / gehn." Dwelling upon the position of "Klage" within this matrix, one wonders whether Rilke's complaint that his "poetry of praise" after the manner of Goethe is endangered does not veil his complacency at having achieved a new rapprochement with the elegiac mode that the breakdown of praise necessitates, a new independence from the ever-beloved objects of praise that need no longer be lamented after the manner of Hölderlin.

IV

Vielleicht hätte ich es gekonnt:
Dinge machen aus Angst.
—Rilke

In the years after Hellingrath's death in 1916, Hölderlin was no longer the conscious focal point of Rilke's interest, but his influence does continue to be evident in the *Elegies* and especially in the *Sonnets*, to which we now turn in pursuing the figure of Orpheus through Rilke's career. Indeed, so fast did the *Sonnets* materialize that it is hard initially to think of them as being subject to any normally human influence at all. Unlike the *Elegies*, with which Rilke struggled for ten years, the *Sonnets* appeared in a month, and Rilke understandably thought of them as "rätselhaftestes Diktat," as having been inspired by some divine agent for which he was the mouthpiece—or pen: "They are, perhaps, even to me the most mysterious and puzzling dictation, in their emergence and their act of commissioning me, that I have ever endured and achieved" (April 1923).[58] A month later he expressed the hope that the *Sonette* would be his most original contribution to an authentic literary tradition:

> The tradition—I don't mean the superficially conventional one—, to preserve and, cleverly or blindly according to inclination, continue the truly originary (even if not *around* us, where the conditions denounce it more and more, so then *in* us) ought to be our . . . resolute purpose. Last year in a few days the impulse to contribute something of my own, comparatively exact, to its fulfillment brought forth a number of sonnets.[59]

In yet another letter a few days later, Rilke made the claim that both in his work and in his life he was now led by the wish to come to terms with his repressions, "everywhere in order to correct our old repressions, which removed us from the mysteries and little by little alienated us."[60] Rilke's familiarity with Freudian terminology and theory make it unlikely that he is speaking of repression in any merely vague sense in this letter to Countess Sizzo. It is especially interesting that in the April letter he should earmark the sonnets as his contribution to a dynamic tradition that anticipates the one envisaged by Harold Bloom. Rilke's manner of speaking would suggest that the "tradition" to which he refers has a thematic as well as a formal component; and because the program of the *Sonnets* is the reconciliation of life and death, it is probable that he has the poetry of German Romanticism at least partly in mind.[61]

As in the earlier poems, the Orpheus of the *Sonnets* is the divine singer whose powers of song are enhanced by his unsuccessful descent and by the loss of Eurydice; but in the *Sonnets* it is not only Eurydice but Orpheus himself who is absent, in most of the sonnets implicitly dismembered already and reabsorbed into the natural cycle. In these poems Orpheus is embodied in a varied group of images and associations that Rilke had toyed with in the previous twenty years. In several of the early *Stunden-Buch* poems he alludes to Orpheus in order to describe the cosmic demiurge around which these poems revolve. In the 1899 "Der Ast vom Baume Gott," the Christ-figure of that poem "ging in Mänteln und Metamorphosen / durch alle steigenden Stimmen der Zeit" (I, 272), resembling Orpheus.[62] Yet more pronounced is the figure in "O wo ist der, der aus Besitz und Zeit" (1903), an evocation primarily of St. Francis but also of a singer whose death is modeled on that of Orpheus; he too is dispersed into nature:

Und als er starb, so leicht wie ohne Namen,
da war er ausgeteilt: sein Samen rann
in Bächen, in den Bäumen sang sein Samen
und sah ihn ruhig aus den Blumen an.   [I, 366]

[And when, so nameless-lightly, he lay dying / he was distributed; his seed ran free / in brooks; in trees his seed was psalmodying / and gazed at him from flowers tranquilly.]   [II, 103–04]

The verb "steigen" in the *Stunden-Buch* poem quoted above is a word Rilke associates particularly with the vocality of Orphic song, a word he subjects to criticism early in his career:

Ich ruhe nicht, bis ich das eine erreicht
Bilder zu finden für meine Verwandlungen.
Mir genügt nicht das steigende Lied.
Einmal muss ich es mächtig wagen,
Weithin sichtbar auszusagen
Was im Ahnen kaum geschieht.   [III, 699]

[I shall not rest, until I've accomplished this— / to find images for my metamorphoses. / The ascending song is not enough for me. / Once I must mightily dare / to declare *quite visibly* / What hardly occurs in the intuition.] {Translation mine}

Here again we are reminded of the way "fallen" for Rilke emphasizes the connection between death and beginnings. In this passage from the early diaries the temporality of song is opposed to a visual poetry which is in some sense material, it is implied, and therefore less fleeting than sound. This is the position reached in conclusion by the *Sonette*: in Part I, Orpheus comprises the ideal of the visionary oracle, a reconciler of life and death who is characterized in terms of song; but gradually the vocal powers of Orpheus are undermined by a new ideal, the "thingness" of *Dinglichkeit* and inscription.

I have mentioned the conflict between voice and writing in Rilke's poetics briefly before, concerning the *Neue Gedichte* (1903–07) and *Malte*; and I would argue now that it is a conflict that leans more often than not toward writing but is never resolved once and for all in his work. Critics have ascribed Rilke's desire for lyric objectification to circumstances in his life, such as his long-standing interest in the plastic values of Rodin. And indeed, Rilke writes vividly of the envy Rodin occasioned him as an artist: "I suffered under the overly great example, which my art offered no means to follow immediately; the impossibility of forming bodily became a pain unto my own body."[63] His letters attest to his desire to make "geschriebene Dinge,"[64] and his Rodin monograph points to Baudelaire as a poet who managed to find verbal equivalents for the materiality of sculpture, with his "Lines, that were like reliefs to the touch, and sonnets, that like columns with intricate capitals bore the burden of a timid thought" (V, 152–53). At the time of Rilke's intensive reading of Hölderlin, the time of "Wendung" and the "Weltinnenraum" poem, there is evident a new interest, critics agree, in "Verinnerlichung," interiorization, which perhaps culminates in the famous line from the Seventh Elegy, "Nirgends, Geliebte, wird Welt sein, als innen" (I, 711). But even as late as 1922, Rilke still speaks of making poetry as "modellieren."[65] As Lou Andreas-Salomé points out, his fascination with translation in later years stemmed in part from his view of the poem to be translated as "material" in Rodin's sense.[66]

But this, as the foregoing cento of conflicting sentiments is meant to indicate, is not Rilke's ultimate poetic belief—nor is his occasional effort to accept a Symbolist poetics, with its project of converting objects into written images. The Symbolist solution may indeed seem close to the notion of "Weltinnenraum," closest perhaps when the Ninth Elegy expresses anew the mandate that the *Neue Gedichte* had long before struggled to fulfill: "Preise dem Engel die Welt. . . . / Sag ihm die Dinge"; "Sind wir vielleicht *hier*, um zu sagen: Haus, / Brücke, Brunnen, Tor, Krug, Obstbaum, Fenster" (I, 719, 718). But especially in the *Sonnets* what Rilke hopes to achieve through poetic transformation is far more concrete and unmediated than what the Symbolists envisioned. E. M. Butler's colorful prose yields insight when she says of the *Sonnets* that "they are like molten lava issuing from the depths of Rilke's mind and ejecting in the process petrified blocks formed during a previous eruption."[67] In my view, the *Sonnets* negotiate a zig-zag course back and forth between the "Innerlichkeit" of the vocal, originary Word, which is espoused by their overt rhetoric, and the assertion that they are formed things, written objects. I shall argue here that Rilke's undiminished rivalry with Hölderlin, whom he continues to play off against Goethe, stands in large part behind his rivalry with Orpheus, whose art he subtly undermines by denying the priority of Orphic singing—the priority, that is, of voice to writing.

Although the reconciliation of opposites—itself a Romantic project—is one aim of the sonnets and antithesis is one of their poetic principles, the antithetical relationship between Orpheus and the speaker of the sonnets seems nevertheless somewhat surprising. While the rhetorical thrust of these poems affirms death in having made it continuous with life, the palpable materiality that reinforces their status as a "Grabmal" would appear at the same time to constitute a monumental defense against time and death. And, from a different standpoint, the poem as "Markstein" plainly marks the site of the dead and even in a sense, by the metonymy of its stoniness, becomes death itself. The tension in "An Hölderlin" between profound admiration of that Orphic poet and the impulse to criticize and surpass him is repeated here. A parallel is discernible between the decline of Rilke's admiration in "An Hölderlin" and his transmutation of Orpheus in the *Sonnets*. (I cannot agree with the tendency of many critics to see Orpheus as a consistently presented figure.) Just as Hölderlin in "An Hölderlin" was first an elegiac yet originary poet, then a belated rival of Goethe, and finally a clone of Goethe with no independent existence—no existence, that is, apart from the organic nature for which Goethe in the Romantic tradition always stands as a symbol—so Orpheus is a vital singer in the first and second sonnets of Part I, a far less vivid presence in the closing sonnet of Part I, and scarcely present at all—significantly, one supposes—in Part II.

At the beginning of the sonnet cycle Orpheus is a "[s]ingender Gott" (I, ii; I, 732). He is part of the "Klage-Welt," the poet whose vocal power is separated from but equal to the things of the world. This is the Orpheus whose unsuccessful attempt to retrieve Eurydice has given him both elegiac inspiration and freedom from her determinate presence. In the first sonnet, his song is represented as a tree: "Da stieg ein Baum. O reine Übersteigung! / O Orpheus singt! O hoher Baum im Ohr!" (I, i; I, 731). No distinction is made in these lines between the actual tree, which we can understand in accordance with the myth to be moved both literally and emotionally by the song, and the figurative tree which is both the song itself and an image within the present song; Rilke's syntax enforces an equivalence between the object and its representation. The equation of song and tree derives from two Rilkean ideas: the song-tree gains its vitality from the underworld of roots that conduct blood upward—the ground of poetry as it is described in "Orpheus. Eurydike. Hermes"—and hence contains, like the poetry of Hölderlin, "death in each line." Also, recalling both Rilke's "Jubel-Baum" and Orpheus's "Klage-Welt," this is a tree of vocal song, both words and music. In this regard it is significant that the tree rising up is like the lengthening, the organic development, of song, its ascent from the ground in the typical Orphic movement of "steigen." Eichendorff had written in 1846 of Goethe's *Naturpoesie*, "thus it grows, carefree, in ascending ("steigender") metamorphosis,"[68] but Rilke only appears to follow Eichendorff here. He pays homage to Goethe by implying that works of art grow organically, but in the same breath he retracts this implication by proclaiming the song's "pure transcendence," transcendence presumably of the natural world and of the temporality with which Rilke always associates the ephemeral sound of voice. Similarly, the listening animals partake paradoxically of the organic and the transcendent at once; they are both animals and the idea of animals, both "Tiere," that is, and "Tiere aus Stille," animals emergent from the timelessness of pure song. Once they have emerged and begin to listen as it were to their own origin, they continue not to be organic but rather become paradigmatic acts of listening, "hören." The poet-speaker in turn exists on these two distinct planes, as a listener in time and as a participant or exemplar of pure transcendence.

In view of Eurydice's implied function at the conclusion of "Orpheus. Eurydike. Hermes," it is not surprising to find that she is a featured object of Orphic song at its most pure and powerful. As the veiled springtime bride, veiled and mysterious like the inspirited nature of the Ancients, she appears to merge with the Persephone whose office it is, in the myth, to relinquish her:

> Und fast ein Mädchen wars und ging hervor
> aus diesem einigen Glück von Sang und Leier
> und glänzte klar durch ihre Frühlingsschleier
> und machte sich ein Bett in meinem Ohr.
>
> Und schlief in mir. Und alles war ihr Schlaf.
> Die Bäume, die ich je bewundert, diese
> fühlbare Ferne, die gefühlte Wiese
> und jedes Staunen, das mich selbst betraf.
>
> Sie schlief die Welt.   [I, ii; I, 731–32]

> [And almost maiden-like was what drew near / from that twin-happiness of song and lyre, / and shone so clearly through her spring attire, / and made herself a bed within my ear./ / And slept in me sleep that was everything: / the trees I'd always loved, the unrevealed, / treadable distance, the trodden field, / and all my strangest self-discovering. // She slept the world.]   [II, 253]

Eurydice's sleep is her death, which makes her as self-contained and inaccessible as the Eurydice of the earlier poem. Here Orpheus's evocation of her absence—her sleep—gives rise to objective images from nature in the mind of the listener-poet, and also arouses, simultaneously with these, the listener-poet's sharply subjectivized responses to them. It is the experience, the *Erfahrung*, of the natural world that she suggests, an experience shared between song and listener in the same way that it is half perceived and half created by the singer: the words and music—both implied by "dies Motiv"— constitute the woman within the receptive listener, whose complementary act of imagination is nevertheless required to locate her specifically in *his* ear, where she becomes, embedded in death, a muse curiously resembling the dead muses of Droste-Hülshoff, and enables the listener to be a singer in his own right. With their confusing mixture of tenses, the last three lines of this sonnet suggest that the listening poet is himself the final creator—the final cause, as it were—of Orphic song:

Wo ist ihr Tod? O, wirst du dies Motiv
erfinden noch, eh sich dein Lied verzehrte?—
Wo sinkt sie hin aus mir? . . . Ein Mädchen fast . . .   [I, 732]

[Where is her death? Oh, shall you find this deep / unsounded theme
before your song expire? / Sinking to where from me? . . . Almost a
maid . . .]   [II, 253]

Significantly, this confusion of authority is expressed in pursuing the theme of death; the use of present, future, and past interchangeably suggests that poetry can fuse life and death by making both past and future constantly present. But this is an abstraction, a trope that makes sense only within the domain of "reine Übersteigung." It is at the moment when the actual event of the young woman's dying must be brought into the song that the imagined singing of Orpheus must break off, as Rilke does not yet claim to be able to follow the descent of Orpheus across the divide between realms: "Ein Gott vermags. Wie aber, sag mir, soll / Ein Mann ihm folgen durch die schmale Leier? (I, iii; I, 732).

The Eurydice figure remains unnamed in the poem, partly because she is also flesh and blood, Rilke's own Eurydice, the young dancer Wera Ouckama Knoop for whose early death the *Sonette* are a "Grabmal." Insofar as the girl in the poem is Wera, her presence within the speaker—"und schlief in mir"—reflects Rilke's poetics of interiorization, the connecting of inner with outer worlds described in "Wendung." This theme merges with the idea, within the fiction of the poem, that it is Orpheus's song about Eurydice to which the speaker is listening. Here too the difficult paradox obtains that Orphic song is at once purely visionary and grounded in nature: "sie erstand und schlief," and it is as though, thus remotely associated with resurrection, the Eurydice seen by the speaker—owing to the song of Orpheus—had acquired a visionary wholeness in which the entire visible world is vicariously present.

In the third sonnet Rilke makes explicit the distance between the divine singer and the mortal poet whose "Sinn ist Zwiespalt" (I, iii; I, 732)—an expression that echoes one of the main themes of the *Elegies*, namely, that consciousness leaves man divided, unwhole, always in a relation of opposition (a "Gegenüber"). Behind this metaphysical theme one can find an allusion to Rilke's specific artistic plight, his sense of being undecided between two poetic models.

He has recourse once more to Schiller's distinction between the Naive and the Sentimental Poet in order to distinguish Orphic song from his own. For the god, "Gesang ist Dasein," song is Being, whereas for the belated poet who attempts to reconcile song with nature, song must remain desire, "Begehr" or "Werbung." But Rilke's mortal poet defies the limitations imposed on the Sentimental Poet by Schiller and persists in hoping to be reunited with the object of his desire, his "Werbung um ein endlich noch Erreichtes." Here is the first hint that Orpheus need not be envied, is perhaps no longer centrally important; and here for the last time Rilke restates the case for the pure transcendence of visionary song, "In Wahrheit singen," which is *spiritus*, an unconditioned, holy breath beyond language entirely, "Ein Hauch um nichts. Ein Wehn im Gott. Ein Wind" (I, iii; I, 732).

With the assertion once made that the object of mediated song can be attained, Orpheus becomes an absent god from the third sonnet on—or else he is transformed into something other than a god. The fifth sonnet, which begins somewhat ominously with the words, "Errichtet keinen Denkstein" (I, v; I, 733), does not relegate Orpheus to an underworld of the dead but rather presents him as the poetic principle per se:

> Errichtet keinen Denkstein. Lasst die Rose
> nur jedes Jahr zu seinen Gunsten blühn.
> Denn Orpheus ists. Seine Metamorphose
> in dem und dem. Wir sollen uns nicht mühn
>
> um andre Namen. Ein für alle Male
> ists Orpheus, wenn es singt. Er kommt und geht.

[Raise no commemorating stone. The roses / shall blossom every summer for his sake. / For this is Orpheus. His metamorphosis / in this one and in that. We should not make // searches for other names. Once and for all, / it's Orpheus, when there's song. He comes and goes.] [II, 255]

This descendental principle, which makes spirit immanent in things and only in things, has been espoused by the poets of many eras, but by each, Rilke realizes, as though he or she were the first to have taken the god out of the sky. "Er kommt und geht" in a natural rhythm resembling the Goethean systole and diastole, but also resembling the way in which this principle itself has come and gone in a succession of poets since Goethe. Hence the inappropriateness of a monument, the aspiration to permanence of which belies the natural coming and going, like the rose, of those poets who have assumed the mantle of Orpheus. By this means Hölderlin in particular is subtly reduced to a transitory phenomenon.

The fifth sonnet is interesting also for Rilke's contention that Orpheus, the poetic principle or word, can transcend "Hiersein," which in Rilke's sense implies something more than that poetry outlasts transitory things. It also implies that when genuine the poetic word participates in death, being grounded in the underworld "wohin ihrs nicht begleitet" (I, v; I, 734)—reminding one again of the genius of Hölderlin as Rilke celebrates it at the beginning of "An Hölderlin." And yet one could read this sonnet from another perspective altogether: the seasonal cycle is a coming and going, and Orpheus shares in this impermanence of the process world. Despite the mystical significance of the rose as a symbol of interiority in Rilke's work, and despite the fact that this sonnet appears to place a higher value on the rose than on a monument or "Denkstein," we must keep in mind that a monument is precisely what Rilke declares his sonnet cycle to be. It is addressed to Orpheus, *"an* Orpheus," but it is also a "Grab-mal," a funerary monument beneath which Eurydice-Wera Knoop may lie entombed but from which Orpheus is therefore, in the logic of the myth, necessarily absent. From this standpoint the fluctuation of nature's creative energies, as embodied in the rose, exists in contrast with the written poetic monument which transcends temporality by constituting an eternal present. Thus "Ein für alle Male / ists Orpheus, wenn es singt" refers not only to spontaneous natural singing and to other poets who have been possessed by Orpheus, but also to those natural things in which the voice of Orpheus is not so much vitally present as hopelessly entrapped. Herein Sonnet I, v anticipates the last sonnet of Part I.

The genius of Orpheus, whatever his limitations, remains his inimitable vertical trajectory. In the sixth sonnet, as conjuror ("der Beschwörende," I, vi; I, 734), Orpheus can penetrate the underworld with his divining rod as well as the world of the living and is thus more than "ein Hiesiger," a Goethean poet. He who has experienced the ground of poetry in death is able to use the weeping willow, the tree of mourning whose branches traditionally help gain entrance to Hades, as a poetic staff with which to plumb the depths: "Kundiger böge die Zweige der Weiden, / wer die Wurzeln der Weiden erfuhr" (I, vi; I, 734). The shape of the willow, with its falling branches, resembles the shape of water rising and falling in a fountain, and both of these images suggest that ascent and descent are necessary to each other, like the slopes of a parabola.

In the seventh sonnet, Orpheus appears after all to be a Goethean poet dedicated to the task of what Rilke had earlier called "Herz-Werk":

> Sein Herz, o vergängliche Kelter
> eines den Menschen unendlichen Weins.
>
> Nie versagt ihm die Stimme am Staube,
> wenn ihn das göttliche Beispiel ergreift.
> Alles wird Weinberg, alles wird Traube,
> in seinem fühlenden Süden gereift.   [I, vii; I, 735]

[Came with his heart, oh, transient presser, / For men, of a never-exhaustible wine. // Voice never fails him for things lacking lustre, / sacred example will open his mouth. / All becomes vineyard, all becomes cluster, / warmed by his sympathy's ripening south.]   [II, 256]

His song converts the world into "das Land, wo die Zitronen blühn," and is itself a fruit, harvest of the natural cycle.[69] At one moment in the cycle, this Orpheus too gains admission to the underworld, this time bearing gifts from the living, bowls "mit rühmenden Früchten." This fruit, his encomiastic song of petition to Pluto and Persephone, is of course much more material and vital than the pure visionary song of the opening sonnets, suggesting again that the poetic principle now being held uppermost is at once the organicism of Goethe and the *Dinglichkeit* with which Rilke himself was recurrently preoccupied.

Again, although I began by assigning an overall movement of thought to the *Sonette*, I do not think that from poem to poem Rilke's vacillation can be said to take a definite course. For example, in contrast with the seventh sonnet, where the "Weinberg" seems to be conceived in opposition to the Hölderlin of "Brot und Wein," Sonnet I, xix seems decisively to pick up ideas and images that Rilke had earlier associated with Hölderlin. This sonnet opposes the idea of stellar song with the counter-sublime movement of "fallen" in language that encompasses both poetry and the things of nature: "alles Vollendete fällt / heim zum Uralten" (I, xix; I, 743), descending together to an origin and reminding one of the words Hölderlin's Empedokles speaks on the day of his death: "Heut ist mein Herbst-tag und es fällt die Frucht / Von selbst" (II, 510). In this sonnet the "god with the lyre" is portrayed as a forerunner suggestive of

Hölderlin, whose "Vor-Gesang" endures in the face of change.[70] Presented in terms that evoke Hölderlin's poetics, Orpheus's song in this sonnet recalls the image of Hölderlin as a moon moving over the nighttime landscape in "Orpheus. Eurydike. Hermes": "Einzig das Lied überm Land / heiligt und feiert."

To summarize, then, Orpheus in these sonnets is clearly a two-sided figure, sometimes embodying the merger of natural with transcendental poetry but more often an unsynthesized grouping of prior poetic solutions—Goethe's, Hölderlin's—over against which Rilke can direct his own pursuit of an ultimate poetic. At one moment Orpheus is Hölderlin as Rilke perceives him—the great elegist—while at another moment he is a Goethe figure, a poet who nearly succeeds in bringing nature into language and whose mode is celebratory rather than elegiac: "Nur im Raum der Rühmung darf die Klage / gehn." (I, viii).

We can further elaborate the Goethean aspects of Rilke's Orpheus by considering two sonnets from Part I in which language and nature are closely aligned. In I, xiii, it is again fruit, a distillation of nature's plenty, which is proffered as a medium, a language, in which death and life find common expression:

> Voller Apfel, Birne und Banane,
> Stachelbeere . . . Alles dieses spricht
> Tod und Leben in den Mund . . . Ich ahne . . .
> Lest es einem Kind vom Angesicht[.]   [I, xiii; I, 739]
>
> [Banana, rounded apple, russet pear, / gooseberry . . . Does not all this convey / life and death into your mouth . . . It's there! . . . / Read it on a child's face any day.]   [II, 259]

Fruit speaks into the mouth, and one can read what it says in the face of a child. If fruit is a language, then it is tempting to say that language conversely can embody fruit; but in fact the authentic speaking of the fruit has the function of pointing away from language toward essence: "Wird euch langsam namenlos im Munde? / Wo sonst Worte waren, fliessen Funde." If a poem is to be like fruit, then, Rilke admonishes the other poets, it must be a language that defamiliarizes words: "Wagt zu sagen, was ihr Apfel nennt." If a poem can fully distill experience, *present* it with no merely representational residue, then it can enter into a symmetrically converse relation with the fruit which in the mouth is "verdichtet," distilled as an intense taste into a *Gedicht*. Although it is not verbal, fruit is still what poetry should be, "doppeldeutig"; its ambiguity however is not the frustrating undecidability that is determined by the mediatory status of conventional language, but rather the Orphic capacity for movement without confusion or liminal obstruction between the two realms of life and death. Like Orpheus, fruit flourishes, then descends to the ground, then is raised up to sing in the mouth—and then is torn apart.

Directness of speech, the return of the arbitrary sign to an unmediated, purely expressive function: this is also the theme of I, xxi, in which the earth is "ein Kind, das Gedichte weiss" (I, xxi; I, 744). Naively but with scrupulous fidelity, the earth each year rehearses the order of the seasons as though it were reciting it:

> O, was der Lehrer sie lehrte, das Viele,
> und was gedruckt steht in Wurzeln und langen
> schwierigen Stämmen: sie singts, sie singts!   {I, 744}
>
> [All she has ever been taught by her teacher, / all that's imprinted in
> roots and soaring / difficult stems,—she sings, she sings!]   [II, 262]

These lines are probably Rilke's most direct appropriation of a text he had read avidly, Goethe's "Metamorphose der Pflanzen."[71] According to Goethe, the whole progress of a plant's life is encoded in its roots and stems; to this Rilke adds the suggestion in this sonnet that the genetic language of the plant is "gedruckt" in the same way that language unfurls itself in a poem. As one critic has pointed out, indeed, "Wurzeln" and "Stämme" belong alike to botany and to grammar.[72] The plant's writing in natural signs, or in any case its imprinted code that enables writing, is revealed to be prior to singing just as roots are prior to flowers.

This key insight, which gains ground as the cycle advances, may help to explain what happens to Orpheus at the end of Part I. The final sonnet comes to terms with Orpheus by burying him. From Ovid we learn that after his unsuccessful attempt to bring back Eurydice, Orpheus shuns the company of women, resisting the advances of the Maenads. Representing those aspects of nature that cannot be reconstituted and reduced to order by song, the Maenads resent the fact that the inspirational estrangement of Orphic consciousness brought about by the loss of Eurydice extends also to them and their domain. They turn nature against Orpheus, throwing sod, stones, and branches at him and thus inverting the power that his song had exercised over precisely these objects. Their wrath culminates in the *sparagmos* of Orpheus; his limbs are scattered over the earth while his head and lyre enter the waters of the Hebron. He thus returns to his original unity with nature, but now pointedly without the power of originary song; henceforth he is no longer a poet but an oracle. In Rilke, however, it is perhaps implied that from the beginning Orphic song understood as the "Ausdruck" of nature is just that, and not in any way an independently originary utterance—this being Rilke's ultimate critique of the Goethean stance. The advantage of this same stance for Rilke, on the other hand, is that even in the face of the chaos wrought by the Maenads, Orphic song remains a civilizing, form-giving influence. Here as elsewhere,[73] one senses a contrast between the Apollonian Orpheus and the Dionysian Maenads: "hast ihr Geschrei übertönt mit Ordnung, du Schöner, / aus den Zerstörenden stieg dein erbauendes Spiel" (I, xxvi; I, 747). By way of Nietzsche's *Birth of Tragedy*, Orpheus the form-bringer is Goethe.

In this sonnet Rilke further emphasizes the idea that the fragmentation of Orpheus exists for us as the coming and going of voice in the poetic tradition. Orpheus must now speak through others, and his song—if one can properly speak of its being originarily his—is no longer a "reine Übersteigung" but rather a *trace*, a "Spur" that is *written* on the material surface of nature:

> während dein Klang noch in Löwen und Felsen verweilte
> und in den Bäumen und Vögeln. Dort singst du noch jetzt.
>
> O du verlorener Gott! Du unendliche Spur! Nur weil dich reissend
> zuletzt die Feindschaft verteilte,
> sind wir die Hörenden jetzt und ein Mund der Natur.[I, xxvi; I, 748]
>
> [sound of you lingered in lions and rocks you were first to / enthrall, in the trees and the birds. You are singing there still. // O you god that has vanished! You infinite track! Only because dismembering hatred dispersed you / are we hearers to-day and a mouth which else Nature would lack.]   [II, 265]

Had it not been for the dismemberment of Orpheus, other poets would not have found a voice, would not subsequently have sung what they found written in nature. The logic of the "Spur" insists that the demarcated absence of Orpheus is what confirms his former presence, but the form of that presence can never now be known. Even while characterizing himself as a listener and epigone, Rilke shows the divine singer himself to have been disabled, wholly subsumed by nature, with the suggestion that only in myth was it ever otherwise. The pointed ambiguity of "Mund" leaves later poets finally wondering whether they are indeed the mouth of nature, its Goethean voice, or whether they are merely its mouthpiece, speakers in its behalf hoping to approximate the mute enigmas posed by its— possibly—hieroglyphic traces.

If the anthropomorphic outline of Orpheus has faded by the end of Part I, in Part II he appears rarely and peripherally in any form at all.[74] In the first sonnet of Part II, conspicuously paralleling the evocation of Orphic song in I, i, Rilke describes his poetics as he now understands them in the context of the *Sonette* as a cycle. Its opening, "Atmen, du unsichtbares Gedicht," recalls the divine breath of I, iii, "Ein Hauch um nichts. Ein Wehn im Gott," and proceeds boldly to undermine the vocality of breath by declaring that the natural object retains its concreteness not when it is sung (formerly Orphic song had been the thing as well as being about it) but when it is expressed in writing. In this poem, Rilke suggests an analogy between the process of breathing, again a Goethean, natural rhythm of expansion and contraction, and the process of writing. Inhalation takes in the natural object and exhalation expresses it in the form of a tree:

> Erkennst du mich, Luft, du, voll noch einst meiniger Orte?
> Du, einmal glatte Rinde,
> Rundung und Blatt meiner Worte.

> [Do you know me, air, still full of my dwelling-places? / You, the one-
> time smooth-skinned / rondure and leaf of my phrases.]   [II, 272]

In this sonnet, with its emphasized concluding possessive, Rilke claims for himself poetic powers similar to those of Orpheus. In order to do this, he turns again to the metaphor of the tree, but here the tree stands for the poem as a written object, its bark no longer smooth because it is inscribed.[75] By thus defining the poem as a verbal object, or at least as an inscription on an object, a funerary monument, Rilke manages at once to connect and to undermine the dominant antithetical interpretations of Orpheus in the *Sonette*: Orpheus the leaning toward visionary poetry, the language of absence, and Orpheus the leaning toward an articulate nature, the language of presence. Emergent as a craftsman, a poet-maker, the poetic self takes the place of Orpheus.

The vocality of song is also undermined by Rilke's celebration of the dance. As early as I, xv, he reverts to the image of the fruit, imagining a dance that is at once the perception of the fruit and the creation of a dancing *experience*, of an "experienced fruit." This dance is an emblem of the way in which the experience of nature enters the work of art: "Tanzt den Geschmack der erfahrenen Frucht! / Tanzt die Orange" (I, 740). He urges the dancers yet further, "Schafft die Verwandtschaft / mit der reinen, sich weigernden Schale," exhorting them to merge their movement with the shape of the fruit and thus to contain its essence. And when Rilke later—in II, viii—uses the expression "Wandung der eigenen Wendung" to characterize the dancer (in this case it is Wera Knoop), he is recalling the "Rundung meiner Worte" of II, i. Like a poem, like the bark of the tree (which is also present in II, viii), the surface created by the movement of the dancer is said to be inscribed, and the dance comes to resemble writing. Rilke frequently recurs, of course, to the sister arts convention in order to describe one art in terms of another.[76] But when he describes the *dance* as though it were writing, he means especially to insist upon the permanence of the transient; the figures inscribed in the air by movement remain transfixed in the mind's eye, just as the writing down of poetry transfixes its images.

Clearly, Rilke's poems *in*scribe their object as much as they *de*-scribe it. Just as the venerable tradition of the *Dinggedicht* survives in the *Sonette*, so too one finds reflected there the closely related tradition of the inscription poem. From the simple inscription on the votive object recorded in the Greek Anthology to the writing of tombstone epitaphs, inscription has always been a metonymy, a proxy, for the object its labeling engraves. In the poetry of Paul Celan, who was much influenced by Rilke, words become stones. If the poet cannot fulfill his wish to recreate the object in its ontological purity, he can at least single it out by marking it commemoratively in the act of writing. Generally speaking, the poetry that aspires toward objecthood for its words—and necessarily falls short of that aspiration—actually does achieve an art of inscription, an incisiveness whereby phenomenal objects do not appear but are effectively re-marked in writing.

In his poetry, Rilke wishes to say that the written text is the equivalent of the natural thing:

Alles ist ausgeruht:
Dunkel und Helligkeit,
Blume und Buch.   [I, xxii; I, 745]

[how rested all things are: / shadow and fall of light, / blossom and book.]   [II, 263]

Light and darkness—or life and death—the things of nature and written things, all exist in quiet equilibrium on a single ontological plane. In defining himself as a poet who makes and inscribes objects, Rilke programmatically parts company once more not only with the Goethean poets who "express" existing objects, but also with Hölderlin and the other visionaries of German Romanticism—such as Novalis, the poet of "Dunkelheit"—for whom, on the authority, again, of Herder, Orpheus was an ancestral model. Rilke's placing "Blume und Buch" side by side rejects the yearning of Hölderlin, in the "Brot und Wein" passage to which I have already referred, for a time when "Worte wie Blumen entstehn," a time when the immediacy of language, not the reconstitutive power Rilke here celebrates, was what made it authentic. Rilke now proclaims the equality of words and things without insisting on their identity. The self-appointed task of poets in the Romantic tradition had always been to convert the mute objects of nature into the articulate, communicable ciphers of metaphor. Stone, tree, flower, star: these are the objects to which the Romantic poets constantly return in the hope, ironically, that naming the auratic names of such objects will bring into being a world that transcends the world of objects.[77] Thus they are limited to a mimetic relationship with nature by the very figures they evoke to carry them toward transcendence. Rilke makes himself vulnerable to just the opposite irony: he uses this same stock of imagery, not for the purpose of transcendence but in rivalry with the things he names, and thus finds himself alienated from nature by the very figures he has designated to dwell among natural things.

In contrast with the dismembered Orpheus who has disappeared into the environment, then, Rilke wishes to stand over against nature and then turn his alienation to creative advantage:

> Und wenn dich das Irdische vergass,
> zu der stillen Erde sag: Ich rinne.
> Zu dem raschen Wasser sprich: Ich bin.   [II, xxix; I, 771]
>
> [And should earthliness forget you quite, / murmur to the quiet earth: I'm running. / Tell the running water: I exist.]   [II, 283]

In these last lines of his last sonnet the poet opposes himself to "das Irdische" in defiance of natural fact; and in asserting the priority of the written word to song, Rilke expresses an opposition to Orpheus and the Romantics that takes a similar form. Orphic song penetrates Nature, perhaps merely *is* nature, but the written word remains apart, separate from but equal to the objects of nature. And, what is equally important to Rilke, "as the non-living representation of voice, writing installs a relation to death within the processes of language."[78] In these ways, by spatializing voice and entrapping it within the poem as a created thing, Rilke strives in the *Sonette* to surpass Goethe, Hölderlin, and the other Romantics, descending deeper than they without following the voice of Orpheus at all.

Chapter Five
The Poetry of
Repetition:
Trakl's Narrow
Bridge

Hölderlin's translations from Sophocles were his last work; in them meaning plunges from abyss to abyss until it threatens to become lost in the bottomless depths of language.
—Walter Benjamin, "The Task of the Translator"

The myth we need as interpreters, and do not have, is that the stars fell into language.
—Geoffrey Hartman, "From the Sublime to the Hermeneutic"

The theme of descent looms large among the poets of the German Romantic tradition because of their common intimation that the origin of their voice is not celestial but deep beneath the surface of the earth or water, locations that are figures for death, the unconscious, the living but estranged mother, the dead but still vital patriarch, and, in the case of Rilke, "writing"— an inscribed code of which voice is the expression. In discussing each poet I have added to these figures still another, one that merges the awful visage of the patriarch with the inscribed code above mentioned, which code understood in its most general sense is simply that priority of language which frustrates the poet's will to originality; the resulting composite figure I have called, following Harold Bloom, the "precursor." In examining the poetry of Georg Trakl, the focus will be almost exclusively on the precursor, but with a difference. Although the influence of prior poets in the Romantic tradition remains important, for Trakl the true precursor, the object of his descent, is the revisionary language of descent itself, the language of exhaustion that all these poets appear to have exhausted. My theme here will therefore be Trakl's complex effort to make that language his own.

Trakl's poetry is opaque by design, willfully fragmented, and always resistant to closure. In the hope of unlocking his hermeticism, many critics have ransacked his life for a key. But what we know of his life is also fragmentary. It was relatively short (1887–1914), and his letters are few and for the most part uninformative. Certain lurid facts do emerge from which the image of Trakl is typically formed: his sanity was precarious, he was addicted to drugs and alcohol, and his relationship with his sister Margarete was almost certainly incestuous—something like a hybrid of Hölderlin, Coleridge, and Byron. The conjunction of Trakl's hermetic poetry with his Romantic life has provoked a number of psychoanalytic studies of varying degrees of competence and interest. There is an essay on Trakl, one of five, in Erich Neumann's *Creative Man*; his Jungian focus on the Great Mother archetype, which appears, he argues, in nearly all the Romantics' experiences of nature and landscape, certainly covers one aspect of the descent theme.[1]

In a recent study, *The Poet's Madness: A Reading of Georg Trakl*, Francis Michael Sharp derives his readings from what he calls Trakl's metanoia, "a shift in the ontological center of the self . . . , a nodal term where poetry and madness have often met,"[2] making the Laingian claim that in order to do justice to Trakl's poetry the reader must enter into his hallucinatory world. Maire Jaanus Kurrik's provocative study correlates changes in Trakl's poetic language with his developing schizophrenia, concluding that Trakl's poetry "leads us ultimately to naked primary process." Kurrik's monograph stresses the peculiar intensity with which Trakl experienced language, and she declares that it was "language, not disease, that made his art,"[3] but Trakl's poetry as she reads it remains by and large a pathological rather than a literary object. It is the language, after all, of a certain tradition and of particular poets to which Trakl responds with such unquestionable intensity; and for this reason the biographical approach to Trakl needs the complement of other emphases.

There is no need to question the image of Trakl as a schizophrenic—and as an addict from an early age—but side by side with these signs of disorder we must place the impression the letters give of a meticulous, very possibly obsessive but still reliable craftsman. He repeatedly pestered his editor Kurt Wolff to make minor changes in punctuation, he was wont to submit lists of typographical errors, and he worried incessantly about arranging his poems in the right order for publication in a volume.[4] All of this bespeaks a strong interest in form and in closure of all kinds. He could never stop revising, as is attested by "the famous café napkins which are the bedevilment of Trakl's editors: layer upon layer of alternative readings."[5] Thus far we remain at least arguably in the domain of obsessive madness, but the idea that Trakl's poetry is an unstructured transformation of illness and excess into language must be supplemented by the frequent, careful, and systematic borrowing from other poets noticed by a number of his interpreters. Perhaps foremost among these is Bernhard Böschenstein, whose essay on Trakl's borrowings from Hölderlin is rich and suggestive. Although he does not stress the point, Böschenstein makes it clear that Trakl sees himself as an heir to Hölderlin deeply preoccupied with the possibility of founding a poetry of his own.[6]

From another perspective, after listing pages of Trakl's borrowings from Rimbaud, Reinhold Grimm notes that Trakl's manner of incorporating Rimbaud's poetry suggests an unusual attitude toward the literary tradition and toward the value of originality; for Trakl, Grimm argues, poetry is no longer the private possession of the poet but is simply verbal material of which anyone can make use.[7] While it is unlikely that any poet could suppress individualism sufficiently to take such a detached view of the poet's function and of his or her predecessors' priority, Grimm's insight concerning existing poetry as verbal material to be appropriated remains a valuable one. If borrowings are taken without regard to context, they are severed from existing poetry and become ciphers or counters of what might be called poeticality. As is yet more obvious in the poetry of Helmut Heissenbüttel, for instance, the accrued meaning of such borrowings is not suppressed but becomes enigmatically immanent and over-rich, simultaneously a homage to tradition and a mockery of its will-to-mean.

Trakl's borrowings, whether they repeat single words, whole phrases, or images and situations, point to themselves *as* borrowings, as quotations bordering on cliché. An obvious example is Novalis's "blaue Blume," which appears everywhere in Trakl's poems. In borrowings of this kind there is an element, to be sure, of the Freudian compulsion to repeat, to gain mastery of a procedure; and there is also, in the wearing down of significance by repetition, what Harold Bloom calls the effort to "undo" the achievement of the poet from whom one borrows.[8] But it is not only a matter of borrowing from other poets; Trakl repeats himself, in poem after poem, with the same mystification through loss of context that accompanies his repeated borrowings from others. Resembling Eichendorff most in this, Trakl moves a highly restricted assemblage of images and verbal material in and out of position like pieces in a board game. The result is a finite set of repetitions and variations—worked out on one napkin or scrap of envelope after another—proceeding not only from draft to draft but also from poem to poem. Walther Killy, who has examined the chaos of manuscripts with painstaking care, has pointed out that in Trakl's work individual words have different meanings in different places ("silbern" is his main example), that variants of the same poem may at least appear to contradict one another, and that what apparently determines a given poem is a grid-like verbal pattern that remains constant from one revision to an-other.[9] The deeper principles governing repetitions of this kind, Killy remains convinced, are inaccessible. He concludes, in the tradition of Hugo Friedrich, that Trakl is more interested in *Sprachmagie* than in meaning.[10]

It is with Friedrich and the more recent scholarly writing based on his ideas that Paul de Man takes issue, in his "Lyric and Modernity," for jumping too quickly to the conclusion that the discourse (especially the lyric discourse) of modernity is programmatically non-referential. In this essay de Man skillfully mediates between the commonsensical awareness (ignored by the school of Friedrich) that all poetry retains some mode of reference and the simultaneous understanding that the very plenitude of reference in the "modern lyric," in excess of any possible configural resolution, is what finally undermines univocal meaning. Most importantly, de Man recommends an approach to the reading of poetry that incorporates "semantic plurality . . . even and especially if the ultimate 'message' is held to be a mere play of meanings that cancel each other out."[11] This is the double awareness the reader of Trakl must be willing to sustain, if only because at least two apparently conflicting impulses are always at work in his poetry: on the one hand the semantically charged desire at once to preserve and undermine in revising the language of the past—especially that of Romantic poetry—by placing it in a new setting, and on the other hand the desire to empty that same language of all content whatsoever in order to release from its constraint the "pure" language that has preoccupied Romantic theorists from Hamann to Walter Benjamin. As we shall see, after the early poems Trakl's poetry simply overrides the contradiction between referential and pure language and strives for both at once.

II

O die Flöte des Lichts, O die Flöte des
Tods.
Was zwang dich still zu stehen auf
Verfallener Stiege, im Haus deiner
Väter?
—Trakl, *Verwandlung des Bösen*

Trakl was an avid reader, and in his early career a brazen literary
thief: other poets' voices appear everywhere without disguise in the
Sammlung 1909, as well as in the *Gedichte 1909–1912*. The seemingly simple yet enigmatic religiosity of the Romantic Clemens
Brentano dominates "Das tiefe Lied" (I, 228); Novalis's *Hymnen an
die Nacht* plainly inform "Gesang zur Nacht" (I, 223) and "Nachtlied
II" (I, 261); "Auf den Tod einer alten Frau" reflects Trakl's familiarity
with the poems and themes of Rilke's *Neue Gedichte*; the posturing of
Heine, his surprising appositions and turns of expression, can be
found everywhere, as in "Ein Komödiant, der seine Rolle spricht, /
Gezwungen, voll Verzweiflung—Langeweile!" ("Confiteor," I, 246);
"Melusine II" is written in obvious imitation of Goethe's "Erlkönig";
Eichendorff's cankered flowers and Baudelaire's flowers of evil appear
variously as "giftige Blumen" ("Das Grauen," I, 220), "blutfarbne
Blüten," and "pestfarbne Blumen" ("Sabbath," I, 222); and Rim-
baud's artificial paradise is represented and subjected to decay in
poems such as "Ermatten" (I, 242).

In these poems, Trakl experiments with a wide variety of poetic
attitudes and a limited number of forms—as one might expect of a
young poet who is at once coming to terms with a poetic tradition
and intent on developing a personal style. But unlike most apprentice poets, Trakl is not just imitative, he is pointedly imitative:
many poems deviate very little from their models, as if with the
intention of learning a technique by rote—one which is then used in
attenuated, distorted form in the more personal poems of the same
period. Other poems reflect a more complex encounter with the
tradition, making a theme of their own borrowing, the resulting
self-consciousness of which then precipitates the business of poetic
revision. In these poems borrowings are easily recognizable, and
serve frequently as vehicles for Trakl's interest in voice—in its role in
prior poetry and as he supposes it to function in his own work. A
poem of this period in which this process works particularly well,
the first in the early group discussed mainly with respect to Trakl's
thematic revisionism, is "Ballade I" (I, 229), which is based in part

on Heine's *Die Nordsee*, a lyric cycle in itself preoccupied with filiality.

The deceptively simple "Ballade I" has much to say about the possession of voice in the German lyric tradition:

Ein Narre schrieb drei Zeichen in Sand,
Eine bleiche Magd da vor ihm stand.
Laut sang, o sang das Meer.

Sie hielt einen Becher in der Hand,
Der schimmerte bis auf zum Rand,
Wie Blut so rot und schwer.

Kein Wort ward gesprochen—die Sonne schwand,
Da nahm der Narre aus ihrer Hand
Den Becher und trank ihn leer.

Da löschte sein Licht in ihrer Hand,
Der Wind verwehte drei Zeichen in Sand—
Laut sang, o sang das Meer.

[A fool wrote three symbols in the sand, / A pale maid stood there before him. / Loudly sang, o sang the sea. // She held a goblet in her hand, / It shimmered to the rim / Like blood so red and heavy. // No word was spoken—the sun disappeared, / Then the fool took from her hand / The goblet and drank it dry. // Then his light extinguished in her hand, / The wind swept away three symbols in the sand— / Loudly sang, o sang the sea.]

In Heine's "Erklärung," a poem in *Die Nordsee*, it is the poet himself, the central figure of the cycle, who writes "Agnes, ich liebe dich" in the sand, only to have the words erased by the waves. And in the darkly ironic "Fragen," a poem in the same cycle, "ein Narr" waits for an indifferent nature to respond to his questions concerning the meaning of life and the nature of the sublime ("Wer wohnt dort oben auf goldenen Sternen?"[12]). In addition, in *Die Nordsee* as in "Ballade I," a beloved, idealized woman holds sway as muse; and a similar figure appears in Heine's *Lyrisches Intermezzo*, of which one is reminded by the simplicity of Trakl's syntax. Heine's presence in the background helps with the interpretation of Trakl's poem; "Erklärung" suggests, for example, that the "drei Zeichen" may be "ich liebe dich," the *Urworte* that all love poetry displaces and elaborates upon.

The seductive pale maiden who lures a lover to death is also in Heine, but she is just as central in Eichendorff and Brentano and is a familiar spirit, indeed, throughout the German tradition. An admirer of Mörike,[13] Trakl would no doubt have been familiar with that poet's enigmatic, strangely decadent rendering of this figure in his "Peregrina," where the maiden similarly hands the speaker "den Tod im Kelch der Sünden."[14] That eroticism and death are always closely linked in Trakl's lyrics can doubtless be referred to his involvement with his sister; but, more important, *Liebestode* of the kind enumerated here—especially given the chosen vocabulary of Trakl, should be referred back to one of Goethe's best-known, if least understood, ballads, "Der König in Thule," sung by Gretchen in *Faust*, Part I. The chalice or "Becher" that is emblematic of the beloved who has given it to the king at her death, at once her sign and the sign of her absence, is fittingly emptied by the king at every meal. But at the same time this chalice represents the king, whose eyes similarly overflow and empty ("Die Augen gingen ihm über"; I, 2765) whenever he drains it. Just before he dies, the cup itself is said to drink ("Trinken, und sinken tief ins Meer"); and at his death his eyes "sink" in imitation of the cup. As understood by his literary descendants, Goethe's poetics renders the "Becher" a "symbol" in which the corporeal presence of the beloved and of the king can be merged across time. The brilliance of the poem is its accomplishment of this burdensome task, a concretely imagined secular communion via the "heilige Becher," without ever calling attention to its symbolic intent. After the golden cup sinks, it becomes a treasure of the depths, for Droste-Hülshoff the vessel of literary inheritance, which only poetic descent can recover. For Trakl too the "Becher" becomes a symbol of literary accomplishment, of Goethe's success in handling symbolism and of his faith in his own power of containment, his control over the evocative compression essential to lyric. "Becher" for Trakl then becomes a verbal talisman, to repeat which is to participate in the genius of Goethe.

In Heine's *Nordsee*, the poet must also come to terms with his literary inheritance. "Die Götter Griechenlands" is clearly as much a confrontation with Goethe and Schiller as with Greek mythology, and it is beautifully staged: at the very moment when Heine arrives at the destruction of the Titans, of fathers by sons—"Doch auch die Götter regieren nicht ewig, / Die Jungen verdrängen die Alten"[15]— he addresses "Jupiter Parricida," alluding, perhaps, to the "Jupiter Pluvius" of Goethe's "Wanderers Sturmlied." (One is reminded as well of Hölderlin's "Natur und Kunst oder Saturn und Jupiter" [I, 78].) And when in "Fragen" the poet besieges nature with questions that go unanswered, when the stars remain indifferent, cold, and inaccessible to interpretation, Heine is simultaneously conceding the belatedness of the poet, the "Narr" who can no longer read natural signs, and directing toward Goethe the shrewd Humanist admonition that metaphors taken from the natural world evade rather than illuminate the concerns of mankind.

Trakl's "Ballade I" repeats Heine's swerve away from Goethe but then somewhat revises Heine's supposition that voice is the medium of the poet even if it is not to be found in nature. In Trakl too, nature is oblivious to the human drama; but his "Narr" is neither a poet who voices questions nor one who, when he writes, merely transcribes the voiced sigh of a lover. He is, much more emphatically than Heine's fool, a writer, one whose signs are not words, as far as we are told, but only marks, and whose silence is as conspicuous as that of Heine's nature: "Kein Wort ward gesprochen." Trakl's nature, by contrast, is what sings, albeit unintelligibly, and sings last and loudest, with a persistence that Trakl acknowledges by making it the theme of a refrain and placing it twice—in the first and last stanzas—in symmetrical contrast with the persistence of human silence. Thus for Heine human voice and the writing that records it are alienated for better as well as for worse from the silence of nature, whereas for Trakl human silence and the hermetic writing that perpetuates it are cut off from the vocality of nature in a state of solipsism to which the values of better and worse are irrelevant.

The very complexity with which Trakl's poem stages itself within the tradition of the written word, at once sharing Heine's confrontation with Goethe and rewriting Goethe's signs of lyric power with almost superstitious reverence, heightens both the distance and the significance of the singing sea in this poem yet further. As if in defiance of the mighty sea, which is also the choral *voice* of a poetic tradition in which the event narrated here has occurred so many times before, Trakl seems to entertain the idea of a poetry that does not issue from voice. But his heresy is only tentative; as his title with its allusion to the oral tradition indicates, he is unwilling wholly to identify with "der Narr." He is not ready to say, as he will in "Nachtlied," "gewaltig ist das Schweigen im Stein" (I, 68). The vocal sea is after all the place into which Goethe's golden cup has been cast; its depths hold the promise of renewed natural communion, and Trakl's homage to the poet of this promise, absorbed into the *sound* of "Becher," is too great to permit open defiance. The refrain goes on, "Laut sang, o sang das Meer," and in repeating this refrain with its inner repetition and its vocative "o," Trakl acknowledges that he remains within the vocal tradition—perhaps too much so, indeed, to accord with his developing interest in the poetics of the pure sign. Whatever the reason, this poem was not published during his lifetime.

In his two "Melusine" poems, Trakl once again associates the theme of an inspirited, vocal nature with Goethe. In what is commonly assumed to be the earlier "Melusine," there exists a deep empathy between the "Meerfee" of the title and the elements other than the sea. The wind cries over her fate, and her passion, figured forth by her fiery hair, finds its reflection in the storm. The narrator, with whose words the poem concludes, keeps himself at a safe distance from this temptress, however, safely protected from her pagan spirit by his Christian faith: "Da spricht für dich, du arme Magd,/ Mein Herz ein stilles Nachtgebet!" (I, 232). All this is conventional enough, and the suggestive confusion of the poem only arises when we attempt to locate voice, the origin of what is spoken, precisely and consistently. Here is the poem:

An meinen Fenstern weint die Nacht—
Die Nacht ist stumm, es weint wohl der Wind,
Der Wind, wie ein verlornes Kind—
Was ist's, das ihn so weinen macht?
O arme Melusine!

Wie Feuer ihr Haar im Sturme weht,
Wie Feuer an Wolken vorüber und klagt—
Da spricht für dich, du arme Magd,
Mein Herz ein stilles Nachtgebet!
O arme Melusine!

[At my windows weeps the night— / The night is mute, it must be the wind, / The wind, like a lost child— / What is it, that makes it weep so? / O poor Melusine! // Like fire her hair streams in the storm, / Like fire passing clouds and lamenting— / Then for you poor maid, / my heart says a silent nighttime prayer! / O poor Melusine!]

The piety of the narrator makes it the more interesting that he would attempt to explain a natural sound by referring it to a nature spirit. There can be no question, apparently, of a natural voice; the night, which is the time Trakl, with Novalis, prefers, is here denied a voice, being mute, "stumm." Like the night, the speaker's prayer is silent, while the poem by contrast ends with a balladic, vocal refrain. The question then is, if it is not part of the speaker's prayer, who speaks this refrain? Is it the anonymous voice of the ballad genre? In the first stanza it might be assigned to the wind, which cries in presumed sympathy with Melusine. But in the second it is plausibly the narrator's voiced, wholly secular and petitionless version of his "stilles Nachtgebet." Or, since Melusine is connected with "klagen," a verb whose antecedent is vague (her hair could stream like tears or bend like a willow, but how could it lament?), perhaps she herself speaks the refrain in self-pity. Finally, and perhaps most convincingly, the closing refrain can be voiced by the wind insofar as it is also Melusine, the "verlornes Kind" to which it is linked in simile. The point of all this ambiguity is, in any case, that voice is now here, now there, but seems never to be the possession of the "speaker"; and the poem's tentative evocation of a nature spirit that in some sense speaks the poet's lines, an anomaly reinforced by the rhyme of "Wind" with "Kind," may have suggested to Trakl the possibility of recasting his poem in the form and rhythms of an earlier ballad about possession, Goethe's "Erlkönig," a poem Geoffrey Hartman has called a "play of voices."[16]

In this ballad of 1782, Goethe dramatizes a struggle for a child between two "fathers," a contest between exhortations, seemingly without physical violence, carried out between rivals for the possession of charismatic authority. The actual father speaks with the voice of enlightened reason and hears nothing but the sound of wind in dry leaves when his rival speaks; and the aspiring father (or lover), the Erlkönig, is at once a nature spirit and the voice of imagination—albeit a regressive, solipsistic imagination. It is easy to view this struggle, whose arena is the mind of the child and whose aim is to shape his view of nature, as a rivalry between literary impulses that were more even than usually at odds in the 1780s, during which the Enlightenment can be said to have lost out, as it does in the poem, to the avatars of the imagination. As Hartman convincingly argues, toward the beginning of the poem the father's voice can still "contain" that of the child;[17] his lines literally frame the child's. But the Erlkönig becomes wholly dominant by the last stanza, with the death of the child—his desertion of the real world for fairy tale and dream—signaling the imagination's victory. Goethe himself can be said however to identify with no one; his is yet another voice in this drama, the impersonal voice of the narrator, or more precisely that of a traditional singer. (The ballad was written for Goethe's *Singspiel, Die Fischerin.*) Here as so often in Goethe, Werther's sensibility being a case in point, the struggle between reason and imagination is distanced, made to seem pseudo-intellectual, by the matter-of-fact simplicity of the ballad form. All voices in "Erlkönig" are framed by the narrator, who speaks the first and last stanzas as though to insist on the insufficiency of any one world view taken by itself, and the impression of superiority achieved by this Olympian perspective is what convinces us that the object of the struggle between mere ideologies is properly a child and not a poet. The object of the *narrator's* seduction is not the child but the reader, a prospective poet who experiences the abrupt end of the narrative, with its implicit indictment of imagination, as a mortal threat to his or her own creative tendencies and rushes into the arms of Goethe himself for continued life.

Why then would Trakl choose a form and a drama of such manifest complexity as a vehicle for his "Melusine" material? In the first version, certainly, being a nature spirit, Melusine does belong to the world of the Erlkönig and his daughters. In the second version, however, she is reduced to natural proportions, attractive but evidently passive and helpless, "mein Kind"; yet it is in this version, the first poem of *Gedichte 1909–1912*, that Trakl faithfully imitates the rhythms of "Erlkönig" and composes a dialogue between two voices, Melusine's and that of another. Trakl has appropriated Goethe's ballad in order to reapportion its roles. The second voice is that of the seducer, an Erlkönig figure, but there are no Olympian perspectives; the role of the father collapses into the repeated banal solicitude of the poet's "mein Kind." There is some confusion of identity in the poem, as Melusine cannot seem to connect the voice she hears with the face she sees, but the second speaker identifies himself definitely with the somewhat jaded sexuality of the burgeoning springtime: "er blühte wohl allzu reich" (I, 259). In the midst of falling blossoms and vampiristic kisses, this assertion makes it clear that the scene described in the second "Melusine" is a scene of seduction and deflowering.

For this feverish view of nature, with its emphasis not only on sex but on perversions vaguely evocative of incest, Trakl typically chooses the poetic vehicle of others, as if to accomplish the same distancing accomplished by Goethe's traditional ballad voice. In "Melusine II" Trakl borrows the camouflage of "Erlkönig" not only in order to neutralize the troubled sexuality of his theme but also in order to replicate formally the questions his poem raises about vocal authority. For his emphasis on overripeness Trakl has a literary fore-runner in Eichendorff, whose sirens, sphinxes, and fallen gardens he takes over in the poem "Blutschuld" (I, 249). But in other poems in addition to the "Melusine" poems, there are indications that the decaying process world is, to be sure, a personal obsession, but also and more interestingly an implicitly pejorative allusion to Goethe's poetics and to the achievement of Goethe's poetry. Goethe's organi-cism, Trakl implies in recasting the seemingly bodiless seduction scene of "Erlkönig," is really a mask for decay and putrefaction. We can sense a similar critique behind such passages as "Wie scheint doch alles Werdende so krank!" ("Heiterer Frühling," I, 50) and "Die Apfelbäume sinken kahl und stad / Ins Farbige ihrer Frucht, die schwarz verdarb" (Im Dorf," I, 63). In this land of corruption, the fiefdom of Goethe, as Trakl implies, he locates voice and song, with their power of seduction and dissimulation. Music and the sister are recurrently linked in Trakl's poetry (his sister was a musician), and he implicates the musicality of his own lines and the seductive beauty of his language in the "Verfall" of the fallen landscape. Probably, then, the two voices of "Melusine II" are one after all.

It has been suggested that Trakl's compulsion to repeat is related to the experience of incest, both a mastery of guilt and a sequential equivalent of the lack of difference in "unnatural" sexuality, and this is probably true. Once more, however, it is important to stress the way in which poetic worlds are informed and shaped by preexisting poetic worlds. "Ballade I" and the "Melusine" poems exemplify the interaction, or better the interfusion, of the personal with the liter-ary. At this point of interfusion the theme that emerges is the poet's effort to overgo the literary past by repeating its forms—its tropes, imagery, and rhythms—repetitions which conceal even while they manifest the poet's will to express his personality as an individual. It is in this accumulated context that we can best understand Trakl's peculiar belief that the Olympian Goethe's poetry was too personal, too confessional, and too freely given over to sensuality;[18] only in the hope that he is the first to suppress personality can Trakl secure his originality. Although "Erlkönig" condemns the regressive paradise of the Elf-king, it does not condemn the power of voice as such but rather glories in it. Rather than celebrating his own skillful control in delaying the outcome of his tale, like Goethe's narrator, Trakl concludes "Melusine II" by drawing down a curtain of night and silence over the scene. As he would say (in one of his many allusions to the conclusion of Hölderlin's "Patmos") in *Verwandlung des Bösen*, "Dem folgt unvergängliche Nacht."

Critics enlist Trakl's same few pronouncements about the writing of poetry in order to make a wide variety of arguments. One such pronouncement, with reference to his early poetry, was prompted by what Trakl took to be the egregious theft of his poetic style by an aspiring poet named Ludwig Ullmann. "Not only," Trakl complains in a letter,

> were certain images and expressions taken over nearly word for word . . . , but also the rhymes of certain verses and their emphases are exactly like my imagistic style, which in four lines welds together four separate images into a single impression, in other words the trappings, the style of my works, so ardently achieved, has been imitated to the smallest detail. [July 1910; I, 478]

It remains open to question, though, whether Trakl himself has at this point in his career achieved a unique style, "heiss errungen." There are Eichendorff poems, such as "Mondnacht," in which quatrains form a single impression with a series of four images. In Trakl's "Musik im Mirabell," which exemplifies this technique, we find Eichendorff's cadences enlisted to express Eichendorff's images and themes: the singing of the "Brunnen" in the evening, clouds in relief against a blue sky, ancestral statues, and, significantly, "der alte Garten." Amid the statuary and the tendency in general to pose things in the scene one is not surprised to find a "Faun mit toten Augen" (I, 18), and Trakl's use of color may also be indebted to Eichendorff: whereas later he would use color in conformance with the Expressionist painters' ideal of representing an "inner reality," here he defers apparently to nature—falling leaves could easily be red—but more probably to the sensuality and sense of danger irradiated by red peonies in Eichendorff. The glowing fire contributes to this mood and, given the "Angstgespenster," the "weisser Fremdling" can easily be viewed as another apparition,[19] a familiar of the decaying hallways in the deserted house. In this poem the extinguishing of the lamp denies vision in favor of audition— "Das Ohr hört nachts Sonatenklänge"—and again the manner in which this preference is expressed (with a certain insincerity, if what has thus far been said about Trakl's mistrust of voice holds true at all) will be familiar to readers of German literature, especially of Mörike's *Maler Nolten*.

Reinhold Grimm argues that this setting with its deserted patriarchal castle is taken from Rimbaud; but as a genre scene it is more persistently linked in the early poetry to Eichendorff.[20] In Eichendorff as in Trakl, the deserted house is connected with the theme of the prodigal son's return, most notably for Eichendorff in "Heimkehr," a poem already discussed as an occasion on which the poet attempts to come to terms with his poetic fathers. Trakl's assertion in "Musik im Mirabell" that "Der Ahnen Marmor ist ergraut" suggests defiance of the fathers, but this defiance is governed by an irony with which we have perforce become familiar, ventured as it is in the voice and manner of one of those fathers, Eichendorff. Similarly, all that remains of the poet's personal self-assertion at this moment of defiance, the erotic situation in the background of "Ballade I" and "Melusine II," is the lingering, intimately melancholy aftersound of a sonata. For a more poetically radical appropriation of these images and themes, the detritus of aristocratic decline nostalgically rendered that is as old as Northern European poetry and still shapes such works of art as "L'Année dernière à Marienbad" and "L'Avventura," we must turn to "Verfall [I]":

Es weht ein Wind! Hinlöschend singen
Die grünen Lichter—gross und satt
Erfüllt der Mond den hohen Saal,
Den keine Feste mehr durchklingen.

Die Ahnenbilder lächeln leise
Und fern—ihr letzter Schatten fiel,
Der Raum ist von Verwesung schwül,
Den Raben stumm umziehn im Kreise.

Verlorner Sinn vergangner Zeiten
Blickt aus den steinernen Masken her,
Die schmerzverzerrt und daseinsleer
Hintrauern in Verlassenheiten.

Versunkner Gärten kranke Düfte
Umkosen leise den Verfall—
Wie schluchzender Worte Widerhall
Hinzitternd über off'ne Grüfte.   [I, 233]

[A wind is blowing! The green lights sing / Extinguishing—large and full / The moon fills the great hall, / In which no more feasts resound. // Ancestral statues smile quietly / And far—their last shadow fell, / The room is humid with decay, / The ravens mutely move in circles. // Lost sense of lost times / Peers out of the stony masks, / Which, contorted with pain and emptied of being / Mourn on in solitudes. // Sick fragrances of sunken gardens / Quietly caress the decay / Like the echo of sobbing words / Quivering over open tombs.]

Here again is the situation of Eichendorff's "Heimkehr": the statuary—"Ahnenbilder"—in the moonlight, the abandoned castle. And here also is another familiar Eichendorff image, the sunken garden which the earlier poet typically renders as a "fallen" garden reflecting the loss of childhood innocence,[21] or as the underworld site of beckoning voices ("der Grund"). "Verfall" obviously belittles the influence of ancestral voices: their laughter is soft and distant, and the "Ahnenbilder" no longer even cast shadows. Such is the irrelevance of their presence, indeed, that they have become ciphers yielding only a trace of intelligible meaning, the pain expressed in their stony faces at having been abandoned. Trakl here accentuates Eichendorff's turn against the fathers: whereas the fathers in "Heimkehr" are drained of authority only when the poet's realization turns them to stone, in "Verfall" they are introduced without preamble as powerless statues. But in their easy dethronement there is a personal cost to the doubly belated poet. Trakl does not repeat Eichendorff's confident ritual of taking up the relinquished sword; he can scarcely carry forward a tradition he has thus consigned to irrecoverable obscurity.

With the opening declaration of his poem, "Es weht ein Wind," Trakl appears to be ushering in an inspiring breath; but instead of exhilarating, the wind uncooperatively snuffs out the lights, making way for the moon, "gross und satt," which fills the empty room. This moment of desublimation, which appears time and again in Trakl's poetry,[22] not only lowers the moon but imprisons it in the empty hall of the fathers. It is rank and overstuffed, Trakl implies, because it has consumed the poets for whom it was an obscure object of desire; and its light is contaminated by its overuse in literature. Moon and moonlight being difficult to tell apart, the light itself may by this time be what is rotting, and the ravens may then bear ironic witness to this fading out of a tradition of which Poe had made them a part. Decay first appears in the poem as that which pervades the room, effecting the merger of two topoi, celestial moonlight and earthy putrefaction, which the Romantic tradition had always kept rigorously separate, except when the former in some Gothic instances was permitted to shine down on the latter. Trakl wants to bring these regions together, as indeed he has already brought them together in the green lights that sing as they are extinguished. In this poem he seems to realize that the props of Eichendorff are less important in themselves than as a means to bring him face to face with the two kinds of metaphor against which his poetry must define itself, the organicism of Goethe (negatively revised as we have seen Trakl revise it elsewhere) and the moonlit interiority of Novalis. These of course would be the oversimplifications of a poet struggling for breathing room; Goethe himself had already brought these regions together in countless ways, they are not always stably polar opposites even in Novalis, Hölderlin's poetry is a struggle to work out their relationship, and their synthesis will be the goal of Rilke's *Sonette an Orpheus*.

The lights extinguished by the wind in "Verfall" are green, and sing a kind of swan song in going out. This synaesthesia, recalling Eichendorff, Baudelaire, and Rimbaud, connects the first stanza with the last, where fragrances are compared with sounds. The "sick" fragrances of the sunken gardens are said to caress the decay within them. In this kind of figure we find embodied at once the fin-de-siècle, the poet's personal life, and the self-consuming conclusion of a poetic tradition; and it must always be borne in mind that for Trakl these moments are inextricably related—as the final two lines demonstrate. They form a metaphor by means of which the fallen garden's fragrances, its residual impressions, are compared with the *echo* of the sobbing words that pass over open tombs. This is the echo of elegy, which is the lyric of belatedness. Just beneath the surface of this concluding metaphor is the Romantic figure of the Aeolian harp, connecting the end of the poem with the beginning, "Es weht ein Wind," in yet another way. Hence at the last moment Trakl acknowledges that his poetry is elegiac after all, and therefore inspired by the residual vocality that arises from the still-open tombs of the dead he had earlier repudiated because they themselves had been, as he thought, irrelevantly elegiac poets.

But because the Aeolian harp figures forth the responsive imagination, not the merely imitative one, Trakl preserves a measure of independence for himself. In admitting at last the echo of other poets' words, Trakl describes the aspect of his poetry that is of special interest to us, and he does not really concede anything to the past: the sounds he echoes are already echoes, tokens of secondariness and absence no more immediate than his own. Poetry results from the passage of poetic language *over*, not from, the tombs of the ancestors, who were as much its mouthpiece merely as he is himself, conjoining inherited language with inherited forms. Only the full implications of the Aeolian harp image, if it is present, allow the possibility of poetic renovation; or else, if the echoes are understood purely as echoes, acoustic repetitions, then poetic language can be purified of mediation and returned to the condition of pure language, which expresses only itself. Here we anticipate the drift of the later poetry; but perhaps the early conviction that it may have been reserved for him to accomplish the repristination of language was what disturbed Trakl so much when he found that Ullmann seemed content simply to echo his own work. In the meantime we have seen that his dawning indifference to the logic of representation, the logic he could imagine the poetic tradition to have worn threadbare, frees him to bring together the realms of the celestial and the earthly and thus to suspend the normal range of their meanings, not by cancelling them out but by keeping them both in play.

A brief look at another poem, "Rondel," may serve to summarize these points:

> Verflossen ist das Gold der Tage,
> Des Abends braun und blaue Farben:
> Des Hirten sanfte Flöten starben
> Des Abends blau und braune Farben
> Verflossen ist das Gold der Tage.
>
> [Over is the gold of days, / Evening's brown and blue colors: / The shepherd's soft pipes died / Evening's blue and brown colors / Over is the gold of days.]

Although he modifies and simplifies the French rondel form, Trakl retains its essential circularity, which becomes his theme. Trakl here reifies the passage of time as the flow of language that evokes it, subtly shifting our attention thereby from experience to its representation; he effects this shift by insisting on the literariness of his topoi, themselves survivors of the passage of time. The replacement of sunlight by the brown and blue of evening is also the replacement of a Golden Age of poetry by Trakl's usual temporal site, the evening land—except that, in the absence of their own verb, the brown and blue seem also to be "verflossen." The third line announces that the pastoral impulse of lyric has died in some indefinite past, and it occurs to the reader that the burden of this poem is simply, over and over, that poetry is dead.

The colon preparing us for the heart of the rondel proves a feint, as that central line simply inaugurates the turn of the poem back on itself without further punctuation, and the more advanced realization dawns that the point of the poem is *not* this message, which would be pivotally declared by the third line only if that line were set off by decisive punctuation, the period that marks an endpoint. Poetry is dead, yes, but a Nietzschean twilight persists in which poetic language seems capable of declaring its demise indefinitely. And indeed, it is the brown night of Nietzsche's poem "Venedig" to which Trakl's second and fourth lines refer.[23] And if Novalis's "blaue Blume" still faintly blooms in these lines as well, more prominently in the fourth line once the very persistence of the twilight has become a kind of momentum, then not only poetry but the spirit of Romanticism lives on. But no longer as elegy, no longer as the pastoral plangency of the Sentimental Poet's wish to recover meaning. The rote repetition of lines, justified by the rondel form, seems to release the last two lines from the responsibility of meaning into pure self-declaration as language and sound. Far from insisting that poetry has died, then, this gesture suggests that pure poetry has not yet been born; and the belated Trakl arrives at the earliness of magic spells and incantations. It is in this sense, to quote Heidegger out of context, that Trakl's "land of descent is the transition to the beginning of the dawn concealed within it."[24]

For Heidegger, Trakl discloses a language that carries him from belatedness back to a new, as yet unborn priority. From this point of view, the poem "Verfall" announces the decay of poetic language, to be sure; but from this decomposition of its given contours—syntax and meaning—a pure essence emerges. Or, as Trakl says in "Herbst des Einsamen," "Ein reines Blau tritt aus verfallener Hülle" (I, 109). The fact that a pure language was a central preoccupation of Romantic theorists as long-buried as Hamann only makes Trakl's choice of metaphor here the more appropriate. And perhaps in part it was the mortal remains of Trakl, his fragmented counters of language taken from other poets, that encouraged Walter Benjamin's description of the task of the translator: "to release in his own language that pure language which is under the spell of another, to liberate the language imprisoned in a work in his re-creation of that work. For the sake of pure language he breaks through decayed barriers of his own language."[25]

III

Du auf verfallenen Stufen:
Baum, Stern, Stein!
—Trakl, *Verwandlung des Bösen*

Not least because they are so quotable, Rilke's pronouncements on Trakl's poetry are deservedly well known. The compressed metaphoricity with which Rilke speaks of the younger poet's "mirror-image world . . . that consisted completely of falling" or his "own descendental language" ("Spiegelbildwelt . . . die ganz im Fallen war" . . . "eigene absteigende Sprache")[26] is typical of Rilke's tendency to conform his critical idiom to the terms of the work he discusses. When he asks for biographical details in this same letter, written shortly after Trakl's death, he hastens to add that he does not expect by this means to "understand" the poetry (the quotation marks are Rilke's own), but rather to have his instincts about it confirmed.[27] Several years later, in a letter to Trakl's closest friend, Erhard Buschbeck, Rilke once again chose the metaphor of falling in his effort to come to terms with Trakl's work; here he characterizes the poetry as being of the most sublime order, adding that "das Fallen [ist] Vorwand für die unaufhaltsamste Himmelfahrt."[28] It is not surprising to find that Rilke's "instincts" about Trakl's writing reflect poetic concerns of his own; his insight, in any case, that for Trakl descent is paradoxically a movement toward the sublime, is central to the present argument. That Trakl himself is aware of this paradoxical movement is facetiously registered in a note written to Buschbeck in August of 1913: "Dear Friend! The World is round. Saturday I'm falling down to Venice. Ever further—to the stars" (I, 523).

Rilke's first encounter with Trakl's poetry coincides with the period of his greatest involvement with Hölderlin, the summer of 1914, when he emphasized the theme of falling, as we have seen, in his "An Hölderlin." There is in fact an aphorism of Hölderlin's that can stand behind this theme in both poets: "Man kann auch in die Höhe fallen, so wie in die Tiefe."[29] While Hölderlin almost certainly intends this remark as a warning—to himself as well as to other poets—not to lose oneself in the aery regions, what he says lends itself readily to an antithetical reading. Neither Rilke nor Trakl knew this aphorism, which was published after both were dead, but both in common appear to sense its provenance in Hölderlin's work and, as it were, to misread it by overlooking its admonitory purpose and asserting in their own work that one can "fall" into the heights with profit.

Rilke's characterization of Trakl's poetry, then, calls attention to their common indebtedness to Hölderlin. In a sensitively argued essay, Bernhard Böschenstein enumerates the ways in which Hölderlin's presence can be registered in Trakl's poetry. To begin with, there are the appearances of a Hölderlin figure as a character. As Böschenstein says, Hölderlin appears variously as "Bruder," "der heilige Bruder," "Krankes," and Daedalus; and he is associated with the personification of "Wahnsinn." Böschenstein also feels that the "Hollunder" or elderberry bush which is common in Trakl's poems may at times be linked with Hölderlin, who was called "Holder"—a variant of "Hollunder"—by his friends.[30]

Of these numerous figurations, that of Daedalus is at once the most surprising and the most instructive. The name "Daedalus," where it occurs, brings with it a change of diction that leans toward Hölderlin's hymnic style. What Böschenstein considers to be Trakl's acknowledged "filial relation to Hölderlin" finds expression in a variant last line of "Gesang einer gefangenen Amsel." The published last line, "Umfängt ein brechendes Herz" (I, 135), had earlier read, at one time, "Umfängt des sterbenden Sturz," and, at another, "Umfing Ikarus Sturz" (II, 239).[31] From this variant Böschenstein infers that Trakl imagines himself to be a failed son of Hölderlin, but makes no further comment about Trakl's choice of this pair from among the various mythological relationships between father and son. It is exceedingly odd, however, that Trakl would identify Hölderlin with Daedalus, a great sculptor but one who was essentially a personification of mechanical genius, one whose inventiveness had practical ends, and whose name means craftsman. As the familiar story has it, the wings that Daedalus fashioned for himself and for his son Icarus carried the father safely to Crete, but Icarus who flew too high, fell into the sea when the sun melted the wax with which the wings were held together. The Icarus figure, which has long been read as a figure of poetic hubris, has tended nevertheless to be admired for his risk-taking nature, while the faint suggestion of an indictment for unimaginative caution has sometimes attached itself to Daedalus, who prudently refused to test the limits of his invention. If the Daedalus figure does indeed represent Hölderlin in Trakl, and Böschenstein offers convincing evidence that he does, then Trakl apparently sees Hölderlin as a craftsmanlike poet in perfect command of his tools—language and meter—who is unwilling to risk flights beyond the range of his medium. This is certainly not the image of Hölderlin envisioned by most readers, but it is one that could certainly embolden and comfort any succeeding poet who entertained it: Hölderlin was not venturesome enough, while I, Icarus, driven to approach the divine fire and heedless of my danger, am a victim of "das Fallen" and have tumbled into the depths for this and only this reason. The myth of Daedalus and Icarus has the further advantage for Trakl, then, of supplying him with a myth of poetic descent, with Icarus characterized, in the "Gesang einer gefangenen Amsel" variants, by his "Sturz" or fall. And finally, the obverse value systems with which the myth can be read lend a discreet ambiguity to the triumph Trakl has wrested from a descent that could have been construed as a defeat: the failure of the language made available by the father to sustain his—the son's— flights of imagination.

Hölderlin's language echoes throughout Trakl's oeuvre, but more often than not deprived of its special resonance. As Böschenstein points out, when the "Trauben und Blumen" of "Brot und Wein" become the "Sommerfrüchte und Gewinde" of Trakl's "Abendmuse" (I, 28), Trakl has conventionalized Hölderlin's imagery. The "Mauern" featured so prominently in "Helian" and elsewhere are beyond a doubt derived from Hölderlin's "Hälfte des Lebens," where the "Mauern . . . / Sprachlos und kalt" signal the end of poetic song in an epochal winter; these "Mauern" as Trakl borrows them then become one token among others of the problem with which Trakl is almost obsessively preoccupied. As this example shows, not only Hölderlin's language but also his themes are likely to be reduced to the status of expressive counters, poetic moves, in Trakl's work.[32] As Böschenstein points out, in three separate poems—and I have found others, including a passage cited earlier from *Verwandlung des Bösen*— Trakl revises Hölderlin's important assertion in the last line of "Patmos," "Dem folgt deutscher Gesang," in the direction of an ensuing silence: "Eh dem Schweigen des Winters folgt," he writes, for example, in "Helian" (I, 71). Böschenstein does not consistently argue, however, that these revisions tellingly undermine Hölderlin, although sometimes he says that they do.[33] His contention that there *are* revisions is in itself salutary, however, and can be corroborated further. To the list of divergences from Hölderlin one could add, for example, that Trakl accepts Hölderlin's belief in poetry's mission to disclose the Holy, but feels that since Hölderlin's time it has become much harder to establish a community of initiates. (But note that self-assertion, the pride of having succeeded at greater odds, would be implicit even in such a concession of belatedness as this.) As Böschenstein notes, in Trakl's "Untergang," the holy night with its Dionysan "madness" in Hölderlin's "Brot und Wein" becomes an eternal night of death and melancholy insanity:[34] the "Nachklang eines trunkenen Saitenspiels" (unpublished variant; II, 195) is an acknowledgment that lyric is a thing of the past couched in Hölderlin's own elegiac rhythm and language.

In Böschenstein's essay, Trakl's reworking of Hölderlin is linked to a similar issue concerning his relationship with Rimbaud. Böschenstein disagrees with Grimm's thesis that Trakl uses the poetry of both Hölderlin and Rimbaud as a quarry of raw materials for his own mosaic configurations; clearly Böschenstein feels, however little willing he is to bring any submerged creative antagonism into focus, that Trakl's relationship at least with Hölderlin is a good deal more complex than that. He argues that Trakl's reading of Rimbaud served largely to shape his reading of Hölderlin; Rimbaud provided Trakl with a more modern set of images with which to modify Hölderlin's ideas about the nature of poetry; Hölderlin, he says further, is perforce the poet of winter in Trakl's imagination largely because Rimbaud had already come to be the (negative and revisionary) poet of summer. The simultaneous reception of Hölderlin and Rimbaud by Trakl, Böschenstein feels, was what initiated Trakl's productive and innovative middle period (roughly the end of 1912 through 1913), but that when he stopped reading Rimbaud the cadences of Hölderlin came more fully to the fore in his work.[35]

Böschenstein's emphases are important and his conclusions convincing; his argument seems limited only in that it points the way toward paths he does not care to explore, leaving several issues unresolved. He does not explain why it is that, as he himself points out, the words and images Trakl associates with Hölderlin he also frequently associates with Novalis, and the two earlier poets seem in some sense to be connected in his mind.[36] He finds reason sufficient in their similar hymnic rhythms and their common exploration of the metaphorical possibilities of night for Trakl's apparently indiscriminate reference to both in such expressions as "das trunkene Saitenspiel." Is this interchangeability an instance of what Walther Killy calls Trakl's structure of "moveable parts"? Or do the two poets merge in Trakl's mind, rather, as a composite precursor? To suppose that they do will help to show why they are figured forth so frequently in Trakl's poems, while no comparable personifications are set aside for any of the other poets from whom he borrows. The best way to resolve this issue is to arrive at Trakl's attitude toward his poetic ancestors by examining the fictions of poetic descent through which he explains his borrowings to himself.

In Trakl there are many images of the access or the difficulty of access to an origin: the crumbling or lost path, "der verfallene Pfad," and two related images, the decaying stairs, "verfallene Stiegen" (sometimes "Wendeltreppe"), and the narrow footbridge, "der Steg." All are ways of going forward, and all at the same time are figures of descent, descent to the world of the dead or to the ancestors, whether they be the "furchtbaren Pfade des Todes" ("Frühling der Seele," I, 141) or "die mondenen Pfade der Abgeschiedenen" ("Gesang des Abgeschiedenen," I, 144). The path is most often crumbling, the steps decayed; the means of access to the underground region or abyss is no longer reliable. Especially notable are the many variations on these themes occurring in fragments connected with Trakl's "Helian":

> über verschüttete Stiegen hinab—purpurner Abgrund. [I, 421]
> Steigt der bleiche Wanderer im Herbst hinab   [I, 421]

> über verschüttete Stiegen hinab wo Böse stehn
> Ein Klang von herbstlichen Zymbeln verklingt
> öffnet sich wieder ein weisser Abgrund.   [I, 422]

> Wo an Mauern die Schatten der Ahnen stehn,
> Vordem ein einsamer Baum war, ein blaues Wild im Busch
> Steigt der weisse Mensch auf goldenen Stiegen,
> Helian ins seufzende Dunkel hinab,   [I, 423]

[downward over buried steps—purple abyss. // The pale wanderer in Autumn descended]

[downward over buried steps where evil ones stand // A crash of autumn cymbals fades to nothingness / A white abyss opens again.]

[Where near walls the shadows of ancestors stand, / Where earlier was a lonely tree, a blue hind in the bush / The white man climbs up on golden steps / Helian down into the sighing darkness.]

This pale wanderer, "der weisse Mensch," like "der weisse Fremdling" of "Musik im Mirabell," is always a figure of the poet, whether of a precursor, of the self, or of the poet per se. The passage concerning the "Mauer" underlines its own indebtedness to Hölderlin's "Hälfte des Lebens" in that the "Schatten der Ahnen" appear near this wall, at the place where the pale wanderer descends into an underground region. While it is true, as most readers of Trakl would insist, that his word associations are frequently linked by sound, it is still worth remarking that in these lines the connection between "Stiegen" and "Steg" is made in proximity to the image of the abyss, more particularly by the borrowing of a Hölderlin passage that a few lines from Trakl's "Die Heimkehr" will call to mind unmistakably:

> O! dort der goldene Steg
> Zerbrechend im Schnee
> Des Abgrunds! [I, 162]

> [O, there the golden footbridge / Breaking in the snow / of the abyss!]

The passage behind these passages is from the famous opening of "Patmos" over which we paused earlier:

> und furchtlos gehn
> Die Söhne der Alpen über den Abgrund weg
> Auf leichtgebaueten Brücken.

> [and fearless over / The chasm walk the sons of the Alps / On bridges lightly built.] [Hamburger, 463]

In short, where there is a downward or narrow passageway in Trakl, Hölderlin is likely to be nearby, not least because these images themselves are Hölderlin's. Only now they are still more fragile: Hölderlin's lightly but adequately constructed bridge, and his much more solid bridges in other poems, become a footbridge or even a plank in Trakl ("Zwischenstück" and "Verbindungsteil" are alternate meanings of "Steg"). If the bridges of the sons of the Alps Hölderlin admires with some envy are easily as well as lightly built ("leichtgebauet"), that is because these sons, literally the offspring of the Alps, have not been estranged from their origin and have no great difficulty returning to it. The sons of the Alps are models for the bridging imagination—and the language to express it—that John confined to his island and the poet isolated in his belatedness have in common. John bridges the sea with the power of his Word, just as Hölderlin wants to bridge the gap, both temporally and culturally, between ancient Greece and the hoped-for Germania. Hölderlin's bridge is meant ultimately to span the intervening darkness, illuminating the "Weltnacht" until the divine again becomes manifestly present on earth. (In "Heidelberg," the poem itself is the bridge on which the speaker stands.) In Trakl's "Heimkehr," by contrast, the footbridge is so fragile that it breaks entirely. The significance of the contrast is clear enough, but it remains to ask whether for Trakl as for Hölderlin the bridge is in fact language, and also to ask what is represented by the abyss.

In "Am Mönchsberg" (second version), from *Sebastian im Traum*, a number of the figures we have discussed appear in high concentration:

Wo im Schatten herbstlicher Ulmen der verfallene Pfad hinabsinkt,
Ferne den Hütten von Laub, schlafenden Hirten,
Immer folgt dem Wandrer die dunkle Gestalt der Kühle

über knöchernen Steg, die hyazinthene Stimme des Knaben,
Leise sagend die vergessene Legende des Walds,
Sanfter ein Krankes nun die wilde Klage des Bruders.

Also rührt ein spärliches Grün das Knie des Fremdlings,
Das versteinerte Haupt;
Näher rauscht der blaue Quell die Klage der Frauen.   [I,94]

Where, in the shade of autumnal elms, the decaying path sinks down, / Far from huts of leaves sleeping shepheds, / Always the wanderer is followed by the dark form of coolness // Over bony footpaths, the hyacinthine voice of the boy, / Softly saying the forgotten legends of the forest, / Softer now, a sick thing, the wild lament of the brothers. // Thus sparse grass touches the stranger's knee, / The petrified head; / Nearer the blue spring rushes the lamentation of women.

Here are the decayed path, the wanderer and the stranger, both self-projections, and the "Krankes" and the brother, both Hölderlin figures according to Böschenstein. Here, as in "Wanderers Schlaf" (I, 391), the footbridge is made of bones. As so often in Trakl, the scene is autumnal; the decaying path descends under the shade of elm trees that are about to shed their leaves. This first scene is drawn in contrast to the idyllic world of pastoral,[37] which is located somewhere in the distance. Insofar as the tenuous world of pastoral is given substantial existence at all (its shepherds are asleep), it is a place apart and seems not to be implicated, as its huts of leaves would suggest, in the seasonal cycle that besets all other states of existence in the poem. The wanderer, a figure who might predictably belong to or at least pass through the world of pastoral, is cut off from this scene and confined to the bridge and path, at best an elegist for a dimly conceived lost unity. The bridge of bone to which he has free access carries him over the river Styx, with the suggestion that he can move without hindrance between the lands of the living and the dead. But for all his apparent command of this terrain, he is always haunted by the formless representations of death that skirt the margins of existence more primordially than he: the dark figure of coolness and the "hyazinthene Stimme des Knaben," which is the voice of the boy Elis wherever it appears in Trakl's poetry.

In "Abendland" (I, 139), a close tie is established between Elis and the underworld of classical mythology. Elis is composed of tears and shadow, and he walks through a grove of hyacinths, seeming gradually to become the whole natural panorama, with lightning playing around his brow. In "Am Mönchsberg," Elis remains a hyacinthine voice, the mournfulness of elegy. (Apollo himself inscribed the hyacinth with the word "io," "alas," after he accidentally killed the young Hyacinth, his dearest companion.) In "Am Mönchsberg," the provenance of the voice of Elis, which speaks "die vergessene Legende des Walds," is ambiguous: Elis on the one hand is merged with the natural world and possesses a voice which, if "hyazinthen," would seem to be like the originary voice for which "Worte, wie Blumen entstehn"; but on the other hand his voice is mediatory, retelling the stories of the holy spirit of the wood, and in this respect recalls Hölderlin's fascination with the "Geist des Waldes."

Indeed, not surprisingly, another voice in this poem is that of Hölderlin. The brother's wild voice madly lamenting is muted now that he has become "ein Krankes"; this latter epithet echoes the language of Hölderlin even as it names him. In effect Hölderlin calms himself, owing perhaps also in part to the proximity of his voice with the voice of Elis issuing from the dead. Because Elis like Adonis can renew life in season, a sparse green growth can touch the stranger's knee and head, which had turned to stone, replacing the earlier "herbstliche Ulmen" with renewed growth; no longer "versteinert," the head of the poet can be vocal again. But we are not quite sure who the "Fremdling" is, beyond knowing that his is a dependent voice. He could be Hölderlin, who lives again through Trakl, his poetry mediated by the voice of Elis; or he could be Trakl himself, empowered to speech in turn by the agency of Elis. With poems in mind such as "Verfall" and "Musik im Mirabell," I lean toward the first reading, because the "Fremdling" is "versteinert" like the ancestral statues in those poems. But the second reading must come into play even if one accepts the first, for if Hölderlin is to speak again it must be through Trakl's reinvigorated voice. Surrounding the promised voice is the rushing of the blue stream, a source ("Quell") that is the natural equivalent of the voice of Elis, together with the wailing of women that reinforces the determination of lyric by elegy, the necessary connection of song with death.

"Am Mönchsberg" is a poem, then, in which Trakl seems to instruct himself about the significance of descent in his imagination: it is the path he follows to recover a lyric voice, a voice however which is necessarily elegiac in mode. The sinking path gives way to the bridge of bone over which the voice of Elis passes from a primal place that is the forgotten storehouse of memory, the ancient underworld, into a place inhabited—apart from the equally ancient world of pastoral—by the modern living and dead alike, including the wanderer and the brother. In order now to interpret the theme of descent in Trakl more concretely, it will be necessary to examine the elusive figure of Elis more closely.

Critical interpretations of Elis are many and diverse. For Heidegger, Elis is the key figure inhabiting the "site" of Trakl's poetry; he is the "early dead" descending into the Evening Land: "the land into which the early dead goes down is the land of this evening . . and [which], as the land of descent into the ghostly night, awaits those who will dwell in it. The land of descent is the transition into the beginning of the dawn concealed within it." Heidegger maintains that the "going under," the "Untergang" or descent which is the endpoint of the crumbling path, is not decay, but a dying into a new origin, a "return into primal earliness."[38] I read Elis somewhat differently, as an emissary from the region, or night, of death, as a figure not of the present poet but of what the poet encounters in his descent. Elis is thus meant to constitute a solution to the crisis of language that faces the poet of the modern age. Trakl's belated imagination in quest of its source finds the path crumbling and decayed, forbidding access; it is at this juncture that Elis, encountered as a voice, is able to pass the power of voice back across the narrow bridge of bone to the estranged imagination—the "Wanderer" or "Fremdling." In associating Elis with the movement of descent, Heidegger unwarrantably merges Elis with the figure of the stranger, oversimplifying Trakl's struggle to come to terms with the determination of the past. But if we recast Heidegger's reading only a little, we can say that the descent into the land of the dead for Trakl does mean a fall downward into an origin and a new poetic beginning. If not precisely the genius loci, Elis is the quality which always precedes the poet, the genius of poetry.

Noting the privileged position of Elis in Trakl's poetry, critics have struggled to understand his name and nature. He has been linked with the Hebrew "el-isch," or "Gott-Mensch,"[39] and also with Elysium,[40] becoming in either case a symbol of redemption. He has also been said to serve a function comparable for Trakl to Hölderlin's vision of Greece.[41] Others point to the possible connection of Elis with Elis Fröbom in Hofmannsthal's dramatization of E. T. A. Hoffmann's *Bergwerk zu Falun*[42]; and indeed, in both these works the character named Elis embodies the Romantic descent into the imagination and the libido. Also suggestive, finally, is Böschenstein's observation that Elis can be seen to represent Novalis— who would then become "Nov[us]- Elis," we might add, ambiguously both prior *and* more recent. Böschenstein points out that in "Am Mönchsberg" the expression "hyazinthene Stimme des Knaben" had earlier read "das weisse Antlitz des Engels, sein erstorbenes Saitenspiel," "erstorbenes Saitenspiel" being in several poems a cipher for Novalis as well as for Hölderlin.[43]

There are additional clues associating Elis with Novalis. Discernible behind the hyacinth of Elis is the "blaue Blume" of Novalis, to which Trakl alludes repeatedly. Hyacinth is also the central character of *Märchen* in Novalis's *Lehrlinge zu Sais*, one whose special gift is the ability to speak the language of nature: "er sprach immer fort mit Thieren und Vögeln, mit Bäumen und Felsen."[44] In Trakl's poetry, Elis is one who has died young, as Novalis did. And insofar as Elis is a figure who appears in the process of descent, he resembles the speaker of the *Hymnen an die Nacht*: "Abwärts wend ich mich zu der heiligen, unaussprechlichen, geheimnisvollen Nacht."[45]

"An den Knaben Elis" (I, 84) is a poem rich in allusions to Novalis. Elis's lips drink "die Kühle des blauen Felsenquells," just as Novalis's Hyacinth drinks from a similar source of mystical insight and imagination, the "krystallenen Quell."[46] Fulfilled in his death, Elis is asked to give up attempting to explain and interpret nature, interpretation no longer being necessary: "Lass . . . / Uralte Legenden / Und dunkle Deutung des Vogelflugs." Accordingly, Elis walks into the night, "Die voll purpurner Trauben hängt," recalling the association of night with "der goldenen Flut der Trauben" in the *Hymnen*[47]—and also, significantly, the petition in Hölderlin's "Brot und Wein" that the night bestow "das Heiligtrunkene." Elis moves in the sphere of the "blue," the zone of imagination not only among the early German Romantics but also for Mallarmé (his *azur*) and, most recently, for Wallace Stevens. Where the celestially visionary eyes of Elis come to rest, they release nature into song: "Ein Dornenbusch tönt / Wo deine mondenen Augen sind."

Of course, the Elis figure also evokes Hölderlin. In this poem, Elis's decaying body, victim of natural process, is compared with a hyacinth into which "ein Mönch" dips his waxen hands. This "Mönch" is a variant on the "heiliger Bruder," one of the figures for Hölderlin that populate Trakl's poems; if Elis is Christ-like in this instance, the monk's dipping his hands in the body is like the participation in the "Brot und Wein" of the Eucharist. For Hölderlin, bread and wine, the gifts of Demeter and Dionysus, are emblems of those gods among whom Christ is the last, emblems both of their presence in the past and of their promised return. The gift of Dionysus especially is the symbol of poetic inspiration, and may thus account for the recurrence of "Brot und Wein" in Trakl's poetry—an attenuated quotation of Hölderlin that becomes a cipher resembling "die blaue Blume."

As in "Am Mönchsberg," then—a name which may itself gather significance in this context—Elis reanimates and inspires a figure who is at once Novalis and Hölderlin. Understanding the monk's *participation mystique* as a scene of inspiration helps explain the sudden transition to silence (line 16) as the silence of the poet today.[48] The focus moves from Elis to "unser Schweigen," a black cave from which occasionally "ein sanftes Tier," a modest, mild creature, perhaps a poem, emerges.[49] The conclusion of the poem returns to the figure of Elis, reasserting his connection both with nature and with the poetic tradition: "Auf deine Schläfen tropft schwarzer Tau, / Das letzte Gold verfallener Sterne." The paratactical structure that Adorno found in Hölderlin and that Trakl learned from the earlier poet leaves open the question whether the black dew and the remains of the stars are one and the same. Both, however, are after-images, the last flicker of decomposition, the former in nature and the latter suggesting a last, "fallen" glimmer of the sublime tradition in poetry.

The theme of song followed by silence and its connection with Elis is further elaborated in the two-part poem "Elis" (I, 85–86), which follows naturally from the poem just discussed, the more so in that in an early draft the two parts of "Elis" were the second and third parts of a poem that began with "An den Knaben Elis." Again there are elements of an idyllic pastoral poem at the horizon of the scene,[50] but at the outset in this case the ordinarily inaccessible golden age is fused affirmatively with the silence of the present: "Vollkommen ist die Stille dieses goldenen Tags." This fusion amounts to a paradox, which the role of Elis confirms: he is at peace, and the blueness of his visionary eyes mirrors "den Schlummer der Liebenden," whose (elegiac) sighs have grown silent "at" his mouth: "An deinem Mund / Verstummten ihre rosigen Seufzer." Here Trakl plays once more on a key passage about the night in *Brot und Wein*:

> Aber sie muss uns auch, dass in der zaubernden Weile,
> Dass im Finstern für uns einiges Haltbare sei,
> Uns die Vergessenheit und das Heiligtrunkene gönnen,
> Gönnen das strömende Wort, das, wie die Liebenden, sei
> Schlummerlos.[51]

> [But to us in her turn, so that in the wavering moment, / Deep in the dark there will be something at least that endures, / Holy drunkenness she must grant and frenzied oblivion, / Grant the on-rushing word, sleepless as lovers are too.]   [Hamburger, 245]

Trakl inverts Hölderlin's simile; instead of being "schlummerlos," his lovers are asleep, indicating that inspired poetic language, "das strömende Wort," does not need to be kept awake and active. If what is mirrored by the visionary eyes of Elis is the perfect peace of the lovers' sleep, their sighs fallen mute, then he must here represent the antithesis, the cancellation, of audible expression. Silence continues to be featured in this first part of "Elis." An old man's dark song dies "an kahlen Mauern." Because this is a recurrent image through which Trakl always alludes to the "Mauern . . . / Sprachlos und kalt" of Hölderlin's "Hälfte des Lebens," one can find in the old man yet another personification of Hölderlin, whose dark song it is that has in that case now been laid to rest. "[D]es ölbaums blaue Stille" sustains the Christian suggestion of the pastoral imagery, reminding us that the "Stille" of Elis is the perfect peace of spiritual resurrection—this in addition to what we have been saying here but not wholly apart from it, as the poetic handling of Christianity is in its turn mediated for Trakl by the example and manner of Hölderlin. Our earlier interpretation of Elis as the privileged occupant of a common ground between the natural world and the poetic tradition is supported—but under the auspices of silence on this occasion—by the conclusion of Part One: "Ein goldener Kahn / Schaukelt, Elis, dein Herz am einsamen Himmel." Even though Elis is not himself the language of poetry, these lines suggest, his heart does serve to replace the traditional moon as a source of inspiration.

Opening the second part of "Elis" is a variant of the "Saitenspiel" that so often in Trakl resonates in the breast of Novalis (in "An Novalis," for example) and also appears together with personifications of Hölderlin: "Ein sanftes Glockenspiel tönt in Elis' Brust / Am Abend." "Am Abend": the second part of the poem presents an apparently more imperfect scene, as the restored golden age unified by the visionary blue of silence in the first part gives way now to the suggestion of decline and death. Blue first appears here as the color of an animal that lies quietly bleeding in the thorny underbrush; the animal is transfigured by the color of imagination because it has been sacrificed, by implication, within a mythological scheme. The thorns suggest of course that the scheme is a Christian one, but again Trakl's poetic Christianity points toward Hölderlin, from whose characterization of the Centaur Chiron—a mirror-image of the poet himself—Trakl takes the word "Wild."[52] The beast is a Christ figure, then, a scapegoat, but also a poet who falls upon the thorns of life and bleeds. No longer merely "ein Greis," he is sacrificed in order to clear a space, albeit a bleak and comfortless one, for Trakl's own poetry. The next image in this revisionary series is the brown tree with barren branches, standing apart from the blue fruits that have already fallen and recalling by contrast both the branches heavy with yellow pears in "Hälfte des Lebens" and the "reifende Frucht" of poetic creativity in Goethe's "Auf dem See." Both the language and the content of earlier poetry lose their meaning as Trakl's figures of descent and dissolution proliferate: "Zeichen und Sterne [now one and the same] / Versinken leise im Abendweiher."

That this apparently calamitous composite loss is actually an accomplishment promising more for the renovation of poetry than the perfect silence of Part One is a matter to which much of what remains to be said in this discussion will be devoted, but for the moment the issues involved will only be sketched. The next line, "Hinter dem Hügel ist es Winter geworden," keeps before us the silent winter world of Hölderlin's "Hälfte des Lebens," while the ensuing image, referring to Elis once more, changes the black dew of "An den Knaben Elis" into an icy sweat, at once a reminder of his last agony and a suggestion that the "Abendweiher" into which poetic meaning disappeared has now become a half-frozen winter pond without ceasing at any stage of its dwindling animation to constitute the genius of Elis. His crystal forehead is the "Quell" from which, even in the present darkness, it is possible for blue doves, messenger-birds of the imagination, to drink. From the barrier of death itself, the "schwarze Mauer" which is the place of silence in Hölderlin, the blue dove resurrected can become the Holy Spirit,

"Gottes einsamer Wind," and emit the perpetual sound—"tönen" brings Part Two full circle—which is, in its absolute priority to the differential sounds of language, the inspirational equivalent of silence in Part One.

We can read "Elis" as an attempt to revise Hölderlin from two different directions, first by installing silence where Hölderlin still sang a "dark song," then by discovering sound in the winter that had fallen silent in Hölderlin. In Part One, Elis, the genius of poetry apart from any and all practitioners and even apart from, prior to, any individual imagination, is the embodiment of the mystical silence to which Novalis would have aspired if he had not been a poet and which can be called "das schweigende Wort" in contrast with Hölderlin's "strömendes Wort." This state recovers the condition of innocent unity with nature in which Trakl's Kaspar Hauser lives ("Kaspar Hauser Lied," I, 95) until God gives him language. But even in denying the spiritual adequacy of Hölderlin's language simply because it *is* language, Trakl repeats that language; it is as though Part Two were meant to suggest what language is like when it exists only for the sake of being repeated. Both signs and their referents sink out of sight, leaving only the sound of repetition, a sound which, in its divinely hermetic refusal to point beyond itself, acquires the perfection of silence. Here we are at the heart of Trakl's revision of Hölderlin: he turns his own belatedness, his imprisonment within the language of Hölderlin, into the achievement of newness; the secondariness revealed by the referential function of Hölderlin's language makes *him* belated, while Trakl's repetition becomes *Ursprache* in giving up that power of signification which is what subordinates language to nature and thought.

In the confluence of "schweigen" and "tönen" Trakl hopes to capture the mystery of the Word, both religious and poetic; and the meaning of that mystery, which is complete only in the fullness of its evocation and finally eludes paraphrase, is the figure of Elis. It is no accident that one finds oneself speaking of meaning after all, that being the paradox, again, on which in Paul de Man's salutary view any reading of the modern lyric must be predicated. What is it that makes Trakl repeat one language as opposed to another (if it is not always the language of Hölderlin it is invariably the language of Romanticism)? Precisely its aura, the fact that it is charged with meaning. In addition to being language it is, as it were, a language-*bearer*, referring to its own nature as well as to nature. The Romantic redoubling of reference is not something that Trakl can undo; he exploits it, rather, by staging its "fall," its collapse under its burden. Romantic suggestiveness becomes incantation, Romantic topicality becomes sheer gratuitous evocation. Underlying even these conversions of theme to mood, however, there remains a coherence that still enables interpretation. This last remaining coherence is conferred by the theme of themelessness; and what Trakl's repetitions repeat therefore is the history of poeticality. In the following sustained reading of a central Trakl poem, "Abendland" (fourth version; I, 139-40), I shall be attempting to elaborate upon these ideas:

1
Mond, als träte ein Totes
Aus blauer Höhle,
Und es fallen der Blüten
Viele über den Felsenpfad.
Silbern weint ein Krankes
Am Abendweiher,
Auf schwarzem Kahn
Hinüberstarben Liebende.

Oder es läuten die Schritte
Elis' durch den Hain
Den hyazinthenen
Wieder verhallend unter Eichen.
O des Knaben Gestalt
Geformt aus kristallenen Tränen,
Nächtigen Schatten.
Zackige Blitze erhellen die Schläfe
Die immerkühle,
Wenn am grünenden Hügel
Frühlingsgewitter ertönt.

2
So leise sind die grünen Wälder
Unsrer Heimat,
Die kristallne Woge
Hinsterbend an verfallner Mauer
Und wir haben im Schlaf geweint;
Wandern mit zögernden Schritten
An der dornigen Hecke hin
Singende im Abendsommer,
In heiliger Ruh
Des fern verstrahlenden Weinbergs;
Schatten nun im kühlen Schoss

Der Nacht, trauernde Adler.
So leise schliesst ein mondener Strahl
Die purpurnen Male der Schwermut.

3
Ihr grossen Städte
Steinern aufgebaut
In der Ebene!
So sprachlos folgt
Der Heimatlose
Mit dunkler Stirne dem Wind,
Kahlen Bäumen am Hügel.
Ihr weithin dämmernden Ströme!
Gewaltig ängstet
Schaurige Abendröte
Im Sturmgewölk.
Ihr sterbenden Völker!
Bleiche Woge
Zerschellend am Strande der Nacht,
Fallende Sterne.

[(1) Moon, as if a dead thing stepped / Out of a blue cave, / And many flowers fall / Across the mountain path. / Silver a sick thing weeps / Near the evening pond; / In a black boat / Lovers moved across into death. // Or else Elis' footsteps ring / Through the grove, / The hyacinthine, / Fading again under oaks. / O shape of the boy / Formed from crystal tears, / Nocturnal shadows. / Jagged lightning illuminates the temple, / Always cool, / When on the greening hill / Spring storms resound. // (2) So quiet are the green forests / Of our homeland, / The crystalline wave / Dying at a decayed wall / And we cried in our sleep. / Wander with hesitant steps / Along the thorny hedge, / Singers in the summer evening, / In holy peace / Of vineyards fading in the distance; / Shadows now in the cool lap / Of night, grieving eagles. / This quietly a moonbeam closes / The purple wounds of melancholy. // (3) You mighty cities / Built of stone / In the plain! / Just as mute / The homeless one with a dark forehead / Follows the wind, / Bare trees on the hill. / You distant rivers, growing dusk! / Violently fear-inducing / Is the ghastly sunset / In the thunder clouds. / You dying peoples! / Pale wave / Breaking on the beach of night, / Falling stars.]

Residual in this poem one finds the seasonal cycle of Georgic; but images of death canker even the springtime setting of Part One. Once again, in one of Trakl's more striking desublimations, the moon is drawn down out of the sky, its pallor suggesting a dead thing emergent from a cave. Or, if the sky itself is the cave, that reading would draw the entire firmament downward, making its infinitude seem confining. The flowering trees of a springtime landscape are represented only by the spent blossoms that litter the path, while the pond seems to exist only to lend its bank to the sick thing—"ein Krankes"—that cries there and to situate the lovers, "die Hinübersterbenden" who once made it a Stygian pond by crossing over it into death. With a rhetorical signal of virtuosity derived from Hölderlin—"oder"—Trakl converts this scene into a hypothesis, suggesting that his landscape filled with dying procreativity is but one possible figuration of a mood or idea. To this end, the scene of the second stanza becomes more definitely mythological, a setting for Elis. As he appears in "Abendland," the figure of Elis, the genius of poetry, takes on an emphatically elegiac character, with the suggestion therefore that lyric is necessarily elegiac, its body formed of crystalline tears like that of Elis, moving through the hyacinthine groves. If we read Trakl's figure literally, the shape of Elis's body is like the shape of a flower, and thus he merges, as usual, with the natural setting. But even though this scene is loaded with the imagery of death, the first section of "Abendland" ends, surprisingly, by evoking sublime strength. During a spring storm, jagged lightning illumines the boy Elis's temple, bringing to mind both the annunciation of Classical heroes in youth and those figurations of Zeus himself in which the thunderer wears a crown of lightning bolts.

The tone of the second section remains unchanged, as a summertime setting is similarly burdened with death. The green forests no longer resound, as they do in the poetry of Eichendorff, but are strangely quiet. A wave "dies" against a decaying wall. The reader is implicated when Trakl says that "we" have cried in our sleep, unconscious as yet that our lives are shaped by sorrow. The syntax is vague enough to extend this "we" forward, making us singers in the summer evening as well, but in that case our lot is still not greatly improved, as we must walk along a hedge of thorns with faltering steps while singing. This allusion to the crown of thorns, which is invariable in Trakl (see, for example, "Im Dorf"—I, 63—which presents "des Heilands schwarzes Haupt im Dornenstrauch"), reminds us at what cost the equally biblical, multiply allusive moment of holy peace with the sun setting over the vineyard has been purchased. Hereafter the singers appear to become shades in the cool lap of night and also, with some increase of nobility but a continued falling away of contentment, sorrowing eagles. Once again, however, a more hopeful—though still disturbing—image concludes a portion of the poem: in allusion to the Passion in which "we" participate, a moonbeam is accorded power to close "the wounds of melancholy." Oddly enough, the moon seems here to gain back the influence of which the opening movement of the poem has deprived it.

The third and concluding section, introducing the stony cities of the plain, extends the sequence of biblical allusions,[53] together with the "Heimatlose" (in whom one can see both the wanderer and the stranger of other poems), who carries the mark of Cain, "mit dunkler Stirne," and, finally, the hill with trees suggesting Calvary. The wintry atmosphere of this conclusion, with its wind and bare branches, stands in contrast with the bleak but still recognizable springtime of the opening, and there is additional symmetry: the "Frühlingsgewitter" of Part One becomes the "Sturmgewölk" of Part Three, while the crystalline beauty of the wave in Part Two pales to become a "bleiche Woge." The rivers darken, while the peaceful sunset of Part Two becomes a terrifying display, a scene of apocalypse. Now the wave crashes against a nighttime beach, while the falling stars mirror and complete the imagery of descent with which the poem opens.

In going through this poem and the above paraphrase, the reader will recognize much that is familiar, and perhaps even feel, understandably, that "Abendland" has the appearance of patchwork, pastiche. The first stanza is replete with the imagery of Romantic nature poetry: the moon and blossoms of Goethe and Eichendorff, the mountain path of Goethe and Hölderlin, the evening pond familiar to readers of Eichendorff, Nikolaus Lenau, and Droste-Huölshoff. It is a set-piece of Romantic lyric, with the important provision that it ironizes, undermines, or empties out the imagery it recycles. In the second stanza, the "Frühlingsgewitter" has a famous antecedent in Klopstock's ode, "Die Frühlingsfeier" (1759–71), while the placement of the "Hügel" near the "Hain" obliquely names the best-known of Klopstock's bardic poems, "Der Hügel und der Hain" (1767). The "grünen Wälder unsrer Heimat" obviously recall Eichendorff's "deutscher Wald," which is in its turn derived from Klopstock, as well as the "Wald" of Hölderlin, which for the latter poet was a site of long-awaited epiphany.[54] "Die kristallne Woge" has its most prominent source in Novalis, especially in the fourth of the

Hymnen an die Nacht, where it is a mystical wave, "die kristallne Woge, die gemeinen Sinnen unvernehmlich,"[55] while the "Mauer" is a cipher for *Sprachlosigkeit* that Trakl derives from Hölderlin's "Hälfte des Lebens." "Heilige Ruh" and "Weinberg" once more recall "Brot und Wein."[56] Given the context of these allusions, the "Adler" evokes the nationalistic poetry of Klopstock, Eichendorff, and Hölderlin, especially Hölderlin's "Germanien." In the third section, the purely literary allusions continue. (I am here excluding allusion to the Bible and the mosaic of self-quotation.) The "Ströme" vividly call to mind the Hölderlin passage to which we have recurred more than once, while "Sturmgewölk" and "Völker" also belong to Hölderlin's vocabulary. Mediating the Bible, the *Hymnen an die Nacht* supply the hill with its trees. The stars are variously displayed in the *Hymnen* as well, but their ubiquity in Romantic poetry refers Trakl's stars most properly to the egregiously hackneyed imagery of Part One.

The intertextuality of "Abendland" produces associations that seem to go off in various directions, apparently frustrating any notion of a governing idea. Perhaps the best place to begin in coming to terms with this problem is with the allusions to Klopstock in Part Two. Klopstock is after all the father of "deutscher Gesang," and it seems fitting to approach the conclusion of a study in which chronology is constantly mocked by the intuition that even the most recent revisionary stratagems were probably accomplished by the first poet—it seems fitting to speak in the long run of the poet who was, if not the first poet, in any case the pioneer of German Romanticism. He is best known in this role (thanks to Werther and Lotte) as the author of "Frühlingsfeier," a poem in which the Classical ode is accommodated to the German language, and thus in a sense an inaugural German poem. Pride in this accomplishment is reinforced by the allusion to "Der Hügel und der Hain," a conversation among poets in which the last word is given to the bard of native German poetry. But when Elis's footsteps echo through a hyacinthine grove, he is in a Greek locale, and his footsteps die away when he comes to pass under the German oaks; here the voice of Klopstock fades, bringing forward the theme of a dying German poetry. In the cluster of allusions to Klopstock there is, then, a miniature history, complete with rise and fall, of the tradition for which Trakl supposes himself to have come too late.

The fading of song is the emergent theme of all the patterns of allusion. To remain in Part Two for the moment, we have remarked that the "grünen Wälder" have grown quiet, not only because nature itself is dying but because in Trakl's view a nationalistic poetry is inappropriate in a war-torn world threatened by nationalism. But apart from the issue of nationalism, groves have always been sacred to the muses, and the theme of the quiet wood raises the question whether poetry of any kind is still possible, pointing at the same time to the unlikelihood of poetic revelation, so different is this silence from "heilige Ruh." Language in fact fails in all settings. Novalis's mystical, visionary wave washes up against a decaying wall, Hölderlin's "Mauern . . . / Sprachlos und kalt." Visionary experience may or may not still be possible, but Trakl imagines that in his time language can no longer capture it. The poets sing in the evening, then die and become shades in the underworld.

One of the many things that Hölderlin inherited from Klopstock was his concern for an indigenous German poetry. Knowing this, Trakl probably understands his "Adler" to symbolize national poetry as well as nationalism. The poem to which the "trauernde Adler" carries us back most directly is "Germanien" (and, less directly, to "Patmos"). In "Germanien," the "Adler, der vom Indus kommt"[57]— from the *Morgenland*, that is—who had earlier given Germania language, "die Blume des Mundes,"[58] urges her now to name the world:

O nenne, Tochter du der heiligen Erd,
Einmal die Mutter. Es rauschen die Wasser am Fels
Und Wetter im Wald und bei dem Namen
Tönt auf aus alter Zeit Vergangengöttliches wieder.[59]

[Once only, daughter of holy Earth, / Pronounce your Mother's name.
The waters roar on the rock / And thunderstorms in the wood, and at
their home / Divine things past ring out from time immemorial.]
[Hamburger, 407]

Through the process of naming Mother Earth and her elements, the divine, long since absent from the earth, will resound again in "der Mitte der Zeit,"[60] midway between the divine past and "Zukünftiges," the promised future. In Trakl's many revisions of the last line of "Patmos," "Dem folgt deutscher Gesang," there is more at stake than a stylistic fascination with inverted word order. The redemptive and curative power of naming is now lost; and the seemingly affirmative conclusion of Part Two, promising the cure of a wound, seems less hopeful when we note that the softness of "[s]o leise" in this place is preconditioned and confused by the fall into silence of "So leise sind die grünen Wälder."

The transitory power of song is also the theme, here still more intricately presented, of Part Three. The three abrupt apostrophes that form a framework for this section seem to test the poet's powers of conjuration; they are verbal spells intended to make "Ihr grossen Städte," "Ihr weithin dämmernden Ströme," and "Ihr sterbenden Völker" vividly present. The first of these objects of attention is traditionally made real by song: the apostrophe evokes not only Sodom and Gomorrah but also the stone walls of Thebes magically built by the song of Amphion. An originary, Orphic musician, Amphion is the type of the poet Trakl hopes to become—if he can only rise above the problem of having inherited his language—and whom he imitates with his own efforts at conjuration. "Der Heimatlose," ordinarily a figure for Trakl himself and suggestive also of Novalis and Hölderlin, is interesting here in seeming no longer to be a subject but an object: as "sprachlos" as the cities of stone, or as Hölderlin's "Mauern," "der Heimatlose" in this case stands in contrast with the speaker of the poem, whose energetic apostrophes seem bent on forging an apocalypse in which the homeless wanderer simply becomes one of the "sterbende Völker." In thus subtly dismantling not only his predecessors but his own customary role as an elegiac poet seeking a lost home, Trakl sets himself apart as a poet-prophet, joining Amphion and the prophets of the Bible. Insofar as his German predecessors had aspired to the role of prophet in their own right—and we have seen that "Germanien" was much on Trakl's mind in Part Two—they are now silenced, their imagery troped by the presentational powers of direct address. Hölderlin's rivers, culture-bearers and emblems of the divine in nature, are now twilit—"dämmernde Ströme"—by Trakl's *Götterdämmerung*. Placed side by side with Trakl's vision of apocalypse, Novalis's visionary wave turns pale and inward, absorbed by the imputed solipsism of his landscape, the "Strande der Nacht." And finally, linked by metonymy with their characteristic visionary objects, the constellated poets of the past, including the poet of the river and the poet of the wave, are now "fallende Sterne," leaving the sky vacant and habitable, free of sidereal influence. Moreover, in another Trakl poem, "Wanderers Schlaf" (I, 391), the lines "Stein und Stern / Darin der weisse Fremdling ehdem gewohnt" suggest a connection between "fallende Sterne" and poetic language to which I shall turn in a moment.

As yet, I have only accounted for a few aspects of Trakl's visionary

Aufhebung in "Abendland." With his tapestry of allusion and direct quotation Trakl elaborates the desire to appropriate the tradition of "vaterländische Gesänge" and visionary song. His homage to Klopstock, Hölderlin, and Novalis is also a challenge to their authority. Humility and vaunting in equal measure inform his implicit insistence on the peril of his historical situation: the world picture has never been so bleak, the poet never so necessary, and the threat of *Sprachlosigkeit* never therefore so deeply felt. (Just here, subject to the irony that always seems to attend proclamations of uniqueness, Trakl faithfully echoes Hölderlin.) To declare oneself the poet of Apocalypse is to say, at the same time, that one is the last poet, speaking on the threshold of ultimate dissolution. This is to grant that one comes after Hölderlin and the rest, but also to claim a privileged intimacy with the sublime in history; not merely in the "Mitte der Zeit" like Hölderlin, Trakl is on the eschatological brink. In this role Trakl is also identifying himself with John of Patmos, something Hölderlin did not dare to do.

And after the Apocalypse, of course, one is no longer the last poet but the first, again one with the divine and blessed with the power of germinating language. Each poet in turn revises the work of predecessors, but Trakl in his mature poetry does this in a radically new way. Still with reference to "Abendland," one can see that the apocalypse Trakl actually effects, as opposed to the one he prophesies, is not the destruction of reality (which it would be absurd in any case to speak of surviving, as the first poet or as anything else) but the destruction of meaning. Hitherto we have read the poem with the assumption that even its borrowings are assembled to communicate themes and images, but these can also be approached in another way. Turning back to Part One, we can now see perhaps more clearly that its function is to deprive the touchstones of Romanticism of both value and significance simply by repeating them out of context, stressing their metalingual character as quotation rather than their semantic resonance. "Mond," "Blüten," "Felsenpfad," "Abendweiher," all present themselves as units of poetic language. Just so, "[d]ie grünen Wälder" and "die kristallne Woge" are not only units of language but units of quotation. No one before Trakl in German had treated the poetic tradition in quite this way, unless Heine's complex manipulation of cliché, at once embracing and rejecting the Romantic tradition is considered a precedent. Others in recent times, however, have shared in Trakl's rebellion against the semantic function of inherited language. It is worth comparing Trakl's practice with the use of quotation in the work of Walter Benjamin as Hannah Arendt understands it.

Arendt suggests that in the early twentieth century "the transmissibility of the past is replaced by its citability."[61] Uncertain about the relevance of past values to his or her present historical situation, the writer cannot approach the texts of the past as vessels of truth. Benjamin's treatment of quotation, which forms a crucial part of his writings, is best compared with his love of collecting; indeed, toward the end of his life the collecting of quotations seemed almost to replace the collecting of books. For him, collecting was clearly an ambiguous activity, on the one hand a way of honoring and protecting cultural traditions, even of preserving their authority, but on the other hand a critique of tradition, even a destruction of it, that takes the form of preserving it in fragments which, as fragments, belie its illusion of ideological adequacy and coherence. Arendt quotes Benjamin on this second function of quotation, which does not afford "the strength to preserve, but to cleanse, to tear out of context, to destroy."[62] As a poetic working-through of an attitude toward tradition, quotation as Trakl lavishly makes use of it has the same double-edged purpose. And, insofar as it puts poetic language on view as language, quotation of this kind also resembles translation as Benjamin recommends that it be practiced: it allows "the pure language, as though reinforced by its own medium, to shine upon the original all the more fully," a language which "no longer expresses anything, but *is*."[63]

As Arendt points out, quoting for Benjamin has the additional function of naming: "For Benjamin to quote is to name, and naming rather than speaking, the *words* rather than the sentence, brings truth to light."[64] In his essay "On Language as Such and on the Language of Man," written under the influence of such Romantic theorists as Hamann and Friedrich Müller, Benjamin contends that "naming, in the realm of language, has as its sole purpose and incomparably high meaning that it is the innermost nature of language itself."[65] If in this context we return briefly to "Abendland" in relation to Hölderlin's "Germanien," we can see how ambiguous, perhaps pointedly paradoxical, Trakl's presentation of the eagle becomes. The eagle exhorts Germania to "name," because in naming "tönt aus alter Zeit Vergangengöttliches wieder." But naming in "Germanien" is strictly the denomination of the natural world, "was

[dir] vor Augen ist,"[66] and is not the *direct* annunciation of the holy. It is circumspect and knowingly metaphorical: "Dreifach umschreibe du es."[67] In one sense, then, Trakl is carrying out the eagle's instructions, although his naming by repetition is perforce mediated to a much higher power than that which Hölderlin appears to have deemed necessary. The divine cannot be named, Trakl implies in agreement with Hölderlin, nor can it be directly presented through the vehicle of nature poetry. From this standpoint Trakl chooses to name, to reconstitute, precisely by forsaking the illusion that he can refer; instead of referring he quotes, emptying what he quotes of its referential power in turn, and suggesting thereby that no predecessor has had any greater success than he in attempting to body forth the world in language. Neither nature nor the poet of nature is the source. Language is the source, and German poetry will issue forth, as Hölderlin says, if the poet will ensure

> dass gepfleget werde
> Der feste Buchstab und Bestehendes gut
> Gedeudet.[68]

[that the solid letter / Be given scrupulous care, and the existing / Be well interpreted.]   [Hamburger, 476]

In sum, quotation honors and preserves earlier texts, but at the same time it makes the text in which it appears still earlier by calling attention to the language of what it quotes as language, thus referring the "language of man," which is indentured in the service of communication, back to the free self-sufficiency of the *Ursprache*, which Benjamin calls "language as such." Thus Trakl's quotations are "allegorical" in Paul de Man's sense of the term: signs that bracket reality by designating other signs. As de Man says of another German poet, one who is in many ways the heir of Rilke and Trakl, "Allegory can only blindly repeat its earlier model, the way Celan repeats quotations from Hölderlin that assert their own incomprehensibility."[69] Although de Man would no doubt have disavowed the imputation of a "Logological" strain in his thinking, one wonders whether this incomprehensibility is not important to him because of its vestigial connection with the Romantics' "pure language," which is a version, of course, of the biblical Word.

It is back toward this inscrutably early mystery, in any case, that the poetry in the tradition I have been considering "descends." What Rilke meant in referring to Trakl's "absteigende Sprache" will be clearer, perhaps, in light of Arendt's brilliant evocation of Walter Benjamin as a pearl diver, which also furnishes a good summary of the themes and metaphors that have recurred in this book— including even the passage beginning "Full fathom five thy father lies" from *The Tempest* that found its way into my discussion of Droste-Hülshoff:

> Like a pearl diver who descends to the bottom of the sea, not to excavate the bottom and bring it to light but to pry loose the rich and strange, the pearls and the coral in the depths, and to carry them to the surface, this thinking delves into the depths of the past—but not in order to resuscitate it the way it was and to contribute to the renewal of extinct ages. What guides this thinking is the conviction that although the living is subject to the ruin of time, *the process of decay is at the same time a process of crystallization*, that in the depth of the sea, into which sinks and is dissolved what once was alive, some things "suffer a sea change" and survive in new crystallized forms and shapes that remain immune to the elements, as though they waited only for the pearl diver who one day will come down to them and bring them up into the world of the living—as "thought fragments," as something "rich and strange," and perhaps even as everlasting *Urphänomene.*[70]

Arendt's relentlessly Romantic reading of Benjamin applies with remarkable precision to Trakl. It is not only that decay and crystallization figure prominently in his poetic landscape, with its rotting organic images and stones resonant with silence; Arendt's formulation also allows us to justify, from our own standpoint, Killy's theory of the "moveable parts" with which Trakl composed and Grimm's related metaphor of the mosaic, the repetition and variation of certain set borrowings. It also shows how Trakl's approach to composition reflects the confluence of two easily confused but normally separate crises: the perceived wearing out of a specific literary tradition and the perceived wearing out of language as such. Trakl honors both tradition and language by consciously repeating "thought fragments," but honors the past even more by (perhaps) unconsciously revising what he seems only to repeat in order to rejuvenate and prolong it.

Most typically Trakl's revisions strip meaning away from traditionally resonant expressions, and one result is the severe attenuation of the Romantic sublime: "Mond, als träte ein Totes / Aus blauer Höhle." Trakl's compensation, however, is the aura he is able to restore to language as such in re-citing it. In a moment of self-knowledge he exhorts the poet to name the words of an earlier poetry: "Du auf verfallenen Stufen: Baum, Stern, Stein!" (I, 97); and he seems to know that the purpose of this naming is the purification of semantic accretion: "Stein und Stern, / Darin der weisse Fremdling ehdem gewohnt" ("Wanderers Schlaf," I, 214). He is certainly aware of the specifically German poetic values attached to these and similar words: most importantly the organically derived "symbol" for Goethe, the attempt at pure metaphor for Novalis, and Hölderlin's longing for an "authentic word that fulfills its highest function in the process of naming,"[71] for the word that originates as the flower does, determined only by its own nature and by no secondary, estranged obligation to refer or communicate. But for Hölderlin the prophetic obligation to communicate was always paramount, and perhaps for this reason he never fully confronted what is entailed in the eagle's exhortation to "name." For better or worse, Trakl more clear-sightedly realized that poetic language descending from poetic language, poem from poem, comes as close to Hölderlin's ideal as it is possible to come.

Notes

CHAPTER ONE

1 I will not here defend the literary-historical latitude either of including Goethe among the Romantics or the implicit claim for the persistence of Romanticism in the poetry written since the time of Novalis, hoping that the treatment of these topics in subsequent chapters will make the case for me. Although German critics on the whole have tended to take a more restricted view of Romanticism, no less a scholar than Friedrich Sengle has anticipated and authorized the view taken here in his crowning work, *Biedermeierzeit*: "Mir scheint, dass man alle Literaturperioden zwischen 1815 und 1945 ohne die mehr oder weniger untergründige Romantiknachfolge nur halb versteht. Sicher aber ist, dass man von der Biedermeierzeit eine völlig falsche Vorstellung bekommt, wenn man die ständige Präsenz der Romantik nicht beachtet" (Sengle, *Biedermeierzeit*, 3 vols. [Stuttgart: Metzler, 1980], I, 244).

2 René Wellek, *A History of Modern Criticism, 1750–1950*, 4 vols. (New Haven: Yale University Press, 1953), I, 211.

3 Johann Wolfgang von Goethe, *Werke: Gedichte und Epen*, 14 vols., ed. Erich Trunz (Hamburg: Christian Wegner, n.d.), I, 373. All further quotations from Goethe's poetry will be cited parenthetically from this edition by volume and page.

4 Klopstock, one of Goethe's literary models, refers to the moon as a "Gedankenfreund" in his ode "Die frühen Gräber" (1764). See Friedrich Gottlieb Klopstock, *Oden: Eine Auswahl* (Stuttgart: Reclam, 1966), p. 75.

5 Brigitte Peucker, "Goethe's Mirror of Art: The Case of 'Auf dem See,'" *Goethe Yearbook* 2 (1984), 43–49.

6 Concerning Goethe's self-confidence in this regard, see Geoffrey Hartman, "Evening Star and Evening Land," *The Fate of Reading and Other Essays* (Chicago: University of Chicago Press, 1975), p. 154; and Harold Bloom, *The Anxiety of Influence: A Theory of Poetry* (New York: Oxford University Press, 1973), pp. 51–56.

7 Here and in the discussion of *Faust* below I am indebted especially to the argument of Neil M. Flax, "The Presence of the Sign in Goethe's *Faust*," *PMLA* 98 (1983), 183–203.

8 Goethe, *Goethes Faust*, ed. Erich Trunz (Hamburg: Christian Wegner, 1966), II, iii, 9901. All citations of *Faust* will henceforth be given parenthetically by part, act (where relevant), and line. Euphorion has himself proclaimed, "Immer höher muss ich steigen" (II, iii, 9821).

9 Unless noted otherwise, I use Walter Arndt's translation here. Johann Wolfgang von Goethe, *Faust*, ed. Cyrus Hamlin, trans. Walter Arndt (New York: W. W. Norton, 1976).

10 Hartman, "Wordsworth and Goethe in Literary History," *The Fate of Reading*, pp. 194–95.

11 *Goethes Briefe*, 4 vols., *Briefe der Jahre 1786–1805*, ed. Karl Mandelkow (Hamburg: Christian Wegner, 1964), II, 60.

12 Heinrich Heine, *Werke*, 4 vols, ed. Paul Stapf (Basel: Birkhäuser Verlag, 1956), IV, 44.

13 Joseph von Eichendorff, *Sämtliche Werke*, vol. VIII/2, ed. Wilhelm Kosch and August Sauer (Regensburg: Joseph Habbel, 1962), p. 182.

14 Novalis (Friedrich von Hardenberg), *Werke in einem Band*, ed. Hans-Joachim Mähl and Richard Samuel (Munich: Hanser, 1981), pp. 149, 175, 177, 177. This edition of Novalis will be cited parenthetically henceforth.

15 Werner Vordtriede, *Novalis und die französischen Symbolisten: Zur Entstehungsgeschichte des dichterischen Symbols* (Stuttgart: Kohlhammer, 1963), p. 49.

16 Georg Trakl, *Dichtungen und Briefe*, 2 vols., ed. Walther Killy and Hans Szklenar (Salzburg: Otto Müller, 1969), I, 325 and 326.

17 As Lawrence Ryan notes, "Der 'Weg nach Innen' des Novalis kehrt in Rilkes 'Weltinnenraum' zwar verwandelt, aber mit erkennbarem Gleichklang wieder" ("Die Krise des Romantischen bei Rainer Maria Rilke," *Das Nachleben der Romantik in der modernen deutschen Literatur*, ed. Wolfgang Paulsen [Heidelberg: Lothar Stiehm, 1969], p. 131).

18 On Fichte's poetics, see Cyrus Hamlin, "The Poetics of Self-Consciousness in European Romanticism: Hölderlin's *Hyperion* and Wordsworth's *Prelude*," *Genre* 6 (1973), 142.

19 In his "Älteste Urkunde des Menschengeschlechts" (1774), Herder argues that nature is the hieroglyph of the divine. See Liselotte Dieckmann, "The Metaphor of Hieroglyphics in German Romanticism," *Comparative Literature* 7 (1955), esp. 309.

20 Wellek, *A History of Modern Criticism*, II, 83.

21 It should be noted, though, that Novalis's teacher figures also evoke another great mentor of his, the "Neptunist" geologist Abraham Gottlob Werner. See John Neubauer, *Novalis* (Boston: Twayne, 1980), pp. 45, 65. One of the literary models of the *Lehrlinge*, however, was certainly *Wilhelm Meisters Lehrjahre*.

22 Friedrich Hölderlin, *Werke und Briefe*, 3 vols., ed. Friedrich Beissner and Jochen Schmidt (Frankfurt am Main: Insel 1969), I, 87. This edition of Hölderlin will be cited parenthetically henceforth by volume and page.

23 As Eudo C. Mason has argued, "Both [Goethe and Hölderlin] have, in spite of all difficulties, so immediate, almost physical an apprehension of a latent harmony in all things, that organic life, the physical universe, and existence within time nearly always appear to them a fully sufficient and appropriate basis for the soul's purest and highest efflorescence, and not as something to be discarded or transcended" (*Hölderlin und Goethe* [Bern: Herbert Lang, 1975], p. 42). Mason thinks that the critical tendency to stress differences rather than similarities between Hölderlin and Goethe reflects an undue stress on the impulse toward transcendence in Hölderlin (see ibid., p. 9). A scholar who does stress Hölderlin's attraction to the underworld, however, is Walther Rehm, both in *Orpheus, der Dichter und die Toten: Selbstdeutung und Totenkult bei Novalis-Hölderlin-Rilke* (Düsseldorf: Schwann, 1950), and "Über Tiefe und Abgrund in Hölderlins Dichtung," *Hölderlin: Gedenkschrift zu seinem 100. Todestag* (Tübingen: Mohr, 1943), pp. 70–133. See also Romano Guardini, *Hölderlin: Weltbild und Frömmigkeit* (Munich: Kösel, 1955).

24 Nägele, *Literatur und Utopie: Versuche zu Hölderlin* (Heidelberg: Lothar Stiehm, 1978, pp. 80, 95.

25 Hamlin, "The Temporality of Selfhood: Metaphor and Romantic Poetry," *New Literary History* 6 (1974), pp. 189–90.

26 Unless otherwise noted I shall use Hamburger's translations of Hölderlin. Friedrich

Hölderlin, *Poems and Fragments*, trans. Michael Hamburger (Cambridge: Cambridge University Press, 1980), pp. 413, 415.

27 See Bernhard Böschenstein, *Hölderlins Rheinhymne* (Zürich: Atlantis, 1968), p. 41.

28 All translations from *Tod des Empedokles* are mine.

29 On the problem of language in this ode, see Emil Staiger, "Hölderlins Ode 'Natur und Kunst oder Saturn und Jupiter,' " *Über Hölderlin*, ed. Jochen Schmidt (Frankfurt am Main: Insel, 1970), p. 39: "Die Wörter der Sprache halten von den wechselnden Dingen ein Bleibendes fest. Der Begriff bezieht sich auf das Viele, das er in sich vereint, und ist nur lebendig in diesem Bezug. Doch eben weil das Viele, immer Flüchtige, im Begriff verwahrt ist, weil es Dauer in ihm gewinnt, löst das Dauernde sich vom Flüchtigen ab und scheint für sich zu bestehn. Dann schaltet der Verstand mit Wörtern als mit eigenständigen Gebilden und fügt die Wörter zusammen, unbekümmert darum, ob auch die mit den Wörtern bezeichneten Dinge sich fügen." Staiger speaks further of the way in which "die Zeichen in der Sprache vom Bezeichneten sich lösen."

30 As Geoffrey Hartman writes, "We come so often on the star/flower theme that it seems to be the founding topos of nature poetry. The gods fell like stars into nature" ("From the Sublime to the Hermeneutic," *The Fate of Reading*, p. 120). But it is still surprising, perhaps, to find this collapse of the transcendent in Hölderlin.

31 Ryan, "Die Krise des Romantischen," p. 136.

32 Before Goethe there is one transcendental voice in German poetry (if even that assertion is not open to debate), that of Friedrich Gottlieb Klopstock—whose upward impulse was so strong that he dared to raise a fallen archangel in his Miltonic epic, *Der Messias* (1748–73).

CHAPTER TWO

1 Theodor Adorno, "Zum Gedächtnis Eichendorffs," *Noten zur Literatur*, vol. 1 (Frankfurt am Main: Suhrkamp, 1958), pp. 105–43.

2 Adorno does not ignore Eichendorff's politics: "Wieviel an Eichendorff aus der Perspektive des despossedierten Feudalen stammt, ist so offenbar, dass gesellschaftliche Kritik daran albern wäre. . . . Seine Überlegenheit über alle Reaktionäre, die heute die Hand nach ihm ausstrecken, bewährt sich daran, dass er, wie die grosse Philosophie seiner Epoche, die Notwendigkeit der Revolution begriff, vor der er schauerte" (*Noten*, p. 113). Adorno's attention may also have been drawn to Eichendorff by Georg Lukács's chapter, "Eichendorff," in *Deutsche Realisten des 19. Jahrhunderts* (Bern: Francke, 1951). pp. 49–65.

3 *Noten*, pp. 124, 121, 119. Oskar Seidlin also notes the distancing from the poetic subject in "Eichendorff und das Problem der Innerlichkeit," *Aurora* 29 (1969), 7–22.

4 Richard Alewyn speaks of Eichendorff's "formulas" and makes the claim "dass es in der gesamten Weltliteratur kein dichterisches *Oeuvre* gibt, das in solchem Ausmass und mit solcher Folgerichtigkeit symbolisch durchkomponiert wäre" ("Ein Wort über Eichendorff," *Eichendorff Heute*, ed. Paul Stöcklein [Munich: Bayrischer Schulbuch Verlag, 1960], p. 17). It is in his essay "Eine Landschaft Eichendorffs," in the same anthology, that Alewyn calls Eichendorff's landscape an "Urlandschaft" (p. 22). Leo Spitzer responds to this latter essay in "Zu einer Landschaft Eichendorffs," *Euphorion* 52 (1958), 142–52.

5 Hermann Kunisch, "Freiheit und Bann—Heimat und Fremde," *Eichendorff Heute*, pp. 131–47. Kunisch speaks of the unity of the inner and outer landscape on p. 141. Marshall Brown refers to the "interpenetration of man and nature" in "Eichendorff's Times of Day," *German Quarterly* 50 (1977), 490.

6 Adorno speaks of Eichendorff's "archaisches Erbe": "Der älteren Tradition der deuts-
chen Dichtung war im Gegensatz zur französischen die unverhüllte Darstellung des
Sexus fremd, und sie hat auf ihrem mittleren Niveau mit Prüderie und idealischem
Philistertum bitter dafür zu büssen gehabt. In ihren grössten Repräsentanten aber
ist ihr das Verschweigen zum Segen angeschlagen, die Kraft des Ungesagten ins
Wort gedrungen und hat ihm seine Süsse geschenkt. Noch das Unsinnliche und
Abstrakte ward bei Eichendorff zum Gleichnis für ein Gestaltloses: archaisches
Erbe, früher als die Gestalt und zugleich späte Transzendenz, das Unbedingte über
die Gestalt hinaus" (*Noten*, pp. 118–19).

7 On the verticality of the Romantic imagination, see Northrop Frye, "The Romantic
Myth," *A Study of English Romanticism* (New York: Random House, 1968), especially
pp. 46–47.

8 I will cite from the following editions of Eichendorff's works parenthetically hence-
forth: Eichendorff, *Werke*, ed. Gerhard Baumann (Stuttgart: Cotta, 1953), vol. I
(Gedichte, Epen, Dramen), vol. II (Romane, Novellen, Märchen); and Eichendorff,
Werke, (Stuttgart: Cotta, 1958), vol. III (Tagebücher) and vol. IV (Vermischte
Schriften). I, 330. All translations in this chapter are mine.

9 The underworld may also be represented by water, as in the complex of poems built
around the figure of the drowning sailor, of which "Die zwei Gesellen" is a notable
example; in these poems "die tausend Stimmen im Grund" are represented by the
songs of the sirens, or "das Meerweib."

10 This "dark side" of the wood stems from the allegorical tradition of Dante's "dark
wood" and, more immediately, from the *Wald* of the German *Märchen*.

11 Vladimir Zernin, "The Abyss in Eichendorff: A Contribution to the Study of the
Poet's Symbolism," *German Quarterly* 35 (1962), 281. See also Richard Benz, "Ei-
chendorffs mythischer Grund," *Medium Aevum Vivum*, ed. Hans Robert Jauss and
Dieter Schaller (Heidelberg: Carl Winter, 1960), pp. 321–39.

12 See Lothar Pikulik, "Die Mythisierung des Geschlechtstriebes in Eichendorffs 'Marmorbild,' " *Mythos und Mythologie in der Literatur des 19. Jahrhunderts*, ed. Helmut
Koopmann (Frankfurt am Main: Klostermann, 1979), pp. 159–72.

13 This allusion has been noticed by Peter Paul Schwarz, *Aurora: Zur romantischen
Zeitstruktur bei Eichendorff*, Ars Poetica, vol. 12 (Bad Homburg: Gehlen, 1970), p.
98.

14 This is reminiscent of Ludwig Tieck's *Die Elfen*, in which the elves, spirits of
nature, sow seeds from which huge flowers bloom forth instantaneously. Eichendorff
greatly admired *Die Elfen* for the way it portrays the "dunkle Mächte." *Geschichte der
poetischen Literatur Deutschlands* (IV, 291).

15 See Horst Meixner, *Romantischer Figuralismus: Kritische Studien zu Romanen von Arnim,
Eichendorff und Hoffmann* (Frankfurt am Main: Athenäum, 1971), who says of "Die
wunderliche Prinzessin": "Das Gespräch über Poesie wird—im wörtlichen Sinne—
selbst Poesie im allegorischen Gedicht der Gräfin Romana" (p. 150).

16 See Robert Mulher, "Der Poetenmantel: Wandlungen eines Sinnbildes bei Eichen-
dorff," *Eichendorff Heute*, pp. 180–203, for discussion of the "Zaubermantel" or
"Poetenmantel" motif. This image undoubtedly derives from "ein Mann aus fremden
Landen" in Novalis's *Lehrlinge zu Sais* who wears "ein wunderliches Kleid mit vielen
Falten und seltsamen Figuren" (*Werke in einem Band*, pp. 215–16). All such images
derive from Plato's representation of the poet as a protean harlequin flourishing in
the democratic body politic, which Plato calls "a garment of many colors" in the
Republic, book 8. Poets resisting Plato's idealist negativity, among them Joseph von
Eichendorff, would also recall that the first coat of many colors was worn by a hero,
the biblical Joseph.

17 Alfred Riemen, "Eichendorffs Garten und seine Besucher," *Aurora* 30/31 (1970–71), 23–33; Dietrich Jäger, "Meditation und Kunst als Beschwörung des Verlorenen," ibid., 34–49; Oskar Seidlin, "Der alte Garten," *Versuche über Eichendorff* (Göttingen: Vandenhoeck und Ruprecht, 1965), pp. 74–98; Walther Rehm, "Prinz Rokoko im alten Garten," *Späte Studien* (Bern: Francke Verlag, 1964), pp. 122–214.

18 See Riemen, "Eichendorffs Garten," p. 23.

19 Quoted by Dieter Lent, *Die Dämonie der Antike bei Eichendorff*, diss., Freiburg, 1964, p. 18.

20 *Werke* 1958, II, 1077. See Rehm, "Prinz Rokoko," pp. 133–34. Paul Stöcklein, in *Joseph von Eichendorff in Selbstzeugnissen und Bilddokumenten* (Reinbek bei Hamburg: Rowohlt, 1963), p. 64, cites a passage that elides the two passages quoted above.

21 Seidlin, *Versuche*, p. 38.

22 Kunisch, "Das Wiedersehen," *Aurora* 25 (1965), 20. There are six Eichendorff poems dedicated to his brother in the collection of 1844: "An meinen Bruder" (1813); "Nachruf an meinen Bruder" (1814); "An meinen Bruder" (1815); "Die Heimat. An meinen Bruder," which Hillach and Krabiel date from the 1830s, not from 1819, as is commonly done (see Ansgar Hillach and Klaus-Dieter Krabiel, *Eichendorff Kommentar, Zu den Dichtungen*, 2 vols. (Munich: Winkler, 1971), I, 93); "Heimweh. An meinen Bruder" (1830s); and "Nachklänge, #6" (1830s).

23 Stöcklein, *Joseph von Eichendorff*, p. 47.

24 See, for this passage and the following, Lent, *Die Dämonie*, p. 21; see also Kunisch, "Das Wiedersehen," pp. 28–29. Ordinarily, though, Lubowitz is "die Heimat" for Eichendorff and Tost is threatening in memory.

25 Kunisch, "Freiheit und Bann—Heimat und Fremde," p. 133.

26 This poem was first published "als Totenklage um eine Geliebte" in 1818; in manuscript it was called "Abendlandschaft, oder Abendwehmuth." See Hillach and Krabiel, *Eichendorff Kommentar*, I, 71.

27 Alexander von Bormann makes an interesting point in "Die ganze Welt zum Bild: Zum Zusammenhang von Handlungsführung und Bildform bei Eichendorff," *Aurora* 40 (1980), 30: "Die Wiederkehr des Verdrängten hat er vielfach beschrieben, und seine Formel '(er)-lösen' meint auch das Bekenntnis zur (Sinnen)welt, zum Strom (in seiner Bilderwelt), der Strom sein muss, um das Meer zu erreichen."

28 Seidlin, *Versuche*, p. 212. See also Kunisch, "Freiheit und Bann," pp. 132–34, for the revisions cited below.

29 Seidlin, *Versuche*, p. 212.

30 See Kunisch, "Das Wiedersehen," p. 30.

31 It might be interesting to examine the fictional moments of these homecoming poems alongside Heine's *Die Heimkehr*, first published in *Die Reisebilder* in 1826.

32 "Es entstand in Lübowitz in einer Zeit der Ungewissheit um das Schicksal des im österreichischen Staatsdienst tätigen Bruders Wilhelms, der nur selten von sich Nachricht gab" (Hillach and Krabiel, *Eichendorff Kommentar*, I, 71).

33 In a letter to Loeben dated August 10, 1814, Eichendorff writes: "Und es fällt mir wohl manchmal gar ein, dass er gestorben. Ich schreibe dies mit tiefen Schauern, denn ich weiss nicht, wie ich ihn überleben soll." Quoted in Kunisch, "Das Wiedersehen," p. 23.

34 As Kunisch puts it in "Das Wiedersehen," "Das aber wird nach dem Gleiten und dem fast süchtigen Verlangen nach dem Versinken nicht recht glaubhaft. Dies Sichhinübergeben in Gottes Führung ist wohl in Wunsch und Gesinnung vorhanden, besitzt aber nicht genügend entzaubernde Kraft" (p. 25).

35 Margaret Homans, *Women Writers and Poetic Identity: Dorothy Wordsworth, Emily Brontë, and Emily Dickinson* (Princeton: Princeton University Press, 1980), p. 155.

36 Kunisch, "Das Wiedersehen," pp. 24, 41.

37 Hermann Lucks, *Wesen und Form des Dämonischen in Eichendorffs Dichtung*, diss. Cologne, 1964, p. 59 (bis).

38 Theresa Sauter Bailliet, *Die Frauen im Werk Eichendorffs: Verkörperungen heidnischen und christlichen Geistes* (Bonn: Bouvier, 1972), p. 34. See also Rudolf Ibel, *Weltschau deutscher Dichter: Novalis, Eichendorff, Mörike, Droste-Hülshoff* (Frankfurt am Main: Diesterweg, 195?), p. 84, speaking of the Venus figure: "Dieses Bild ist durchzogen von den mythischen Elementen germanischer Sagen und Märchenwelt. Da ist der Leben gebärende Weiher und die aus ihm auftauchende Nixe als Gestalt des Lebengeheimnisses, Geliebte und Mutter zugleich."

39 See Pikulik, p. 161: "Das revolutionäre Neue, das im *Marmorbild* über den Eros verschlüsselt enthüllt wird, liegt darin, dass er nicht als etwas Physisches, sondern als etwas Psychisches begriffen wird. Dies ist für die damalige Zeit etwas völlig Ungewohntes."

40 Quoted by Kunisch, "Das Wiedersehen," p. 30.

41 Gerhard Möbus, *Der andere Eichendorff: Zur Deutung der Dichtung Joseph von Eichendorffs* (Osnabrück: A. Fromm, 1960), p. 31: "Erschliesst sich der Sinn dieses Werkes, das der Dichter selbst ein Märchen genannt hat, dann eröffnet sich mit ihm zugleich der Zugang zum Gehalt des Gesamtwerkes."

42 Prinz Romano, the object of satire in *Viel Lärmen um Nichts*, has a very similar experience; as he watches, "ein Schwan, den Kopf unter dem Flügel versteckt, beschreibt auf einem Weiher stille, einförmige Kreise" (II, 460).

43 On this issue, see Paul H. Fry, "Oedipus the King," *Homer to Brecht: The European Epic and Dramatic Traditions*, ed. Michael Seidel and Edward Mendelson (New Haven: Yale University Press, 1977), pp. 186–87.

44 Joseph Kunz, *Eichendorff: Höhepunkt und Krise der Spätromantik* (Darmstadt: Wissenschaftliche Buchgesellschaft, 1967), p. 154.

45 See Jean Laplanche and J.-B. Pontalis, "Narcissism," *French Freud: Structural Studies in Psychoanalysis*, *Yale French Studies* 48 (1972), 194–96.

46 Rilke's "Die Laute," in the *Neue Gedichte, Anderer Teil*, is one of his most sexual poems; it begins "Ich bin die Laute. Willst du meinen Leib / beschreiben, seine schön gewölbten Streifen: / sprich so, als sprächest du von einer reifen / gewölbten Feige."

47 Eichendorff called Goethe's Werther "ein moderner Narziss" (IV, 713). The passage from *Das Marmorbild* reads: "Ich warf mich in das tiefste Gras und sah stundenlang zu, wie die Wolken über die schwüle Gegend wegzogen" (II, 337). It is again tempting to say that the father in this scene, as in others, is Goethe.

48 See, e. g., Kunz, *Eichendorff*, p. 188.

49 Brisman, *Romantic Origins* (Ithaca: Cornell University Press, 1978), p. 31.

50 On the sphinx, see Rehm, "Prinz Rokoko," pp. 140–43.

51 Paul Stöcklein (*Eichendorff*, p. 37) mentions his mother's anger at having been caricatured as Frau von A. in *Ahnung und Gegenwart*, for which she never quite forgave him. Stöcklein says later (p. 46): "Die Spannung zur Mutter wird später ein 'Thema' werden; wenn er ihre Erwartungen enttäuscht; mit seinem langen Berufsweg, mit seiner Schriftstellerei; mit seiner Heirat." At the very least, such evidence may help to establish the mother as a powerful presence in the imagination of the son.

52 He styles himself a prodigal son, the "dark brother," in "An meinen Bruder" (1813): "Mich irrte manches Schöne" (I, 141).

53 Frye writes: "In Romanticism the main direction of the quest for identity tends increasingly to be downward and inward, toward a hidden basis or ground of

identity between man and Nature. It is a hidden region, often described in images of underground caves and streams . . . that the final unity between man and his nature is most often achieved" ("The Romantic Myth," p. 33).

54 Adorno, *Noten*, pp. 124, 127.

55 This conversion is Eichendorff's more orthodox equivalent of the transformation by poets of Neoplatonic leanings of the earthly Venus into the celestial Venus.

56 Numerous Eichendorff poems evoke the national poetry of Klopstock—which does not prevent Eichendorff from satirizing "Vaterländerei" in "Hermanns Enkel" (IV, 480).

57 Eichendorff disapproved, however, of what he took to be Klopstock's equal love of Teutonic and Christian myth. See "Die geistliche Poesie in Deutschland" (IV, 480).

58 Of course there are other Romantic influences on Eichendorff as well, primarily that of Tieck; *Das Marmorbild*, for instance, has much in common with Tieck's *Runenberg*. Schwarz (*Aurora*, pp. 53, 85), briefly mentions the influence of Brentano as well. But Tieck's work is in turn derivative from that of Novalis, who remains the central figure among the Romantics in Eichendorff's imagination.

59 From Eichendorff's standpoint the word "Romantik" *tout court* refers to all literature in the Christian tradition.

60 Novalis's connection with the Jena circle and Friedrich Schlegel and his early death in 1801 would alone suffice to make him the first poet under consideration. See also Gerhard Möbus, "Eichendorff und Novalis," *Eichendorff Heute*, ed. Stöcklein, pp. 165–79. Unfortunately, this is a limited and general comparison. Paul Stöcklein quotes an interesting passage from the "Wiener Zeitschrift für Kunst, Literatur, Theater, und Mode," Jan. 26, 1847, which contains the following remark: "Eichendorff zählt jedenfalls zu den subjektiven Dichtern, und daher wohl auch jene wohltuende Innerlichkeit, die uns so gern bei ihm verweilen lässt. Seine Schriften in Prosa erinnern an Novalis" (*Eichendorff*, p. 141).

61 "über die ethische und religiöse Bedeutung der neueren romantischen Poesie Deutschlands" (IV, 447).

62 Eichendorff's aspirations for poetry were more limited, clearly, than those of Friedrich Schlegel, envisioning only a "neue *christliche* Mythologie" (IV, 448; italics mine).

63 From an 1810 letter quoted by Stöcklein, *Eichendorff*, p. 71.

64 Möbus, *Der andere Eichendorff*, p. 68.

65 Quoted in ibid., pp. 39–40.

66 In criticizing Friedrich Weschsta (for other reasons), Möbus summarizes Weschsta's argument about the marked similarities between *Das Marmorbild* and *Heinrich von Ofterdingen*, but these parallels are restricted to plot, image, and verbal echo, and draw no conclusions about the nature of Eichendorff's appropriations: "Augenfällig sind die Übereinstimmungen in der Darstellung des Festes, vor allem auch in der Rolle der beiden Sänger Fortunato und Klingsohr. Auffällig klingt die Schilderung der Träume Florios und Heinrichs einander an. Bis zur wörtlichen Übereinstimmung geht die Szene, in der Florio wie Heinrich nach dem Fest und Garten einer Frauengestalt begegnet, deren Gesang er belauscht. Ein Entwurf Eichendorffs bringt die Fahrt auf dem Strom wiederum bis in den Wortlaut übereinstimmend; ein weiterer enthält die Szenerie des golden sprühenden Springbrunnens, des entzückten Tauchen in das Wasser, und vor allem des fernher tönenden, einfachen Liedes" (ibid., pp. 32–33). All this in fact bespeaks a conscious turning away from Novalis.

67 Seidlin, *Versuche*, p. 249.

68 Ibid., pp. 193, 251. Seidlin makes an interesting point about "Jagdlied": "Denn auf die verräterischen Zeilen, die die todestrunkene Versunkenheit in grüne Nacht

feiern, folgt eine Schlusswendung von einer so herzhaften Harmlosigkeit, dass man . . . über ihre entwaffnende Banalität nur fassungslos staunen möchte." (p. 193).

69 Frye, "The Romantic Myth," pp. 41, 33.

70 Schwarz asserts it to have been proven that Novalis was influenced in turn by Edward Young's *Night Thoughts* (*Aurora*, p. 26).

71 Ibid., p. 29. Schwarz also mentions (ibid., p. 44) that Görres's interpretation of Runge's *Tageszeiten* associates the night with the "Mysterium der Empfängnis."

72 Schwarz recognizes that night in Eichendorff is a "Dimension der Tiefe": "Die nächtlich laut werdenden Stimmen und Klänge scheinen all aus einem chthonischen Zentrum aufzusteigen und in dieses hinein zu locken" (ibid., p. 95); but his argument about the influence of the *Hymnen* restricts it primarily to Eichendorff's night poems.

73 Lucks, *Wesen und Form*, p. 90.

74 "Der Einfluss der 'Götter Griechenlands' (1788), auf den Fritz Strich verweist, und das Wechselspiel von philosophischer und dichterischer Mythendeutung bezeugen Schelling, Hegel, Hölderlin, und Novalis," writes Herbert Anton, "Romantische Deutung griechischer Mythologie," *Die deutsche Romantik*, ed. Hans Steffen (Göttingen: Vandenhoeck und Ruprecht, 1967), p. 280. Max Kommerell makes the connection between Novalis's fifth *Hymn* and Schiller's poem in "Novalis' 'Hymnen an die Nacht,' " *Gedicht und Gedanke*, ed. Heinz Otto Burger (Halle: Max Niemeyer, 1942), p. 224.

75 See Kommerell, " 'Hymnen,' " p. 225.

76 Schiller, *Sämtliche Werke*, 5 vols., ed. Gerhard Fricke (Munich: Carl Hanser, 1965), I, 167 (1. 146).

77 As Anton says, "Die romantische Idee einer *neuen Mythologie* ist eine Konsequenz ihrer ästhetischen Deutung der griechischen Götterwelt, und sie wiederum empfängt ihre Impulse aus der Idee einer *neuen* Mythologie. Das bedeutet: sowohl die Deutung der griechischen Mythologie als auch die Hoffnung einer 'künstlichen Herstellung jenes mythischen Zustandes' sind ästhetische Utopien einer mythologischen Funktion" ("Romantische Deutung," p. 281).

78 See Dieckmann, "The Metaphor of Hieroglyphics," p. 309. Herder's section of *Älteste Urkunde des Menschengeschlechts*, "Unter der Morgenröte," evokes Jakob Böhme's *Aurora*.

79 See Bailliet, *Die Frauen im Werk Eichendorffs*, p. 131.

80 See Hillach and Krabiel, *Eichendorff Kommentar*, p. 139.

81 As Meixner says, "Im Sinne Friedrich Schlegels lassen sich Eichendorffs Romane als poetische Reden von der Poesie verstehen, als eine Selbstdarstellung der Poesie in einem unendlichen Gespräch über Poesie" (*Romantischer Figuralismus*, p. 146).

82 Quoted in Stöcklein, *Eichendorff*, p. 64.

83 See Alewyn, "Ein Wort über Eichendorff," pp. 17–18, and Seidlin, "Eichendorffs symbolische Landschaft," *Eichendorff Heute*, pp. 240–41. It is hard to avoid noticing that Eichendorff's swan, a sign of the imagination, essentially static in the repetition of its circular motion, becomes even more motionless when it becomes Mallarmé's swan in "Le Cygne."

84 See also: "Es schrieb mit feurigen Lettern / Der Herr, und sprach in Wettern" ("Der brave Schiffer," 1835, I, 159).

85 Lothar Pikulik is somewhat off course here: "Der Buchstabe ist dem Geist zuwider, denn wenn der Geist lebendig und beweglich ist, so hat der Buchstabe den statischen Charakter der Norm. Der Buchstabe raubt dem Geist somit den Lebensnerv. Das flüssige Element des Geistes in Lettern zu verfestigen, bedeutet eben jenes tödliche Festhalten" (*Romantik als Ungenügen an der Normalität: Am Beispiel Tiecks,*

Hoffmanns, Eichendorffs [Frankfurt am Main: Suhrkamp, 1979], pp. 492–93). Precisely. Seidlin (*Versuche*, p. 33) sees this question somewhat differently; since he realizes that Nature is tainted for Eichendorff, he is eager to distinguish between a "true" Book of Nature conception and what he calls "nicht eine zweite Offenbarung, durch die der Geist sich offenbar enthüllt, nicht heilige Schrift, sondern die *Tafel*, auf der die Inschrift erscheint."

86 As did Herder, Wackenroder, Friedrich Schlegel, and Görres, among others. See Meixner, *Romantischer Figuralismus*, p. 147.

CHAPTER THREE

1 Quoted by the editors in Annette von Droste-Hülshoff, *Sämtliche Werke*, 2 vols., ed. Gunther Weydt and Winfried Woesler (Munich: Winkler, 1973), I, 749 (translation mine). The review was published in the *Beilage zur Allgemeinen Zeitung*, Augsburg, #331, 11–26–1844. I shall quote Droste-Hülshoff from the edition cited here parenthetically by volume and page number.

2 Schücking, "Fünf Droste-Rezensionen, 1838–60," *Jahrbuch der Droste Gesellschaft* 5 (1972), 83. This passage is from "Eine Charakteristik," 1847.

3 See Heselhaus, *Annette von Droste-Hülshoff: Werk und Leben* (Düsseldorf: August Bagel, 1971), pp. 197–98.

4 Erwin Rotermund, "Die Dichtergedichte der Droste," *Droste-Jahrbuch* 5 (1962), 78.

5 See Staiger, "Annette von Droste-Hülshoff, Festrede bei der Jahrhundertfeier am 24. Mai 1948 in Meersburg," *Droste-Jahrbuch* 2 (1950), 51. Of her poetry he writes that "ihren Fabeln fehlt die Idee" (p. 71).

6 Staiger, *Annette von Droste-Hülshoff, Wege zur Dichtung*, ed. Emil Ermatinger (Zürich: Münster Presse, 1933), pp. 79, 80.

7 Staiger does not seem to have been aware of the poet's original intention to open the entire 1844 collection with this poem, not just the section called "Gedichte Vermischten Inhalts." We owe it to Schücking's intervention that she did not do so. See Heselhaus, *Werk und Leben*, p. 17.

8 Staiger, *Annette von Droste-Hülshoff*, p. 10 (translation mine). His bibliography cites only two women critics, Bertha Badt and Gabriele Reuter, neither of whom can be said to have a feminist orientation.

9 Ibid., p. 22.

10 See, e. g., G. Guder, "Annette von Droste-Hülshoff's Conception of Herself as a Poet," *German Life and Letters* 11, no. 1 (Oct. 1957), 14.

11 Droste-Hülshoff, *Ausgewählte Werke*, ed. Huch (Leipzig: Reclam, 1932), p. 5.

12 See the introduction to Droste-Hülshoff, *Auswahl aus ihrem Werk und aus dem Lebensbild von Levin Schücking*, ed. Malechow (Leipzig: Koehler und Amelang, 1955), p. 11.

13 See Böschenstein-Schaefer, "Die Struktur des Idyllischen im Werk der Annette von Droste-Hülshoff," *Kleine Beiträge zur Droste-Forschung* 3 (1974–75), 25–49.

14 *Die Briefe der Annette von Droste-Hülshoff*, 2 vols., ed. K. S. Kemminghausen (Darmstadt: Wissenschaftliche Buchgesellschaft, 1968), I, 165. Letters cited henceforth parenthetically by volume and page number from this edition, called "*B*."

15 See Heselhaus, *Werk und Leben*, p. 31.

16 One of the first of the letters in the Kemminghaus collection speaks of her "sehr aufgeregte Phantasie" (*B* I, 13), and in one of the last she says, "meine Phantasie arbeitet mir zu schwer" (*B* II, 525).

17 *B* I, 198, 211, 216 312; *B* II, 43. It is still hard to say what her illness was. At times during her life it was thought that she had tuberculosis, but this opinion was reversed (*B* II, 158), and shortly before her death doctors could find nothing amiss (*B* II, 528).

18 De Beauvoir, *The Second Sex*, trans. H. M. Parshley (New York: Alfred Knopf, 1953), p. 594.

19 Among them "Johanna von Austen," who is Jane Austen turned German Klopstock enthusiast, and "die Briesen," probably a satiric portrait of the Fräulein von Bornstadt who haunts her letters.

20 Staiger, *Annette von Droste-Hülshoff*, pp. 98, 101.

21 Gundolf, *Romantiker* (Berlin: Heinrich Keller, 1931), p. 132. Similar epithets abound in the criticism; she is called *Seherfrau, Norne, Sibylle, Spinnerin, Hexe*—all somewhat ambivalent names for the female artist.

22 Ibid., pp. 196, 210. See also Bernhard Böschenstein, "Drostische Landschaft in Paul Celans Dichtung," *Kleine Beiträge zur Droste-Forschung* 1 (1972–73), 7–24. Böschenstein notes that in particular Droste-Hülshoff and Celan have a common obsession with death, and implies that for this reason they emphasize the *Dinglichkeit* of their landscapes.

23 Sengle, *Biedermeierzeit*, III, 637–38, 624–25, 611.

24 See Heinz Schlaffer, *Lyrik im Realismus: Studien über Raum und Zeit in den Gedichten Mörikes, der Droste, und Liliencrons* (Bonn: Bouvier, 1966), p. 94.

25 See Gundolf, *Romantiker*, p. 199, and Heselhaus, *Werk und Leben*, p. 108.

26 Heselhaus, *Werk und Leben*, p. 95.

27 See Huch, ed., *Ausgewählte Werke*, p. 11.

28 Gundolf, *Romantiker*, p. 198.

29 See Bertha Badt, *Annette von Droste-Hülshoff: Ihre dichterische Entwicklung und ihr Verhältnis zur englischen Literatur* (Leipzig: Quelle und Meyer, 1909), p. 13. Badt claims (p. 13) that Schlüter translated Coleridge, but I have never seen this mentioned elsewhere.

30 As, for example, in a letter to Chr. B. Schlüter, Dec. 12, 1838: "Leider bin ich mit Malchen in allem, was Kunst und Poesie betrifft, [nicht einer] Meinung, da sie einer gewissen romantischen Schule auf sehr geistvolle, aber etwas einseitige Weise zugetan ist" (*B* I, 316–17).

31 The issue is summarized by Heselhaus, *Werk und Leben*, p. 111.

32 Harold Jantz, "Sequence and Continuity in Nineteenth-Century German Literature," *The Germanic Review* 38 (1963), 32–33.

33 See Staiger, *Annette von Droste-Hülshoff*, p. 22.

34 Heselhaus, *Werk und Leben*, pp. 109–10.

35 Heselhaus, *Annette von Droste-Hülshoff: Die Entdeckung des Seins in der Dichtung des 19. Jahrhunderts* (Halle: Max Niemeyer, 1943), p. 157.

36 Guder, "Droste-Hülshoff's Conception of Herself," p. 16.

37 Von Wiese, "Die Balladen der Annette von Droste," *Droste-Jahrbuch* 1 (1947), 28 (translation mine).

38 Schücking, "Fünf Droste-Rezensionen," pp. 93, 100.

39 Sandra M. Gilbert and Susan Gubar, *The Madwoman in the Attic: The Woman Writer and the Nineteenth-Century Literary Imagination* (New Haven: Yale University Press, 1979), p. 37.

40 See ibid., p. 57.

41 Ibid., pp. 76, 77.

42 The peculiar gifts of Droste-Hülshoff were so openly manifest to the Westphalian peasants that they called her a "Sternjungfrau," "ein Mädchen das nicht zum Lieben bestimmt und deswegen mit seltsamen Heil und Wunderkräften begabt ist." See Walter Nigg, *Wallfahrt zur Dichtung* (Zürich: Artemis, 1966), p. 26.

43 Schücking, *Annette von Droste: Ein Lebensbild* (Leipzig: Amelang und Koehler, 1942), p. 80.

44 Ibid., p. 81.

45 See Joyce Hallamore, "The Reflected Self in Annette von Droste-Hülshoff's Work: A Challenge to Self-Discovery," *Monatshefte* 61 (1969), 63. Most recent Droste-Hülshoff scholarship deals mainly with *Die Judenbuche*, but the following articles are concerned also with her poetry: Rudolf Haller, "Eine Droste-Interpretation: 'Das Spiegelbild,' " *Germanisch-romanische Monatsschrift* 37 (1956), 253–61; Walter Silz, "Problems of 'Weltanschauung' in the Works of Annette von Droste-Hülshoff," *PMLA* 64 (1949), 678–700; Christa Suttner, "A Note on the Droste-Image and 'Das Spiegelbild,' " *German Quartery* 40 (1967), 623–29.

46 Concerning the child, see Böschenstein-Schaefer, "Die Struktur des Idyllischen," p. 48.

47 I do not feel that the self-doubt expressed in this poem is in any way inconsistent with the more declamatory, affirmative moments in Droste-Hülshoff's work in which she justifies herself as a woman writer—as in "Mein Beruf."

48 Bachelard, *L'eau et les rêves: Essai sur l'imagination de la matière* (Paris: José Corti, 1942), pp. 111, 113. I have chosen the name "Ophelia" even though the poet never does so herself. For related ideas, see Bernhard Blume, "Das ertrunkene Mädchen: Rimbauds 'Ophelie' und die deutsche Literatur," *Germanisch-romanische Monatsschrift* 35 (1954), 108–19.

49 See Friedrich Götz's introduction to Günderode, *Gesammelte Dichtungen*, ed. Götz (Mannheim: Friedrich Götz, 1857), p. vii. Günderode's suicide was less smoothly accomplished than the similar act of Virginia Woolf. She poised herself to fall into the river and pierced her heart with a dagger, but the thrust threw her backward rather than forward; otherwise she would have sunk to the bottom under the weight of the rocks she had bound to her person. Later, in obvious fascination, both Bettina von Arnim and Christa Wolf were to use the materials of Günderode's life in *Die Günderode: Ein Briefwechsel* (1840) and *Kein Ort, Nirgends* (1979), respectively.

50 Sigmund Freud, "The Uncanny," *On Creativity and the Unconscious: Papers on the Psychology of Art, Literature, Love, Religion*, ed. Benjamin Nelson (New York: Harper & Row, 1958), p. 151.

51 See Heselhaus, *Werk und Leben*, p. 26.

52 The sisters Berta and Cordelia, and later Ledwina and Therese, have much in common with Annette and her sister Jenny. Heselhaus speaks of Annette's "Leben in der Phantasie," which made her "fremd, wunderbar, und unverständlich" to her family (*Werk und Leben*, p. 23).

53 De la Motte Fouqué's *Undine* (1811) is the first longer Romantic fiction concerning this nymph; he cites as his main source the *Liber de Nymphis* of Paracelsus.

54 Hallamore, "The Reflected Self," p. 67.

55 Walter Hinck interprets "Gespenst" to mean a person in "extremer menschlicher Situation" and sees the expression as evidence for the poet's "balladische[r] Realismus" (*Die deutsche Ballade von Bürger bis Brecht* [Göttingen: Vandenhoeck, 1968], p. 81).

56 In *Hamlet* V: i, the clowns make much of the point that Ophelia is given a Christian burial under circumstances that normally prohibit one.

57 See Heselhaus, *Werk und Leben*, p. 25.

58 Apart from the analysis of this passage, I have been concerned chiefly with female doubles—and only those that are reflected in mirrors and bodies of water. Setting this matrix aside, perhaps the best-known appearance of the double in Droste-Hülshoff's work is in the *Judenbuche*; there are other instances as well. See Hallamore, "The Reflected Self," and Silz, "Problems of 'Weltanschauung.' "

59 Especially in Meyer's "Eingelegte Ruder" (*Gedichte* [Stuttgart: Reclam, 1973], pp. 10–11).

60 In my view, the male personification of "Weiher" is only grammatically gender-determined: *"der* Weiher." For a Freudian interpretation of this cycle, see Böschenstein-Schaefer, "Die Struktur des Idyllischen."

61 This poem is not included as such in the Woesler edition. I shall quote it by page number from Annette von Droste-Hülshoff, *Sämtliche Werke,* ed. Clemens Heselhaus (Munich: Hanser, 1966).

62 In the late fragment *Bettina und Syri,* Droste-Hülshoff roundly condemns Bettina von Arnim's admiration for Goethe. Bettina is represented here as a rose whose turning toward the sun—toward Goethe—breeds in her the "Würmer des Bösen," because in turning to Goethe rather than to Christ she is guilty of heresy. Needless to say, there is something of Droste-Hülshoff's own relationship to Goethe in *Bettina und Syri,* and for this reason her horror of unhallowed influence is all the greater. This is perhaps one of the motives of the frequent retreat to religious orthodoxy in her work. See Bernd Kortländer, *Annette von Droste-Hülshoff und die deutsche Literatur: Kenntnis—Beurteilung—Beeinflussung* (Münster: Aschendorff, 1979), pp. 146–47.

63 Kirsch, *Zaubersprüche* (Berlin: Aufbau 1973), p. 55.

64 I refer to the original first stanza, which Keats rejected, together with the published first stanza beginning "No, no, go not to Lethe."

65 Heselhaus, *Entdeckung des Seins,* p. 150.

66 Rudolf Ibel has called several of Droste-Hülshoff's poems "Gedichte der Entsinkung." I derive the term "poems of descent" from Ibel, but I have expanded his category and its definition. See Ibel, *Weltschau deutscher Dichter* (Frankfurt am Main: Moritz Diesterweg, n.d.). Böschenstein-Schaefer ("Die Struktur des Idyllischen," p. 47) refers to the poet's "Totenlandschaft" and says "Es errübrigt sich, auf die Häufigkeit und Bedeutung des Todesmotivs bei der Droste ausführlicher einzugehen." Sengle too (*Biedermeierzeit,* p. 637) makes a point of the involvement of Droste-Hülshoff's imagination with the subject of death in calling "Im Grase" "ein Totengedicht."

67 Bloom, *A Map of Misreading* (New York: Oxford University Press, 1975), p. 92.

68 Homans, *Women Writers and Poetic Identity,* p. 100. Droste-Hülshoff is certainly writing in this tradition, as the poem "Die Elemente," with such expressions as "Natur schläft—Ihr Odem steht / Ihre grünen Locken hangen schwer" (I, 63) sufficiently indicates.

69 Böschenstein-Schaefer, "Die Struktur des Idyllischen," p. 47.

70 Von Wiese, "Die Balladen der Annette von Droste," p. 32. Writing in the same vein, Lotte Köhler says: "Aus dunklen Tiefen sah sie unheimliche Traumgestalten aufsteigen und erlebte den Einbruch des Irrationalen auf so bedrängend greifbare Weise, dass die Angst zu einer wesentlichen Komponente ihres Lebensgefühls wurde" ("Annette von Droste-Hülshoff," *Deutsche Dichter des 19. Jahrhunderts: Ihr Leben und Werk,* ed. Benno von Wiese [Berlin: Erich Schmidt, 1979], p. 228).

71 This second letter was written to Schücking's wife Luise; Droste-Hülshoff's jealousy of Luise may explain the air of forced gaiety about the letter, but it does not account for its imagery.

72 Like the famous dash in Kleist's *Marquise von O . . . ,* the line of division in "Die Vogelhütte" implies reticence about the event it passes over.

73 A passage from a letter to Wilhelm Junkmann (Aug. 26, 1839) is pertinent here: "Es wird mir zuweilen ganz wunderlich, wenn ich manche Stengel oder Muscheln genau in der Form, wie sie damals der Augenblick verbogen hat, wieder hervortreten sehe, gleichsam in ihrer Todeskrümmung. Ich wollte, ich träfe einmal auf ein lebendiges Tier im Stein! Was meinen Sie, wenn ein Mensch mal so aus seiner viertausendjährigen Kruste hervorkriechen könnte? Was müsste der nicht fühlen!

Und was zu fühlen und denken geben! Seltsam bleibt's immer, dass man nicht wenigstens *versteinerte* Menschen findet" (*B* I, 375). The poet is not concerned in such passages with natural history or human history alone; the image of man buried and petrified in itself agitates her imagination.

74 This brief epic ends on a humorous note stressing the lack of historical understanding involved in the misidentification of bones:

> Am Moore nur trifft wohl einmal
> Der Gräber noch auf rost'gen Stahl,
> Auf einen Schädel; und mit Graus
> Ihn seitwärts rollend, ruft er aus:
> "Ein Heidenknochen! Schaue, hier schlug
> Der Türke sich im Loener Bruch!"   [I, 421]

> Only in the moors perhaps does the digger / Sometimes come upon rusty steel, / Or upon a skull; and rolling it / Aside with horror, he calls out: / "A heathen's bone! Look, the Turks / Fought here in the Loener Bruch!"

75 In the notes to "Die Mergelgrube," Weydt and Woesler list the articles that take up this issue (I, 758).

76 This speaker is an insomniac, like the Fräulein von Rodenschild and like Ledwina; and, like Ledwina, she perceives that "hell gezeichnet von dem blassen Strahle / Legt auf mein Lager sich des Fensters Bild" (I, 460). The double dissolves just as it had when Ledwina gazed upon the water.

77 See Abrams, *The Mirror and the Lamp: Romantic Theory and the Critical Tradition* (New York: Norton, 1958).

78 Schücking, *Lebensbild*, pp. 23–24.

79 Huch, ed., *Ausgewählte Werke*, pp. 5–6.

80 Böschenstein-Schaefer, "Die Struktur des Idyllischen," p. 29.

81 Naturally the affair with Schücking had to be played down for home consumption; Droste-Hülshoff asked Schücking to address her as "Sie" in his letters for fear that her mother would intercept them and discover intimacy in his address. Droste-Hülshoff went to great lengths to be the first to open her own mail. (See *B* II, 13, 45, 343.)

82 Böschenstein-Schaefer, "Die Struktur des Idyllischen," p. 38.

CHAPTER FOUR

1 See Andreas-Salomé, *Rainer Maria Rilke* (Leipzig: Insel, 1928), p. 7.

2 See Simenauer, *Rainer Maria Rilke: Legende und Mythos* (Bern: Paul Haupt, 1953), and Butler, *Rainer Maria Rilke* (Cambridge: Cambridge University Press, 1941), p. 29.

3 Ibid., p. 335.

4 See Ibid., p. 374.

5 Blanchot, *The Space of Literature*, trans. Ann Smock (Lincoln: University of Nebraska Press, 1982), p. 126.

6 See Rilke's letter to Hermann Pongs of Aug. 17, 1924, quoted in Hermann Kunisch, *Rainer Maria Rilke: Dasein und Dichtung*, 2d ed. (Berlin: Duncker und Humblot, 1975), p. 414. Blanchot has suggested that Rilke took the idea of a personal death from his reading of Nietzsche (*The Space of Literature*, p. 121).

7 Blanchot, *The Space of Literature*, p. 124.

8 Hartman, *The Unmediated Vision* (New Haven: Yale University Press, 1954), p. 72.

9 Allemann, *Zeit und Figur beim späten Rilke: Ein Beitrag zur Poetik des modernen Gedichts* (Pfullingen: Neske, 1961), p. 193.

10 Ibid., p. 195.

11 See Steiner, *Rilkes Duineser Elegien*, 2d ed. (Bern: Francke Verlag, 1969), p. 240.

12 All references to Rilke's poetry, henceforth cited parenthetically, will be from the following edition: Rainer Maria Rilke, *Sämtliche Werke*, 6 vols. (Wiesbaden: Insel, 1957). I, 726.

13 All translations of Rilke poems are from Rainer Maria Rilke, *Selected Works*, J. B. Leishmann, trans., 2 vols. (London: The Hogarth Press, 1960), II, p. 248.

14 See Simenauer, "R. M. Rilke's Dreams and his Conception of Dream," *Rilke: The Alchemy of Alienation*, ed. Frank Baron, Ernst S. Dick, and Warren R. Maurer (Lawrence, Kans.: The Regents Press, 1980), pp. 246, 252–53.

15 Rainer Maria Rilke, *Briefe aus den Jahren 1907 bis 1914*, ed. Ruth Sieber-Rilke and Carl Sieber (Leipzig: Insel, 1933), p. 150.

16 Letter to Andreas-Salomé, Jan. 24, 1912, ibid., p. 180.

17 See Simenauer, "Rilke's Dreams," p. 257.

18 Andreas-Salomé, *Rilke*, p. 14; Simenauer, "Rilke's Dreams," p. 246.

19 Cited by Carol Jacobs, *The Dissimulating Harmony: The Image of Interpretation in Nietzsche, Rilke, Artaud, and Benjamin* (Baltimore: The Johns Hopkins University Press, 1978), p. 48.

20 Blanchot, "The Gaze of Orpheus," trans. Lydia Davis, in Blanchot, *The Gaze of Orpheus and Other Literary Essays*, ed. P. Adams Sitney (Tarrytown, N.Y.: Station Hill Press, 1981), p. 99.

21 Ovid, *Metamorphoses*, trans. Mary M. Innes (Middlesex, England: Penguin Books, 1955), p. 226.

22 Blanchot, "The Gaze of Orpheus," p. 99.

23 See Frye, "The Romantic Myth," pp. 33–34; and Walter A. Strauss, *Descent and Return, The Orpheus Theme in Modern Literature* (Cambridge, Mass.: Harvard University Press, 1971), pp. 12–13. The Tenth Elegy also makes use of the "Bergbau" metaphor in its description of the land of death, the "Leidland."

24 De Man, "Intentional Structure of the Romantic Image," *Romanticism and Consciousness, Essays in Criticism*, ed. Harold Bloom (New York: Norton, 1970), p. 76.

25 See, for instance, Kurt Oppert, "Das Dinggedicht, eine Form bei Mörike, Meyer und Rilke," *Deutsche Vierteljahresschrift* 4 (1926), 747–83.

26 Harry Mielert, "Rilke und die Antike," *Die Antike* 16, i (1940), 58. In writing "Orpheus. Eurydike. Hermes," Rilke drew upon a marble relief that he saw in Naples in June 1904. See Hans Berendt, *Rainer Maria Rilkes "Neue Gedichte," Versuch einer Deutung* (Bonn: Bouvier, 1957), p. 179.

27 Paul de Man sees the interest that the Orpheus myth holds for Rilke from another perspective in *Allegories of Reading: Figural Language in Rousseau, Nietzsche, Rilke, and Proust* (New Haven: Yale University Press, 1979), p. 46: "The poem explicitly describes the poetic vocation by means of a thematized version of chiasmic reversal, source of Rilke's affinity with the myth of Orpheus."

28 In her insightful study of Rilke's middle period, Judith Ryan has this to say about the turning of Orpheus: "Bei ihm [Orpheus] geschieht sogar eine doppelte Wendung: erstens seine Reise in die Unterwelt und seine Rückkehr auf Erde, zweitens das fatale Umkehren durch das er Eurydike auf immer verliert. Eurydike selber verkörpert in reinster Form die Umkehr" (*Umschlag und Verwandlung: Poetische Struktur und Dichtungstheorie in Rainer Maria Rilkes Lyrik der mittleren Periode (1907–1914)* [Munich: Winkler, 1972], p. 124).

29 De Man, *Allegories of Reading*, p. 47.

30 Plato, *Cratylus, The Collected Dialogues*, ed. Edith Hamilton and Huntington Cairns, Bollingen Series (Princeton: Princeton University Press), p. 444.

31 See Strauss, *Descent and Return*, p. 33.

32 For a discussion of the differences between the kind of "inwardness" that Novalis espouses and that of the later Rilke, see Richard Jayne, "Rilke and the Problem of Poetic Inwardness," in *Alchemy*, ed. Baron, Dick, and Maurer, p. 192ff.

33 Hölderlin, *Werke und Briefe*, I, 176.

34 See de Man, "Intentional Structure," p. 70.

35 See the Fifth Hymn of the *Hymnen an die Nacht* in Novalis, *Werke in einem Band*, p. 169.

36 Hermand, "Rilkes 'Gesang der Frauen an den Dichter,' " *Monatshefte* 56, ii (Feb. 1964), 51.

37 See Herbert Singer, *Rilke und Hölderlin* (Cologne: Böhlau, 1957), p. 11.

38 See Kunisch, *Dasein und Dichtung*, p. 249.

39 See Singer, *Rilke und Hölderlin*, p. 11.

40 Rilke held out particularly against the reading of Goethe. Although it is known that he read Goethe intensively until he was twenty-one, he later claimed scarcely to have read him at all. See Eudo C. Mason, *Rilke und Goethe* (Cologne: Böhlau, 1958), p. 24.

41 Ibid., pp. 77–78.

42 Quoted by Singer, *Rilke und Hölderlin*, p. 32.

43 See ibid., p. 33.

44 Rilke, *Briefe aus den Jahren 1907 bis 1914*, p. 372.

45 Singer, *Rilke und Hölderlin*, p. 32.

46 Ibid., p. 44.

47 Singer, *Rilke und Hölderlin*, p. 45.

48 See the letter to Frau von Hellingrath, Oct. 26, 1914, in Rilke, *Briefe aus den Jahren 1914 bis 1921*, ed. Ruth Sieber-Rilke and Carl Sieber (Leipzig: Insel, 1937), p. 22.

49 Michel, *Hölderlins Wiederkunft* (Vienna: Gallus, 1943), p. 17.

50 See Norman O. Brown, *Hermes the Thief: The Evolution of a Myth* (Madison: University of Wisconsin Press, 1947), p. 32.

51 See Brigitte Peucker, "The Poem as Place: Three Modes of Scenic Rendering in the Lyric," *PMLA* 96 (1981), pp. 909–10.

52 Michel, *Hölderlin's Wiederkunft*, p. 29.

53 Allemann, *Zeit und Figur*, p. 240.

54 Letter to Countess Sizzo-Noris-Crouy, Jan. 6, 1923, quoted by Allemann, *Zeit und Figur*, p. 197.

55 Singer cites a passage from *Hyperion* that is also relevant: "Ich bin wirklich nicht mehr, der ich sonst war, Diotima! Ich bin Deines gleichen geworden, und Göttliches spielt mit Göttlichem jetzt, wie Kinder unter sich spielen" (*Rilke und Hölderlin*, p. 48).

56 Rilke's "Fünf Gesänge" (Aug. 1914) are commonly acknowledged to be much influenced by Hölderlin. They were written in Rilke's copy of the Hellingrath edition, vol. IV.

57 In *Literatur und Utopie*, Rainer Nägele speaks of Hölderlin's self-conscious "Regress zum Ursprung," and of "die notwendige Loslösung von den Bindungen an den Ursprung" which becomes one of the most important moments in the dialectics of the later poetry (pp. 141, 95).

58 Letter to Xaver V. Moos, Apr. 20, 1923, in Rilke, *Briefe aus Muzot, 1921 bis 1926*, ed. Ruth Sieber-Rilke and Carl Sieber (Leipzig: Insel, 1935), p. 195.

59 Letter to Leopold v. Schlözer, May 30, 1923, ibid., p. 190.

60 Letter to Countess Sizzo-Noris-Crouy, Jan. 6, 1923, in Rilke, *Briefe*, 2 vols., ed. Karl Altheim (Wiesbaden: Insel, 1950), II, 406.

61 Concerning Rilke and Romanticism, see Lawrence Ryan, "Die Krise des Romantischen."

62 See also "Du bist der Arme . . ." (1903; I, 356–58).

63 Quoted by Andreas-Salomé, *Rainer Maria Rilke*, p. 39.

64 Letter to Andreas-Salomé, Aug. 10, 1903, in Rilke, *Briefe aus den Jahren 1902 bis 1906*, ed. Ruth Sieber-Rilke and Carl Sieber (Leipzig: Insel, 1930), p. 119.

65 See letter to Countess Sizzo-Noris-Crouy, March 17, 1922, in Rilke, *Briefe*, ed. Altheim, II, 341.

66 Andreas-Salomé, *Rainer Maria Rilke*, p. 89.

67 Butler, *Rainer Maria Rilke*, p. 340.

68 Eichendorff, *Werke und Schriften*, IV, 241.

69 In this connection, see the letter of Dec. 16, 1923 to Countess Sizzo, in which Rilke speculates about the iconographic significance of the lemons he has frequently seen in female portraits of the seventeenth and eigthteenth centuries. A friend, he says, believes the lemon to signify that the woman has already died. "Ist das wirklich die Bedeutung der mitgegebenen Citrone," he muses, "so bleibt es ja immernoch unerklärt, wie diese Frucht zu dieser bildlichen Anwendung kam. Ich wüsste nicht dass sie in irgend welchen Toten-Kulten eine Rolle gespielt haben sollte; ist es diese Verbindung von letzter Bitterkeit und Reife, die sie zum Zeichen des Verstorbenseins machen konnte—das käme mir schon fast zu abgeleitet und ausgeklügelt vor. (Ihr Duft übrigens, der Duft dieser Frucht, hat für mich eine unbeschreibliche Eindringlichkeit.)" *Briefe*, ed. Altheim, II, 426.

70 As Martin Heidegger writes, "Hölderlin ist der Vor-Gänger der Dichter in dürftiger Zeit" ("Wozu Dichter?" *Holzwege* [Frankfurt: Klostermann, 1977], p. 320).

71 See Mason, *Rilke und Goethe*, p. 69.

72 See Hans Egon Holthusen, *Der späte Rilke* (Zürich: Die Arche, 1949), p. 117.

73 See Sonnet I, iii: "An der Kreuzung zweier / Herzwege steht kein Tempel für Apoll" (I, 732).

74 Never mentioned by name, in II, xvi "der Gott" Orpheus "[ist] die Stille, welche heilt" (I, 761). and in II, xxvi, just once, he is the "singender Gott" (I, 769.) II, xxix (I, 770), which purports to be addressed to someone else, admittedly, could be addressed to Orpheus.

75 See my reading of this poem in "The Poem as Place: Three Modes of Scenic Rendering in the Lyric," *PMLA* 96, v (Oct. 1981), 911. Holthusen has pointed out that Rilke's language lays stress upon spatial contours in a number of ways—in its emphasis on rhythmic pattern, its use of verbs as nouns, and in the radical insistence with which its metaphors enforce identity (see *Der späte Rilke*, pp. 54, 153, 142). Likewise the sonnet form, although it is continuously varied by Rilke, helps to suggest the fixity and substantiality to which Rilke aspired.

76 In "Der Berg" (*Neue Gedichte*, II; I, 638), the painter is said to "write" the mountain; and in an earlier poem, "Eingang" (*Buch der Bilder*, I, 371), the first brush stroke on an empty canvas is also the first mark of writing on an empty page.

77 See de Man, "Intentional Structure," p. 75.

78 John Brenkman, "Narcissus in the Text," *Georgia Review* 30 (1976), 317.

CHAPTER FIVE

1 Neumann, *Creative Man: Five Essays*, trans. Eugene Rolf, Bollingen Series, vol. LXI, 2 (Princeton: Princeton University Press, 1979), esp. p. 195. For another Jungian approach to Trakl, see Theodor Spoerri, *Georg Trakl: Strukturen in Persönlichkeit und Werk: Eine psychiatrisch-anthropographische Untersuchung* (Bern: Francke, 1954).

2 Sharp, *The Poet's Madness* (Ithaca: Cornell University Press, 1981), p. 40.

3 Kurrik, *Georg Trakl, Columbia Essays on Modern Writers*, no. 72 (New York: Columbia University Press, 1974, pp. 3, 9.

4 See the letters in Georg Trakl, *Dichtungen und Briefe*, ed. Walther Killy and Hans Szklenar (Salzburg: Otto Müller, 1969), especially I, 538. All references to Trakl's poetry and letters will be made henceforth to this edition, cited parenthetically by volume and page.

5 Howard Stern, "Verbal Mimesis: The Case of 'Die Winzer,'" *Studies in Twentieth-Century Literature* 8, i (1983), 27.

6 See Böschenstein, "Hölderlin und Rimbaud, simultane Rezeption als Quelle poetischer Innovation im Werk Georg Trakls," *Salzburger Trakl Symposion*, ed. Walter Weiss and Hans Weichselbaum (Salzburg: Otto Müller, 1979), pp. 9–27.

7 Grimm, "Georg Trakls Verhältnis zu Rimbaud," *Germanisch-romanische Monatsschrift* 9, iii (1959), 312–13.

8 See Bloom, *The Anxiety of Influence: A Theory of Poetry* (New York, Oxford University Press, 1973), p. 80.

9 Killy, *Über Georg Trakl* (Göttingen: Vandenhoeck und Ruprecht, 1967), pp. 91, 60, 63, 76.

10 Ibid., pp. 94–95. See Friedrich, *Die Struktur der modernen Lyrik* (Hamburg: Rowohlt, 1956).

11 De Man, *Blindness and Insight: Essays in the Rhetoric of Contemporary Criticism* (New York: Oxford University Press, 1971), p. 179.

12 Heinrich Heine, *Gedichte*, ed. Georges Schlocker (Stuttgart: Philipp Reclam, 1965), p. 95.

13 See Christa Saas, *Georg Trakl* (Stuttgart: Metzler, 1974) p. 44.

14 Eduard Mörike, *Sämtliche Werke*, 2 vols. (Munich: Winkler, 1968), I, 746.

15 Heine, *Gedichte*, p. 92.

16 Hartman, "Wordsworth and Goethe in Literary History," p. 191.

17 Ibid.

18 In *Georg Trakl* (p. 44), Saas quotes Szklenar's report of Trakl's assertion that "'Goethe sei schamlos oft, voll Ausspruch, voll Bekenntnis und doch gab er sich der *Sinnlichkeit* hin.'"

19 Böschenstein ("Hölderlin und Rimbaud," p. 18) associates "der Fremdling" with Hölderlin, pointing out that "Fremdling" belongs to his stock of images. I shall take up Trakl's recurrent figurations of Hölderlin at a later stage in this discussion.

20 Grimm, "Trakls Verhältnis zu Rimbaud," p. 309. It must be borne in mind that the period of Trakl's greatest interest in Rimbaud was later, 1911–12, and that although his French was excellent, the verbal influence of Rimbaud seems to have been mediated for Trakl by the translation of K. L. Ammer.

21 For another variation on this theme in Trakl, see his poem "Schwesters Garten," I, 317.

22 The celestial is nowhere dragged down more decisively than in "Ruh und Schweigen" (I, 113): "Hirten begruben die Sonne im kahlen Wald. / Ein Fischer zog / In härenem Netz den Mond aus frierendem Weiher."

23 As Saas tells us (*Georg Trakl*, p. 30), Trakl was an avid reader of Nietzsche.

24 Heidegger, "Language in the Poem: A Discussion of Georg Trakl's Poetic Work," trans. Peter D. Hertz, *On the Way to Language* (San Francisco: Harper and Row, 1971), pp. 175, 194.

25 Benjamin, "The Task of the Translator," trans. Harry Zohn, *Illuminations*, ed. Hannah Arendt (New York: Schocken, 1969), p. 80.

26 Quoted by Joachim Storck, "Arbeitsgespräche: Trakl und Rilke," *Salzburger Trakl Symposion*, ed. Weiss and Weichselbaum, p. 154.

27 Letter to Ludwig von Ficker, Feb. 8, 1915, *Briefe aus den Jahren 1914 bis 1921*, p. 35.

28 Feb. 22, 1917, ibid., p. 126.

29 Hölderlin, *Werke und Briefe*, III, 242.

30 Böschenstein, "Hölderlin und Rimbaud," p. 20.

31 See ibid., p. 15.

32 For these examples, see ibid., p. 21.

33 See, for example, ibid., p. 13, where Bösechenstein says concerning the revision of Hölderlin in "Helian": "Gewiss ist hier der negative Bezug auf *Patmos* nicht unbedingt als reflektierte Auseinandersetzung mit Hölderlin zu verstehen, aber die Umwertung ist Trakl zweifellos bewusst."

34 Ibid., p. 15.

35 Ibid., p. 27.

36 See ibid., p. 16.

37 I cannot pursue the topic here, but I believe that the remnants of pastoral and Golden Age topoi in Trakl's work, which obviously lend themselves to Christian allegory, come to him in part from Hölderlin. The seasonal structure of his poems and his interest in times of day have Hölderlin as a source, in any case, but also entail the revision of Eichendorff, whose optimistic springtime morning setting becomes the "Abendland" of Fall in Trakl.

38 Heidegger, "Language in the Poem," pp. 194, 190.

39 Erich Bölli, *Georg Trakls "dunkler Wohllaut": Ein Beitrag zum Verständnis seines dichterischen Sprechens* (Zürich: Artemis, 1978), p. 121.

40 Jost Hermand, "Der Knabe Elis: zum Problem der Existenzstufen bei Georg Trakl," *Monatshefte* 51, v (1959), 229.

41 Eduard Lachmann, "Trakl und Hölderlin. Eine Deutung," *Georg Trakl: Nachlass und Biographie*, ed. Wolfgang Schneditz (Salzburg: Otto Müller, 1949), p. 209.

42 Klaus Simon, *Traum und Orpheus: Eine Studie zu Georg Trakls Dichtungen* (Salzburg: Otto Müller, 1955), p. 167; and Clemens Heselhaus, "Die Elis-Gedichte von Georg Trakl," *Deutsche Vierteljahresschrift* 28, iii (1954), 387.

43 Böschenstein, "Hölderlin und Rimbaud," p. 16. See Trakl, *Dichtungen und Briefe*, II, 94.

44 Novalis, *Die Lehrlinge zu Sais, Werke in einem Band*, p. 214.

45 Ibid., p. 149.

46 Ibid., p. 217.

47 Ibid., p. 153.

48 It should be pointed out that silence is already featured in Hölderlin's poetry, as the "Mauern . . . / Sprachlos und kalt" will attest; indeed, critics have repeatedly and variously remarked on this fact. Adorno refers to Hölderlin's "Ekel vor der Kommunikation" ("Parataxis. Zur späten Lyrik Hölderlins," *Über Hölderlin*, ed. Schmidt, p. 356); Max Kommerell says that "[d]as Verschweigen, das Verstummen ist mit dabei in Hölderlins Sprechen" ("Hölderlins Empedokles-Dichtungen," ibid., p. 221); and Cyrus Hamlin speaks of "the climactic moment of intuited transcendence, which always manifests itself as an epiphanic silence, a sustained gap (Lücke) in time" ("The Temporality of Selfhood," p. 193).

49 For readers of Rilke, this passage will bring to mind the first of the *Sonette an Orpheus*, where "Tiere aus Stille" can be read as the motifs of Orpheus's song.

50 The two pastoral figures in this poem, the fisher of men and the good shepherd, are presented in a specifically Christian context which I shall touch upon only briefly here.

51 Hölderlin, *Werke und Briefe*, p. 115.

52 See Böschenstein, "Hölderlin und Rimbaud," p. 18.

53 Theodore Fiedler identifies the source of these apostrophes as Hölderlin's "Lebensalter," pointing out that Trakl "adapted its three opening apostrophes, yet another type of Hölderlin's hyperbatic syntax, to fuse images and imagistic scenes from the repetitive second and third versions of 'Abendland' and transform them, as it were, into an apocalyptic vision of the Occident, indeed of the Cosmos itself" ("Hölderlin and Trakl's Poetry of 1914," *Friedrich Hölderlin: An Early Modern*, ed. Emery E. George [Ann Arbor: University of Michigan Press, 1972], p. 101). As an aside here, Trakl also wrote a poem called "Lebensalter" (I, 352) which recalls the first stanza of Hölderlin's "Hälfte des Lebens." It contains the lines "Es reicht ein Greis mit edlen / Händen gereifte Früchte," in which Trakl seems to imagine Hölderlin giving the gift of poetry to him, which he then returns.

54 See Böschenstein, "Die Dunkelheit der deutschen Lyrik des 20. Jahrhunderts," *Der Deutschunterricht* 3 (1969), 57.

55 Novalis, *Werke in einem Band*, p. 155.

56 The scene of Trakl's poetry is often laid in the first section of "Brot und Wein." A clear-cut example is "Träumerei am Abend" (I, 290), but there are many less obviously derived settings.

57 Hölderlin, *Werke und Briefe*, I, 154.

58 Ibid., I, 155.

59 Ibid., I, 156.

60 Ibid.

61 Arendt, "Introduction: Walter Benjamin, 1892–1940," in Benjamin, *Illuminations*, ed. Arendt, p. 38.

62 Arendt, "Introduction," p. 39, translates and quotes Benjamin's *Schriften* (Frankfurt am Main: Suhrkamp, 1955), II, 192.

63 Benjamin, "The Task of the Translator," *Illuminations*, pp. 79, 80.

64 Arendt, "Introduction," p. 49.

65 Benjamin, *Reflections: Essays, Aphorisms, Autobiographical Writings*, ed. Peter Demetz (New York: Harcourt, 1978), p. 318.

66 Hölderlin, *Werke und Briefe*, I, 155.

67 Ibid., I, 156.

68 Ibid., I, 183. The location of authenticity in intertextuality by this poetics prompts the thought that Klopstock is as prominent as he is in "Abendland" because in "Patmos," where the idea of German song as a following, a literary imitation, concludes the poem, there are an unusual number of allusions to Klopstock's *Messias* (see ibid., III, 112).

69 De Man, *Blindness and Insight*, p. 186.

70 Arendt, "Introduction," pp. 50–51.

71 De Man, "Intentional Structure of the Romantic Image," p. 67.

Index